WELL BEGUN BUT NOT YET DONE

Titles in the Equity and Development Series

The Equity and Development Series addresses the distributional consequences of macroeconomic policies and showcases techniques for systematically analyzing the distributional consequences of policy reform. Titles
in this series undergo internal and external review under the management
of the Research Group in the World Bank's Development Economics Vice
Presidency.

Free access to titles in the Equity and Development Series is available at
https://openknowledge.worldbank.org/handle/10986/2160

WELL BEGUN BUT NOT YET DONE

Progress and Emerging Challenges for Poverty Reduction in Vietnam

Valerie Kozel, Editor

WORLD BANK GROUP

Washington, DC

Contents

Figures

Maps

Tables

Foreword

Vietnam has built a remarkable record of economic growth and poverty reduction over the last two decades. Using a poverty line set in the 1990s and since updated, Vietnam's poverty rate fell from 58 percent in the early 1990s to 14 percent by 2008 and had fallen to well below 10 percent in 2010. Vietnam has also made substantial progress in other dimensions of well-being, ranging from high primary and secondary school enrollment rates to improvements in health outcomes and reductions in morbidity and mortality. Consequently, Vietnam has achieved—and in some cases surpassed—most of the Millennium Development Goals (MDGs).

Despite such remarkable progress, the task of poverty reduction is still not complete. Although tens of millions of Vietnamese households have escaped from extreme poverty, many continue to have incomes very close to the poverty line, leaving them vulnerable to poverty due to shocks from droughts, floods, job loss, and illness. Almost one-sixth of the population still lived on less than two dollars a day in 2010. Moreover, the standards that applied to Vietnam as a low-income country in the 1990s are no longer relevant to modern day, middle-income Vietnam. Citizens now have higher expectations and aspirations, and they expect more from their leaders than in the past.

Despite Vietnam's success at lifting millions of people out of poverty, there are still major challenges in reaching the remaining poor who face isolation, few assets, limited education, and poor health status. Although Vietnam's 53 ethnic minority groups make up less than 15 percent of the population, they accounted for nearly half of the remaining poor in 2010, compared with only 29 percent in 1998. So while the living conditions for Vietnam's 53 ethnic minority groups have improved over time, that improvement has been at a much slower pace than for the majority Kinh. And while Vietnam has achieved or surpassed many of the MDGs, the quality of education and health services remain a problem for many of its people, while access to water and sanitation, especially in rural areas, still falls short of the MDG targets.

This book presents the key findings from a new Poverty Assessment for Vietnam, led by the World Bank and the Vietnam Academy of Social

Sciences (VASS), working in collaboration with the General Statistics Office (GSO). It takes a fresh look at the constraints and opportunities facing the poor men, women, and children who are working to escape poverty. Building on a rich body of analytical work, this assessment has three aims. First, it proposes revisions to Vietnam's poverty monitoring system—including better data, updated welfare aggregates, and new poverty lines—to bring the system more in line with the economic and social conditions of today's Vietnam. Second, it revisits the stylized facts about deprivation and poverty in Vietnam and develops an updated profile and diagnostic of poverty, drawing on information from the 2010 Vietnam Household Living Standards Survey and new qualitative field studies. Third, it aims to forge a consensus around some of the key challenges Vietnam faces—including high and chronic poverty among ethnic minorities, persistent vulnerability, and rising inequality in outcomes and opportunities—in reducing poverty and promoting shared prosperity over the next decade.

Axel van Trotsenburg
Vice President,
East Asia and Pacific region
The World Bank
Washington, DC
August 2014

Acknowledgments

The 2012 Vietnam Poverty Assessment was prepared in partnership by the World Bank and the Center for Analysis and Forecasting, Vietnam Academy of Social Sciences (CAF/VASS), with substantial inputs and comments provided by national researchers and experts, as well as international partners, including the United Kingdom (DFID), the United Nations (UNDP, UNICEF, UNFPA, UN Resident Coordinators Office), the European Commission, Ireland (IrishAid), and Oxfam GB.

The Poverty Assessment was prepared by a team led by Valerie Kozel (principal author) under the overall guidance of Victoria Kwakwa, World Bank Country Director in Vietnam; Sudhir Shetty, Poverty Reduction and Economic Policy Sector Director; and Deepak Mishra, Lead Economist, Vietnam Country Program. Core team members include Nguyen Thang (Director, CAF), Reena Badiani (World Bank), Bob Baulch (RMIT University), Loren Brandt (University of Toronto), Nguyen Viet Cuong (National Economics University), Vu Hoang Dat (CAF), Nguyen Tam Giang (World Bank), John Gibson (Waikato University), John Giles (World Bank), Ian Hinsdale (World Bank), Pham Thai Hung (Indochina Research), Jae Kyun Kim (World Bank), Peter Lanjouw (World Bank), Marleen Marra (World Bank), Vu Van Ngoc (CAF), Nguyen Thi Thu Phuong (CAF), Paul Schuler (UC San Diego), Hoang Xuan Thanh (Ageless Consulting Ltd), Le Dang Trung (University of Copenhagen), Phung Duc Tung (Indochina Research), Linh Hoang Vu (World Bank), and Andrew Wells-Dang (Oxfam GB). The team from the General Statistics Office included Nguyen Phong (ex-Director, Social and Environmental Statistics Department), Do Anh Kiem (Director, Social and Environmental Statistics Department), Lo Thi Duc, and Nguyen The Quan. Additional inputs were provided by Paul Van Ufford and the team at UNICEF/Hanoi (on child poverty), Ingrid Fitzgerald (UN Resident Coordinators Office, Vietnam), and Michaela Prokop (UNDP/Hanoi) on the Human Development Index and multidimensional poverty indicators. Peter Lanjouw and Nguyen Viet Cuong were lead authors for Chapter 4; Andrew Wells-Deng was the lead author for Chapter 5; and Reena Badiani was the lead author for Chapter 6.

Diane Stamm provided able editorial support, and Tuyet Thi Phung, Lynn Yeargin, Mildred Gonsalvez (all World Bank), and Vu Van Ngoc (CAF) provided effective and much appreciated administrative support over the course of the project. Tuyet Thi Phung and Vu Van Ngoc also were responsible for organizing numerous consultations and dissemination events in Vietnam.

Background papers prepared for the Poverty Assessment include works by the following: Ian Hinsdale, Valerie Kozel, and Nguyen Phong, on an updated 2010 poverty line and poverty profile; Bob Baulch and Vu Hoang Dat on ethnic minority poverty; Andrew Wells-Dang on qualitative research on ethnic minority poverty and inequality; Nguyen Viet Cuong and Pham Thai Hung on poverty in the northern mountains; Le Dang Trung, Phung Duc Tung, and Nguyen Viet Cuong on sources of risk and shocks in rural areas; Hoang Xuan Thanh on perceptions of inequality; Nguyen Thi Thu Phuong on intergenerational gaps in perceptions of inequality; John Gibson on the spatial cost of living indicators and poverty measurement; Nguyen Tam Giang (in collaboration with Oxfam GB) on long-run drivers of poverty reduction; Peter Lanjouw, Marleen Marra, and Nguyen Viet Cuong on 2009 poverty maps; Peter Lanjouw and Marleen Marra on urban poverty and city size; Marleen Marra on subjective measures of poverty, also on economies of size and scale in consumption.

The Poverty Assessment benefited from extensive review and inputs at the concept phase, and the team very much appreciates the many suggestions received at the World Bank concept review meeting and three early consultations workshops (in Hanoi and HCMC) organized by VASS in 2011. The work benefited as well from comments received at two seminars sponsored by the World Bank office in Hanoi in March and June, 2012, and a technical workshop organized by VASS in June, 2012, to discuss the background papers and an early draft of the book. The team is grateful for comments received at the World Bank decision review in June, 2012, including from peer reviewers: Dominque van de Walle; Michael Woolcock; and Salman Zaidi (all from the World Bank); and Dr. Nguyen Thi Lan Huong (Director, ILSSA). More generally, the team would like to acknowledge comments received throughout preparation from members of the Vietnam country team as well as staff in East Asia Poverty Reduction and Economic Management (PREM) department, including Mette Bertelsen, Christian Bodewig, Quang Hong Doan, Kari Hurt, Steve Jaffee, Andrew Mason, Nguyen Thi Thu Lan, Trang Van Nguyen, Son Thanh Vo, and Myla Williams.

A second and final round of consultation workshops was organized by VASS and the World Bank in HCMC and Hanoi in August, 2012, on the revised draft of the Poverty Assessment. The team is grateful for comments and suggestions provided by participants at both workshops, including written comments provided in advance of the HCMC workshop by

Dr. Jonathan Pincus (Fullbright Program, HCMC); Dr. Huynh Thi Ngoc Tuyet (former researcher from Southern Institute of Sustainable Development); Dr. Nguyen Hoang Bao (HCMC University of Economics); and Dr. Le Thanh Sang (Southern Institute of Sustainable Development). Written comments were received in advance of the Hanoi workshop from Dr. Le Dang Doanh (former Economic Advisor); Dr. Nguyen Hai Huu (MOLISA); Mr. Do Anh Kiem (GSO); Bert Martens (Oxfam/HK); and Dr. Trinh Cong Khanh (CEMA). We are also grateful for comments and suggestions provided at the consultation workshops by Nguyen Tien Phong (UNDP); Pham Quang Ngoc (ADB); Madame Pham Chi Lan (former Vice President of VCCI); and Dr. Dang Kim Son (IPSARD).

The Poverty Assessment was initially released in English and Vietnamese as World Bank Report 70798-VN. The manuscript was subsequently revised for wider dissemination in the World Bank's Equity and Development series.

The team gratefully acknowledges financial support provided by the United Kingdom Department for International Development (DFID) under the GAPAP trust fund, and would like to specifically thank Renwick Irvine and Huong Than Thi Thien, DFID staff in Hanoi, for their ongoing support. We would also like to acknowledge TFESSD donors for their financial support for new work on perceptions of inequality.

We would like to thank the General Statistics Office for providing excellent logistical assistance as well as timely access to the 2010 VHLSS and other sources of data. This book is one of many products emerging from the long and fruitful collaboration between the World Bank, VASS, and the GSO on poverty measurement, monitoring, and poverty reduction policies and programs.

The advice of many others, both from inside the World Bank as well as outside, who provided valuable inputs and suggestions throughout the process of preparing background papers and this book is acknowledged and appreciated.

About the Contributors

Valerie Kozel is Senior Economist with the Global Practice on Poverty at the World Bank. She worked previously on poverty reduction and social protection with the East Asia, South Asia, and Africa regional teams, as well as with the World Bank's Development Research Group. She has published numerous articles in academic and development journals, and was co-editor and contributor to *The Great Indian Poverty Debate* (Macmillan, 2005). Her main research interests include welfare and poverty (with a focus on extreme poverty), social identity and exclusion, migration, social welfare, and vulnerability. She holds a PhD from Massachusetts Institute of Technology and an MS from Northwestern University.

Reena Badiani-Magnusson is an economist with the Social Protection and Labor Unit in the Southeast Asia team of the World Bank's East Asia and Pacific region; before that she was with the World Bank's Poverty Reduction and Economic Management Unit. She has published articles in academic economic and development journals, and has experience working on social protection design and delivery, poverty and inequality, labor markets, and impact evaluations in Vietnam, Thailand, Myanmar, India, and the Democratic Republic of the Congo. Her main research areas include education, evaluations of social assistance policies, electricity pricing, and the drivers of inequality. She holds a PhD in Economics from Yale University and a DEA from the University of Social Sciences, Toulouse, France.

Bob Baulch is Associate Professor of Economics and Research Coordinator at RMIT University Vietnam. He is also an Adjunct Professor at Tan Tao University (Vietnam) and a Senior Research Fellow with the Brooks World Poverty Institute at the University of Manchester (UK). Baulch's research interests include poverty dynamics, household surveys, and food price analysis, and he has worked in 20 developing countries in Africa, Asia, and the Pacific. He holds a PhD from Stanford University.

Loren Brandt is Professor of Economics at the University of Toronto specializing in the Chinese economy. He is also a research fellow at the The Institute for the Study of Labor (IZA) in Bonn, Germany. He has published widely on the Chinese economy in leading economic journals, and has been involved in extensive household and enterprise survey work in both China and Vietnam. He was co-editor and contributor to *China's Great Economic Transformation* (Cambridge University Press, 2008), which provides an integrated analysis of China's unexpected economic boom during the past three decades. His current research focuses on issues of industrial upgrading in China, inequality dynamics, and economic growth and structural change.

John Gibson is Professor in the Department of Economics, University of Waikato, and a Senior Research Associate of Motu Economic and Public Policy Research. He taught previously at the University of Canterbury, and the Economics Department and Center for Development Economics at Williams College. Since receiving his PhD from Stanford University, he has worked mainly in East Asia and Pacific countries on issues related to food policy, migration, and poverty. Many of his research publications can be found at: http://ideas.repec.org/e/pgi12.html.

Ian Hinsdale graduated from Georgetown University with a BA in Economics and Philosophy. He is founder and CEO of Wynno, Inc., which focuses on the intersection of economic forces and political life. While this report was being drafted, he worked as a consultant to the World Bank in Hanoi and Washington, DC. He has also worked as a research assistant at the International Monetary Fund.

Hoang Xuan Thanh is Managing Partner and Senior Consultant at Ageless Consultants in Hanoi, Vietnam. He has worked extensively on impact evaluation and participatory and qualitative research, and he has led studies and impact evaluations for a wide range of research organizations, international partners and NGOs in Vietnam, including the World Bank, DFID, UNDP, SNV, and Oxfam GB. He holds a degree from the Technology Institute of the Army in Hanoi.

Jaekyun Kim is a consultant in the Poverty Reduction Unit of the World Bank's East Asia and Pacific region. He has worked on the Pacific Islands Hardship Study, Myanmar IHLCA deep dive data analysis, and has done regional work on inequality and mobility in the unit. His interests and work experience are in poverty analysis, disaster risk management, humanitarian assistance, and social protection. He holds an MA from the Institute of Development Studies, University of Sussex, UK.

Peter Lanjouw is Research Manager of the Poverty Group in the Development Economics Research Department of the World Bank. He completed his doctoral studies in economics at the London School of Economics, and then joined the World Bank in 1992. His research has focused on rural development, notably the study of a village economy in rural India and the broader analysis of rural nonfarm diversification, as well as methodological questions in the measurement of poverty and inequality. He has taught at the Vrije University in Amsterdam, UC Berkeley, University of Namur, the Foundation for Advanced Study of International Development in Tokyo, and he is an Honorary Fellow of the Amsterdam Institute of International Development. He is an associate editor of the World Bank Economic Review and a past editorial board member of the Journal of African Economies. In 2015 he will take up the position of Professor of Economics at the Vrije (Free) University of Amsterdam.

Trung Dang Le is a postdoctoral fellow in the Department of Economics, University of Copenhagen, where he is doing research on development economics; he holds a PhD in Economics from the same university. His research interests cover applied microeconomics and econometrics in such areas as the economics of disasters, household economics, labor economics, and economic development. He has published in academic journals such as *Oxford Development Studies* and *Journal of Agricultural Economics*.

Lo Thi Duc is Senior Statistician at the General Statistics Office (GSO) of Vietnam. Her work focuses on the Household Living Standard Surveys (VHLSS), poverty, and inequality. She is also tasked with the design, supervision, training, and analyses of many large-scale surveys conducted by GSO. She directed the Vietnam Government Poverty Lines during 2006–10 and 2011–15 periods, and participated in the GSO-World Bank 2002–12 poverty lines. She has joined the Core Technique Group, which is setting up the multidimensional poverty methodology for Vietnam. She graduated from the Ha Noi National Economics University and holds an MBA from the Asian Institute of Technology (AIT).

Marleen Marra is a consultant with the Development Economics Research Department of the World Bank. She carried out research on issues related to the measurement of poverty and inequality, nonfarm development and urban poverty, and the effectiveness of a randomized controlled trial. In addition to her extensive research on Vietnam, her country work experience includes Nepal, Malawi, and Burkina Faso. She is an Economics PhD candidate at University College London, UK, and holds an MSc in Economics from Tilburg University (the Netherlands). Her current research focuses on early childhood development and econometric identification of a skill technology function.

Nguyen Viet Cuong is Senior Lecturer and Researcher at the National Economics University, and Mekong Development Research Institute, Hanoi, Vietnam. He holds a PhD and an MSc in Development Economics from Wageningen University (the Netherlands). His main interests are impact evaluation, poverty analysis, ethnic minorities, and education and health. He has worked in Vietnam, Lao PDR, and South Africa. His recent studies have been published in journals such as *American Political Science Review, World Bank Economic Review, Journal of Comparative Economics, Health Economics, World Development,* and *Journal of Development Studies.*

Giang Tam Nguyen is a consultant with the World Bank in Vietnam. He has a PhD in Development Sociology from the Royal Holloway College, the University of London, UK, and an MA in Globalization, Development, and Transition from the University of Westminster, UK. His research interests include vulnerability and poverty, migrant labor, social protection, and children's rights. He has authored many development reports commissioned by international nongovernmental organizations in the UK and Vietnam, with a strong focus on poverty reduction.

Nguyen Phong is retired Director of the Social and Environmental Statistics Department of the General Statistics Office of Vietnam. The Department is and has been in charge of designing and implementing Vietnam Household Living Standards Surveys (VHLSS) and many other nationwide household surveys, including the National Health Survey, the National Family Survey, the Multi Cluster Indicators Surveys (MICS), the Survey and Assessment of Viet Nam Youth (SAVY), the Family Violence Survey, the Young Life Surveys (YL), and the Global Adult Tobacco Survey (GAT). He has more than 30 years of experience working on social statistics, data collection, and data analysis of household surveys, especially regarding living standards and poverty. He holds a PhD from the University of South Australia and an MBA from Bentley University, Massachusetts, United States.

Nguyen Thang is a senior research fellow and the Director of the Centre for Analysis and Forecasting (CAF) of the Vietnam Academy of Social Sciences (VASS). His areas of expertise include macroeconomics, trade, competitiveness, labor markets, and poverty. He has worked on various policy reports on poverty assessments and human development in Vietnam, and he has published in Vietnamese and international journals. He received a PhD in Economics from the Moscow Institute of National Economy and an MSc degree in Economics from the London School of Economics and Political Science.

Nguyen Thi Thu Phuong is an economist at the Centre for Analysis and Forecasting under the Vietnamese Academy of Social Sciences. She was the team leader of Vietnam Rapid Impact Assessments of global economic crises on Vietnamese firms, workers, and households, which has been conducted several times a year since early 2009. She has expertise in combined quantitative and qualitative research in ethnic minority poverty assessment, social inclusion and empowerment for vulnerable groups, labor dynamics and migration, social protection, and governance. Phuong has focused on the perceptions of households and household businesses regarding a number of topics, such as inclusive growth, social inclusion, empowerment, and price impacts. Phuong completed her MA at the Vietnam-Netherlands Economics Development Program, Vietnam National Economics University. She is currently a PhD candidate at Paris University of Dauphine.

Tung Duc Phung is Director of Mekong Development Research Institute. He holds a PhD in Economics from the Institute of Development and Agricultural Economics, Leibniz University of Hannover, Germany. Dr. Phung has a strong background in econometrics, impact evaluation, survey design, and implementation. He was the lead consultant in various impact evaluation projects for international agencies and line ministries. He has 17 years of experience working in development and poverty reduction. His work has been published in international peer-reviewed journals such *American Economic Journal* and *World Development*; his research focuses on poverty reduction, socioeconomic development for ethnic minorities, social welfare, and vulnerability to poverty.

Michaela Prokop is Policy Advisor at United Nations Development Programme in Vietnam focusing on inclusive growth related issues. Previously she worked as an economist for the Asian Development Bank and on various assignments for the European Union, the World Bank, and the UN in Asia, Africa, and the Pacific. She holds a PhD in Political Economy from Durham University, U.K.

Vu Hoang Dat is a researcher at the Centre for Analysis and Forecasting (CAF) within Vietnam Academy of Social Sciences (VASS). He works mainly in the areas of productivity analysis and poverty assessment, and he is a contributor to several publications. Recently his research has focused on the impacts of trade liberalization on Vietnam's labor market. He is a PhD candidate at the University of Paris, Dauphine, France. He holds an MA in Development Economics from the Vietnam-Netherlands Program.

Andrew Wells-Dang is Senior Technical Advisor for Oxfam in Vietnam. He has lived in Vietnam since 1997 and has worked as a researcher, evaluator, and representative of several international NGOs. Andrew holds a PhD in Political Science from the University of Birmingham, UK, and an MA in International Development from Johns Hopkins SAIS, Washington, DC. He is the author of *Civil Society Networks in China and Vietnam: Informal Pathbreakers in Health and the Environment* (Palgrave Macmillan, 2012) and is a frequent contributor to books and journals on governance and politics in Southeast Asia.

Abbreviations

AC	Agricultural Census
ADB	Asian Development Bank
ASEAN	Association of Southeast Asian Nations
CAF	Center for Analysis and Forecasting
CBN	Cost of Basic Needs
CPI	Consumer Price Index
CPRGS	Comprehensive Poverty Reduction and Growth Strategy
CPS	Country Partnership Strategy
CSA	Country Social Analysis
DFID	Department for International Development (UK)
DOLISA	District-level MOLISA staff
DPT1	Diptheria, Pertussis, and Tetanus, first immunization
EA	Enumeration Area
EAP	East Asia and Pacific
ELL	Elbers, Lanjouw, and Lanjouw
FDI	Foreign Direct Investment
FGT	Foster-Greer-Thorbecke
FGT0	Poverty headcount
FGT1	Poverty gap
FGT2	Squared poverty gap
GAPAP	Governance and Poverty Policy Analysis and Advice
GDI	Gender Development Index
GDP	Gross Domestic Product
GSO	General Statistics Office
HCMC	Ho Chi Minh City
HCR	Headcount Rate

HDI	Human Development Index
HOI	Human Opportunity Index
ILSSA	Institute of Labour, Science, and Social Affairs
IMF	International Monetary Fund
MCP	Monetary Child Poverty (rate)
MDCP	Multi-dimensional Child Poverty (rate)
MDG	Millenium Development Goal
MICS	Multi-Indicator Cluster Survey
MOC	Ministry of Construction
MOET	Ministry of Education and Training
MOH	Ministry of Health
MOLISA	Ministry of Labor, Invalids, and Social Affairs
MPI	Ministry of Planning and Investment
MPI	Multi-dimensional Poverty Index
NGO	Nongovernmental organization
NHDR	National Human Development Report (UNDP)
NSS	National Sample Survey
NTP-PR	National Targeted Program for Poverty Reduction
NTP-SPR	National Targeted Program for Sustainable Poverty Reduction
PA	Poverty Assessment
PAPI	Public Administration Performance Index
PM	Prime Minister
POVCALNET	PovcalNet, the WB's online poverty analysis tool
PPA	Participatory Poverty Assessment
PPP	Purchasing Power Parity
PREM	Poverty Reduction and Economic Management
PRSP	Poverty Reduction Strategy Paper
RAFC	Rural Agriculture and Fishery Census
RCS	Ravallion, Chen, and Sangraula
RIM	Rural Impact Monitoring
SCOLI	Spatial Cost of Living Index
SEDP	Socio-Economic Development Plan
SEDS	Socio-Economic Development Strategy
SOE	State-owned enterprise

SPB	Social Policy Bank
TFESSD	Trust Fund for Environmentally and Socially Sustainable Development
UNDP	United Nations Development Programme
UNFPA	United Nations Population Fund
UNICEF	United Nations Children's Fund
USAID	United States Agency for International Development
VASS	Vietnam Academy of Social Sciences
VBA	Vietnam Bank for Agriculture
VDR	Vietnam Development Report
VHLSS	Vietnam Household Living Standards Survey
VLSS	Vietnam Living Standards Survey
VPHC	Vietnam Population and Housing Census
WDI	World Development Indicators
WHO	World Health Organization
WTO	World Trade Organization

OVERVIEW

Vietnam has had a remarkable record on economic growth and poverty reduction over the last two decades. Using a basic-needs poverty line initially agreed in the early 1990s,[1] the poverty headcount fell from 58 percent in the early 1990s to 14.5 percent by 2008 and to well below 10 percent by 2010. Similar progress in the face of steadily rising incomes is evident when assessed by "global" standards of US$1.25 and US$2.00 per person per day (2005 purchasing power parity, PPP). Progress has also been substantial in other dimensions of well-being, including high rates of primary and secondary school enrollment, improved health status, and lower morbidity and mortality. Vietnam has achieved—and in some cases surpassed—most of the Millennium Development Goals.

Despite remarkable progress, the task of reducing poverty in Vietnam is not finished. Vietnam's basic-needs poverty line, agreed in the early 1990s, is low by international standards, and the methods used to monitor poverty since then are outdated: the poverty standards that applied to Vietnam's emerging economy in the 1990s are no longer relevant to modern-day, rising middle-income Vietnam. In addition, although tens of millions of Vietnamese households have risen out of poverty, many have incomes very close to the poverty line and remain vulnerable to falling back into poverty as a result of idiosyncratic and related economy-wide shocks, including the adverse effects of climate change on rainfall and temperatures, human and animal influenza pandemics, and impacts of the 2008–09 global financial crisis. Economic growth has faltered in recent years as a result of continuing macroeconomic instability accompanied by sharp bouts of inflation; the economy grew at a decade low of 5.3 percent in 2012, with similar levels expected over the next several years. Vietnam's leadership faces the daunting task of responding to citizens' rising aspirations for greater security and economic prosperity in the context of slowing growth and difficult economic conditions.

In important respects, the task of poverty reduction has become more difficult, because Vietnam's success has created new challenges. The remaining poor are harder to reach and face the challenges of isolation, limited assets, low levels of education, and poor health status. At the same time, poverty reduction has become less responsive to economic growth. Poverty among the country's ethnic minorities is a growing and persistent challenge. Although Vietnam's 53 ethnic minority groups make up less than 15 percent of the population, they accounted for 47 percent of the poor in 2010, compared to only 29 percent in 1998.

Rapid structural transformation and Vietnam's ongoing transition to a market economy have given rise to new patterns of development that bring additional challenges for poverty reduction. Inequality in incomes and opportunities are rising, underpinned by continuing disparities in human development between urban and rural areas and widening disparities within rural areas and across socioeconomic groups. Poorer areas are still not well connected to markets. While coverage of local infrastructure and basic services is good in most regions, reliability (for example, of electricity) and quality of services are uneven. Vietnam's push toward modernization and industrialization has had mixed impacts on the overall quality of life. The pace of urbanization is accelerating, and increasing numbers of rural workers are migrating to cities in search of jobs in industry and services. Many of these jobs are informal and lack the benefits historically provided by the public sector and state-owned enterprises. There is growing demand for young, skilled workers, but many older workers do not have the training or skills to compete for jobs in the expanding modern economy.

A new poverty assessment for Vietnam, entitled *Well Begun, Not Yet Done: Vietnam's Remarkable Progress on Poverty Reduction and the Emerging Challenges*, was finalized in December 2012. It was led by the World Bank (WB) and the Vietnam Academy of Social Sciences (VASS), working in collaboration with the General Statistics Office (GSO) and a team of local and international consultants. This new poverty assessment—presented in this book—takes a fresh look at the lives of poor men, women, and children and explores the constraints and opportunities they face in rising out of poverty. Building on a rich body of poverty analysis and an excellent base of knowledge from previous poverty assessments (in 1995, 2000, 2003, and 2008), it has three aims. First, it proposes revisions to Vietnam's poverty monitoring system—including better data, updated welfare aggregates, and new poverty lines—to bring the system more in line with economic and social conditions in present-day Vietnam. Second, it revisits the stylized facts about poverty and deprivation in Vietnam and develops an updated profile of poverty using data from the 2010 Vietnam Household Living Standards Survey (VHLSS) and new qualitative field studies. Third, it aims to forge a consensus around some of the key challenges for poverty reduction in the next decade, including changing regional patterns of poverty and wealth, high and persistent poverty among ethnic minorities, and rising inequality in outcomes and opportunities.

Improved systems for monitoring poverty

Vietnam has used two very different approaches to measuring poverty and monitoring progress over time. Both were initiated in the early 1990s, and both have evolved since then.

The first approach was developed by the Ministry of Labor, Invalids, and Social Affairs (MOLISA), the agency assigned primary responsibility for Vietnam's poverty reduction programs and policies in the early 1990s. MOLISA is tasked with proposing official urban and rural poverty lines at the beginning of each five-year Socio-Economic Development Plan (SEDP) and with setting the initial-period poverty rate. Using official lines, MOLISA is responsible for assessing changes in poverty and updating the official list of poor households on an annual basis, using a "bottom-up" mix of local surveys and village-level consultations to count the number of poor at the local (commune) level. These local counts are then aggregated up to estimate provincial and national poverty rates. Progress is assessed against poverty reduction targets set in the SEDP. The MOLISA lines were initially derived on the basis of rice equivalents, but since 2005 they have been calculated using a cost-of-basic-needs (CBN) methodology similar to the approach led by the General Statistics Office, which is described next. The official lines are typically not adjusted for annual inflation; they are only revised after five years. MOLISA uses the official lines and resulting provincial poverty estimates to set budget allocations and determine eligibility for targeted poverty reduction programs, most notably the National Targeted Program for Sustainable Poverty Reduction, but other programs as well (for example, free health insurance).

The second approach, which is led by the GSO, measures poverty and monitors progress on the basis of a series of nationally representative household surveys. The GSO uses two methods to measure poverty—one based on official poverty lines (adjusted for inflation) applied to per capita incomes and one based on per capita consumption using a poverty line, developed by a joint GSO and World Bank team in the late 1990s. The original GSO-WB poverty line was constructed using the standard CBN methodology, based on a reference food basket for poor households anchored in nutritional norms plus an additional allocation for essential nonfood needs. Unlike Vietnam's official poverty lines, the GSO-WB line has been kept roughly constant in real purchasing power since the late 1990s and been applied to per capita consumption measured in successive rounds of Vietnam's living standard surveys to estimate poverty at the national, urban-rural, and regional levels. The original GSO-WB methodology has been used widely in Vietnam and in international forums to monitor changes in poverty, beginning with two rounds of the Vietnam Living Standards Survey (VLSS) in 1993 and 1998 and then continuing under the GSO's leadership with an expanded Vietnam Household Living Standards Survey (VHLSS), conducted in 2002, 2004, 2006, and 2008. The national poverty rates reported in figure O.1 are based on the original GSO-WB poverty line.

FIGURE 0.1 **Economic growth and poverty reduction in Vietnam: Two decades of progress, 1993–2008**

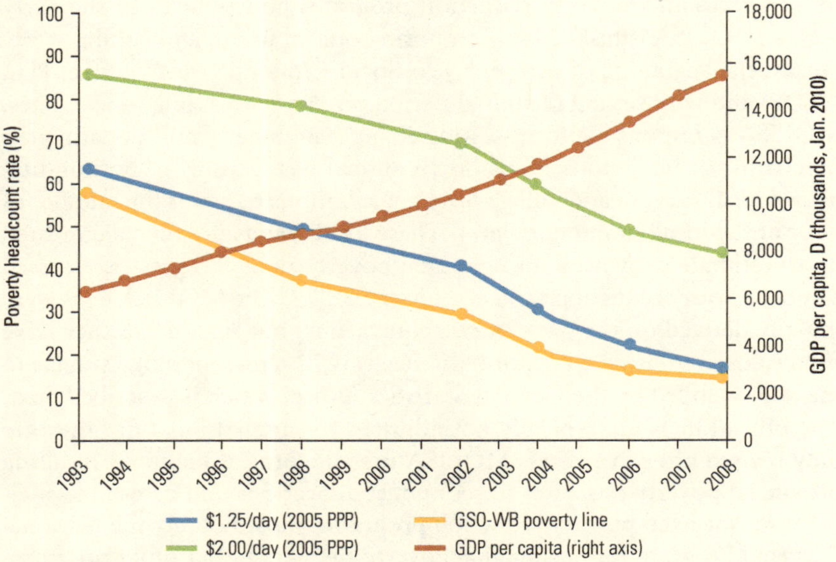

Source: Estimates based on the original GSO-WB poverty line.
Note: PPP = purchasing power parity.

The two separate systems for measuring and monitoring poverty produce widely different poverty estimates, and their continuing use has, at times, complicated the dialogue between the development community and local researchers (who typically use the GSO-WB approach) and the government (which uses the official methodology). While the poverty trends from the two monitoring systems are similar—both show excellent progress—the poverty levels are different, reflecting differences both in methodology and in intended use. Vietnam's official poverty lines and the methodology used by MOLISA are fundamentally influenced by the availability of resources; they are revised every five years in the work leading up to the Socio-Economic Development Plan and are used over the plan period to target scarce public resources to those most in need. In contrast, the GSO-WB poverty lines are independent of budget considerations and are used primarily to monitor changes in poverty over time.

Updating the GSO-WB poverty monitoring system

Consistency in methodology and comparability over time are two of the great strengths of Vietnam's poverty monitoring system. However, by the end of the 2000s, key aspects of the system had become outdated. The methods used to measure household well-being and construct the original GSO-WB poverty line were based on economic conditions and the consumption patterns of poor households in the early 1990s. The country has changed dramatically since then, and the Vietnamese people live very differently today than they did more than two decades ago.

Beginning in 2009, a team from the World Bank worked closely with local and international experts and in collaboration with the GSO to update Vietnam's poverty monitoring system. The design of the 2010 VHLSS (and subsequent rounds) was improved, and a new sample frame was developed on the basis of the 2009 Housing and Population Census. The definition of the consumption aggregate was revised to make it a more comprehensive measure of well-being. New spatial cost-of-living indexes (SCOLIs) were calculated using a special survey of consumer prices carried out in conjunction with the 2010 VHLSS. A new poverty line was then constructed using an approach similar to that of the original GSO-WB poverty line, but based on a more comprehensive measure of well-being, updated consumption patterns of the poor (from the 2010 VHLSS), and the new SCOLIs.

The new GSO-WB poverty line for 2010 was D 653,000 per person per month (US$2.26 per person per day), which is substantially higher than the original GSO-WB poverty line (all US$ in this paragraph are 2005 PPP). The increase reflects improvements in the quality of the food reference basket (fewer calories from rice, more consumption of proteins, vegetables, and fats) and a higher allocation for spending on essential nonfood products, including housing and durable goods. A new "extreme poverty" GSO-WB line was also calculated to replace the previous food poverty line: its value in 2010 was D 435,000 per person per month (US$1.50). The new GSO-WB poverty lines compare to Vietnam's official poverty lines for the current SEDP (announced in September 2010) of D 400,000 per person per month (US$1.29) for rural areas and D 500,000 per person per month (US$1.61) for urban areas.

Using the new GSO-WB poverty line and improved methodology, 20.7 percent of Vietnam's population were still poor in 2010, including 27 percent of the population living in rural areas and 6 percent living in urban areas, and 8 percent were extremely poor (table O.1). The official poverty rate, based on Vietnam's official urban and rural poverty lines, was 14.2 percent. Although the regional distribution of the poor is similar between the two approaches, poverty levels are substantially higher in aggregate according to the GSO-WB methodology. However, official estimates suggest that poverty is higher in urban areas and in the north-central and south-central coastal regions. The GSO-WB approach indicates substantially higher levels of poverty in rural areas, in part due to differences between the official poverty lines and the new GSO-WB poverty line, but

TABLE 0.1 New poverty estimates for Vietnam, by region and urban or rural areas, 2010
Percent

| Indicator | GSO-WB poverty estimates | | | | Official poverty estimates | | Share of total population |
| | Poverty | | Extreme poverty | | | | |
	Rate	Contribution to total	Rate	Contribution to total	Rate	Contribution to total	
All Vietnam (national)	20.7	100	8	100	14.2	100	100
Urban	6	9	1.5	6	6.9	6	30
Rural	27	91	10.7	94	17.4	94	70
Red River Delta (Hanoi)	11.4	12	2.8	8	8.34	13	22
Northeastern mountains	37.3	21	17.9	26	24.2	20	11
Northwestern mountains	60.1	9	36.5	14	39.4	9	3
North-central coast	28.4	16	9.7	15	24	20	12
South-central coast	18.1	7	5.9	6	16.9	10	9
Central highlands	32.8	10	17	13	22.2	9	6
Southeast (Ho Chi Minh City)	8.6	7	3.1	7	2.3	4	18
Mekong Delta	18.7	17	4.8	11	12.6	17	19

Sources: 2010 VHLSS.

also due to important differences in methodology. The GSO-WB poverty rate was calculated using the 2010 VHLSS and detailed measures of household welfare; in contrast, MOLISA's official poverty rates were calculated at the commune level using a combination of short-form questionnaires and local consultations and then aggregated up from the commune level to the provincial and national levels.

Neither methodology is inherently better than the other. Rather, they are designed to serve different and equally valid objectives. The strength of the GSO-WB approach lies in its consistent measurement over time and space and its independence from budgetary or political considerations. It serves an important monitoring function. In contrast, Vietnam's official poverty lines and bottom-up methodology are intended to support the setting of targets and the determination of resource allocations for the government's poverty reduction and social protection programs and policies.

Revisiting the facts about poverty and the poor

The new GSO-WB poverty line was used to construct an updated profile of poverty based on the 2010 VHLSS, complemented by new information collected through participatory poverty assessments and qualitative field studies. The poverty rate—defined as the proportion of the population living below the poverty line—is a widely understood and frequently reported measure of poverty. But it ignores the fact that all poor people are not the same: some have incomes or consumption levels very close to the poverty line, while others live in much poorer conditions, well below the standards set by the poverty line. The new 2010 poverty profile differentiates between the *total poor* (individuals living below the GSO-WB poverty line) and the *extreme poor* (individuals living below two-thirds of the GSO-WB poverty line). In 2010, 20.7 percent of the population were poor, and just over one-third of these (8 percent of the population) were extremely poor.

The updated poverty profile shows that many of the factors that characterized Vietnam's poor in the 1990s still characterize the poor today: low educational achievement and limited job skills, heavy dependence on subsistence agriculture, physical and social isolation, specific disadvantages linked to ethnic identity, and exposure to natural disasters and risks. Over the past decade, rising levels of education and diversification into off-farm activities have been powerful forces for poverty reduction. The remaining poor still reside predominately in rural areas, and their livelihoods depend primarily on agriculture and related activities.

But some of the stylized facts about poverty in Vietnam have changed. Concerns about ethnic minority poverty were only beginning to emerge in the late 1990s; these concerns have become much greater today as the gap continues to widen between minority populations and the Kinh majority. The report documents great diversity across Vietnam's 53 ethnic minority groups and finds encouraging signs of progress for some minority groups in some regions. But the concentration of minorities among the poor has continued to rise; in 1993, poverty was widespread, and minorities constituted only 20 percent of all poor households. By 1998, the share of minorities among the poor had increased to 29 percent, and by 2010 minorities accounted for 47 percent of the total poor and a resounding 68 percent of the extremely poor. The gap in living standards between ethnic minorities and the Kinh majority is very large: 66.3 percent of ethnic minorities were still poor in 2010, compared to only 12.9 percent of the Kinh, and a substantial 37.4 percent of ethnic minorities were still extremely poor, compared to only 2.9 percent of the Kinh.

The majority of poor ethnic minorities continue to live in more isolated and less productive upland regions of Vietnam, and most (three-quarters) of their total income comes from agriculture and allied activities. In contrast, poor Kinh have more diversified labor and earnings portfolios and live in coastal and delta regions. The depth and severity of poverty are much less for poor Kinh than for poor ethnic minorities.

Our analysis suggests that agriculture will continue to be an important source of income for the poor in Vietnam, including but not limited to ethnic minorities. Compared to many other countries, agricultural land is equitably distributed in Vietnam, and the continuing shift out of subsistence agriculture and into more commercial activities has been an important driver of poverty reduction. This has been accompanied by a rapid expansion in opportunities for off-farm employment and income diversification over the last decade. Despite this, the link between landlessness and poverty has increased, particularly in the Mekong Delta.

Vietnamese today are far better educated and better skilled than they were a decade ago. Primary school completion rates were already high by the end of the 1990s. Since then, there has been a rapid increase in enrollments at lower- and upper-secondary levels, leading to a substantial increase in the number of students who attend colleges and universities. Nevertheless, lack of education continues to be an important determinant of poverty: in 2010, 46 percent of poor households and 58 percent of extremely poor households were headed by persons who had not completed primary school. Worrisome gaps persist between enrollments for children from poor and better-off households. Most primary-school-age children—rich and poor, minority and majority—are enrolled in school. But enrollments among (poor) minorities drop off at the lower-secondary level, and children from lower-income households are much less likely to be enrolled in upper-secondary schools than children from better-off households, perpetuating intergenerational poverty. Differential enrollments also contribute to rising inequality. According to the 2010 VHLSS, 40 percent of persons 21 years and older in the richest quintile had completed a university degree; in contrast, less than 2 percent in the poorest quintile were university graduates. In fact, more than a quarter of those in the poorest quintile had not even completed primary school by 2010.

The impacts of demographic factors on poverty have changed since the late 1990s. Child poverty continues to be a concern, although less so than in the 1990s, when poor rural households had many children and struggled to feed and educate them. As a result of family planning policies initiated in the early 1990s, most households now have only one or two children, and many of the adult children from the large families of the 1990s are helping to support their parents and siblings. Aging is a new demographic risk. Vietnam's population is aging, and our analysis suggests that the elderly, particularly those living alone, may be increasingly at risk of future poverty. Although targeting is good, existing poverty and social protection programs provide only partial coverage and limited benefits to poor and at-risk individuals. In 2010, only half of the extreme poor (measured in terms of the GSO-WB methodology) reported that they were eligible to receive benefits from MOLISA's poverty reduction programs.

Emerging challenges: Changing spatial patterns of poverty and rising inequality

New poverty maps were developed based on the 2009 Housing and Population Census and the 2010 VHLSS. The maps show that poverty is becoming more concentrated in upland regions of Vietnam, including the northeast and northwest mountains and parts of the central highlands (map O.1). In contrast, complementary household "wealth" maps[2] indicate that better-off households are concentrated primarily in the Red River Delta (near Hanoi) and the southeast (near Ho Chi Minh City) and in urban centers along the coast. Although poverty rates are low in urban areas, lower-income residents struggle to cope with the rising cost of living (including rising electricity rates, water tariffs, and fuel prices), and many work in the informal sector without social protection or employment benefits. Urban poverty is most prevalent in Vietnam's small cities and towns, which lag behind Vietnam's larger cities in terms of basic infrastructure and public services.

Ethnic minorities make up 15 percent of the population in Vietnam and nearly half of the remaining poor. They are concentrated in upland regions, which have more difficult growing conditions, less infrastructure, and much poorer connectivity. However, location is only one factor that accounts for the large gap in living conditions between ethnic minorities and the majority Kinh. As shown on map O.2, even in the same (upland) districts, poverty is substantially higher among ethnic minorities (by a factor of four to six) than among the Kinh majority. The persistent gap con-

MAP 0.1 **Poverty rates in Vietnam, by region, 1999 and 2009**

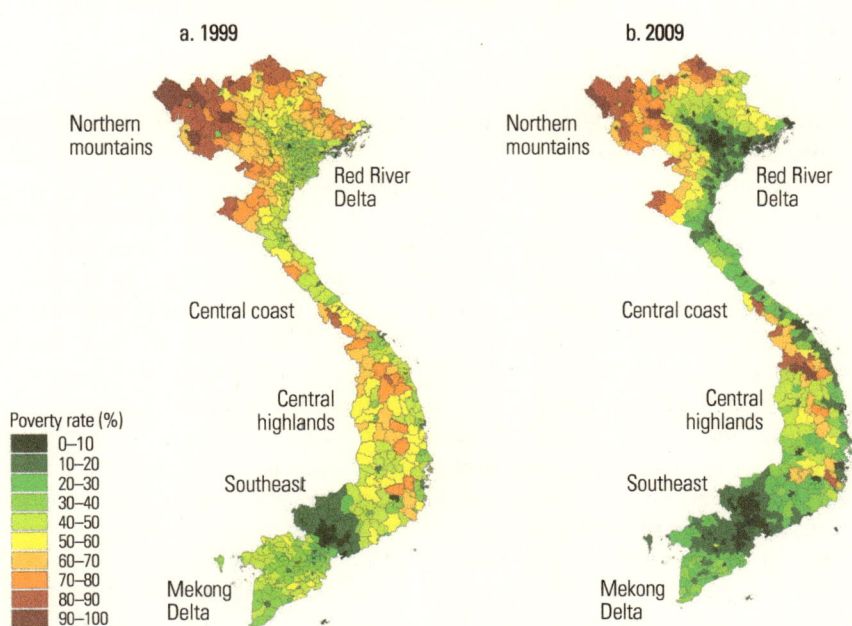

Sources: GSO 2009 (estimates based on the 2009 Population and Housing Census and the 2010 VHLSS). The 1999 poverty rates are from Minot, Baulch, and Epprecht 2003.

MAP O.2 Poverty rates in Vietnam, by ethnicity, 2009

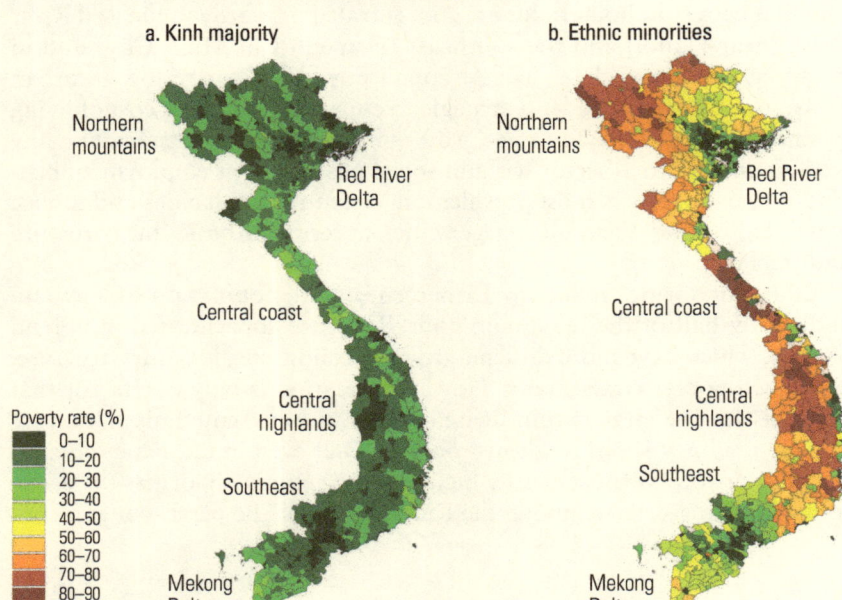

Source: Estimates based on the 2009 Population and Housing Census and the 2010 VHLSS.

tributes to very high levels of inequality in poor regions with substantial minority populations.

The book looks at inequality through two lenses—the first based on empirical analysis of various rounds of the VHLSS and the second drawing on findings from a new qualitative field study of "perceptions of inequality" that was carried out in sites throughout Vietnam. The perceptions study draws on a diverse and rich set of individual interviews and focus group discussions that highlight which types of inequalities are considered as unacceptable by Vietnamese people and provide information on less easily measured inequalities, such as inequalities in connections, voice, and influence. It documents widespread concerns across the population about rising inequality. The quantitative analysis examines the factors driving the rise in inequality, including geographic and sectoral variations in growth processes and disparities in education by ethnic identity. The rise in income inequality reflects, in part, a growth process that has altered the relative returns to assets, such as education and productive capital in the economy. Growth has interacted with existing inequalities in opportunities—inequalities in education and access to good jobs, patterns of social exclusion, and geographic disparities—to increase income inequality and widen the welfare gaps between rich and poor households. The persistent and rising gap between the incomes and living conditions of ethnic minorities and the Kinh majority contributes in important ways to rising inequality.

Our analysis identifies important avenues for future research. More work is needed to understand old and new sources of vulnerability, including urbanization and changing patterns of employment, as well as aging and health shocks. In addition, Vietnam's targeted poverty reduction policies and programs should be analyzed in more depth, focusing on policies designed specifically to reduce poverty among ethnic minorities, where challenges clearly remain. Although Vietnam has successfully eradicated extreme poverty and hunger in all but a few isolated areas, there are widespread concerns about rising inequality in opportunities and outcomes. New work is needed to understand the various sources of inequality and, more important, to facilitate discussion in Vietnam on what is the appropriate role of public policy in addressing them.

Emerging policy and program implications

The poverty assessment focused primarily on poverty and inequality diagnostics; as such, it aimed to support a better-informed debate on policy and program responses among stakeholders in Vietnam, including government ministries, the National Assembly, local researchers and research institutes, domestic and international nongovernmental organizations, international partners, and the wider research community. Building on these diagnostics, work is under way with the Vietnam Academy of Social Sciences and other stakeholders in Vietnam to develop a more comprehensive policy framework for poverty reduction. The emerging framework has four areas of focus.

First, to put Vietnam back on the path of high and sustained economic growth, it is essential for Vietnam to reduce volatility and macroeconomic instability and to undertake the complementary structural reforms—restructuring state-owned enterprises, reforming the financial sector, raising the effectiveness of public investments, and moving to a more transparent and open development process. But the quality of growth matters as much as the rate of growth.

Second, measures are needed to make Vietnam's future economic growth more inclusive—for example, supporting productivity and growth in the rural sector by improving connectivity, strengthening skills, improving the investment climate, expanding access to basic services, and improving the targeting of agriculture-support measures (for example, credit, agricultural extension, and market information) to the needs of poor and ethnic minority farmers. Support for labor-intensive industries and small and medium enterprises in both formal and informal sectors can also contribute to inclusive growth, including better access to credit and training, expanded vocational training for youth in poor and ethnic minority areas, and incentives for local enterprise development to provide more diversified employment options in local communities. The occupational and geographic mobility of labor should be enhanced: migration of rural workers to Vietnam's rapidly growing cities has been a powerful force for growth and poverty reduction in the past. It is also important to reduce inequality of opportunities, including improving the quality of education and promoting skills development, particularly in rural areas and for ethnic minority groups. Improving governance through greater transparency and accountability will help to increase local participation and reduce existing inequalities in voice and power that work to undermine inclusive growth.

Third, policies to promote growth must be complemented by effective social insurance and social assistance policies. It is essential for Vietnam to protect social spending and social assistance in the process of economic restructuring. Social benefits and the official poverty lines used to target these benefits should be indexed to inflation, adjusted to capture differences in the spatial cost of living, particularly between rural and urban areas, and to ensure that these take account of the basket of goods and services consumed by the poor. Better measures are needed to protect poor and vulnerable households from the rising cost of basic services, including, for example, rising electricity costs in the context of the planned phase-out of the energy subsidy. Migrant workers have been particularly hard hit by the rising cost of living in urban areas; they need to have equal access to basic services, portable benefits (including health insurance), and better access to social protection programs in their new place of residence.

Finally, Vietnam's poverty monitoring system should be updated on a regular and more frequent basis so that it provides a reliable source of information for policy making in Vietnam's rapidly changing economy. To this effect, objective resource-independent poverty lines (like the new GSO-WB poverty line) should be used in parallel with resource-linked targeting lines (like Vietnam's official poverty lines and the poverty lines used by authorities in Hanoi and Ho Chi Minh City), and the source and appropriate application of the two types of poverty lines should be communicated clearly to policy makers, practitioners, and the public. Future poverty profiles and poverty estimates should be constructed in an open and transparent way; making more data on poverty, inequality, and social programs publicly available would facilitate better monitoring of progress by independent experts and the public at large.

Notes

1. The General Statistics Office–World Bank (GSO-WB) poverty line was constructed in the late 1990s using data collected in the 1993 Vietnam Living Stan-

dards Survey; it was presented in the 2000 Vietnam poverty assessment, entitled *Attacking Poverty*, carried out by the joint government, donor, and nongovernmental organization Poverty Working Group.
2. Defined as the share of individuals in the top 15 percent of per capita consumption.

References

GSO (General Statistics Office of Vietnam). 2009. *Population and Housing Census Vietnam 2009*. Hanoi: GSO.

Minot, Nicholas, Bob Baulch, and Michael Epprecht. 2003. "Poverty and Inequality in Vietnam: Spatial Patterns and Geographic Determinants." Final report of Project Poverty Mapping and Market Access in Vietnam, conducted by the International Food Policy Research Institute and the Institute of Development Studies, Washington, DC.

CHAPTER 1

Vietnam's Growth and Poverty Reduction Record: Remarkable Success, but Big Remaining Challenges

Vietnam has made remarkable progress at reducing extreme poverty and promoting shared prosperity over the last two decades. But the task of poverty reduction is not yet finished: promoting inclusive and sustained growth, addressing ethnic minority poverty, and reducing vulnerability and inequality are major challenges going forward.

Vietnam experienced high and sustained rates of economic growth over the last two decades, driven by a series of market-oriented reforms launched in the late 1980s. Initial progress was the result of reforms in the rural economy, which led to a highly egalitarian distribution of agricultural land to rural households and on-farm diversification. Early reforms provided the right incentives for higher farm production and export orientation in the agriculture sector. In recent years, job creation in the private sector has become a driving force behind Vietnam's high economic growth, complemented by greater integration of agriculture in the market economy and further opening of the Vietnamese economy to global trade and investment. Vietnam's accession to the World Trade Organization (WTO) in early 2007 created opportunities for a new round of reforms and the potential for additional changes in the policy and business environment. These changes have had major implications for future economic growth and poverty reduction. But the opportunities have been accompanied by new challenges and risks. Growth has slowed in recent years, and Vietnam has struggled with periods of macroeconomic instability and bouts of high inflation.

Vietnam's historical growth patterns have been remarkably pro-poor; growth in per capita gross domestic product (GDP) averaged 6.1 percent a

FIGURE 1.1 Growth and poverty reduction in Vietnam, 1993–2008

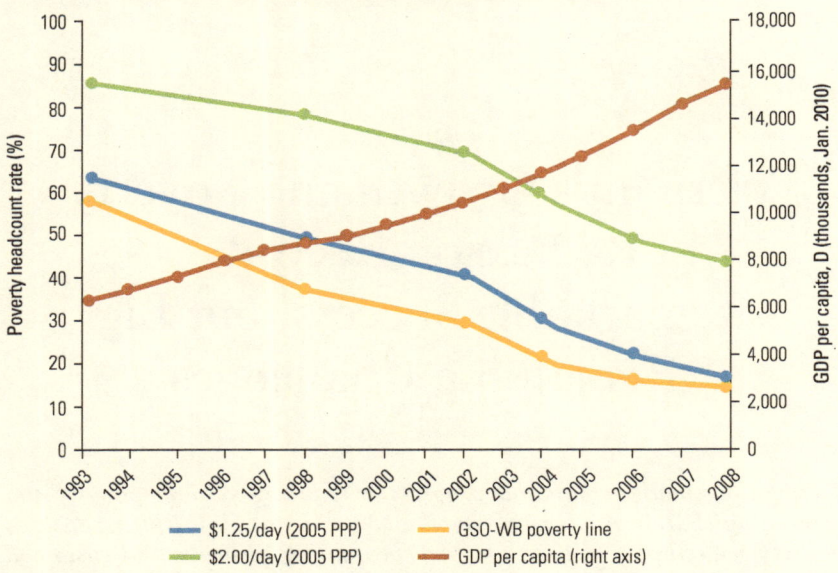

Source: GSO-WB poverty headcount calculated using the 1993 and 1998 Vietnam Living Standards Survey (VLSS) and the 2004–10 Vietnam Household Living Standards Survey (VHLSS). Dollar-a-day poverty rates are reported by the World Bank at http://iresearch.worldbank.org/povcalnet/index.htm.

year between 1993 and 2008, and poverty fell an average of 2.9 percentage points a year (figure 1.1).

Despite remarkable progress, Vietnam's task of poverty reduction is not finished, and in important respects it has become more difficult. This chapter takes stock of Vietnam's past record at reducing poverty and improving living conditions—which is remarkable judged by any standard—and highlights several remaining and new challenges. It argues that the task of poverty reduction is by no means complete and that it will become more difficult in the face of growing affluence and rising aspirations, as Vietnamese society becomes more heterogeneous, market-oriented reforms continue, and Vietnam becomes more integrated into the global economy.

Rapid growth and structural transformation of the Vietnamese economy

Comprehensive economic reforms were launched in the second half of the 1980s under *Doi Moi* and have accelerated over the last two decades. As a result of the reform process, the economy has been liberalized both internally and externally. Passage of the revised Land Law in 1993 and introduction of the Enterprise Law in 2000 were among the most important domestic reforms. The accession of Vietnam to the WTO is widely recognized as a key milestone in the country's external liberalization. Vietnam announced an ambitious plan to restructure the economy and shift to a new growth model in 2011, taking an important step in its ongoing transition toward a market economy.

The Land Law of 1993 marked the continuation of a program of agricultural reforms that were initiated in 1988 with implementation of Resolution 10. Resolution 10 radically changed the incentive system in the rural sector by recognizing, for the first time, households as the basic production unit of Vietnam's agrarian economy and granting them five basic rights: to transfer, exchange, inherit, rent, and mortgage their land. The law also extended the lease term to 20 years for annual cropland and 50 years for perennial cropland. The implementation of this law resulted in an extensive land titling program. In terms of scale and speed of implementation, it was one of the largest rural land titling programs in the developing world (Iyer and Do 2008). Resolution 10 and the Land Law of 1993 together played a crucial role in boosting agricultural growth in the 1990s, thus enabling Vietnam to stop being a food-deficit country in the 1980s and to become one of the world's largest rice exporters by the end of the 2000s.

A series of additional policy reforms outside the agriculture sector helped to lay the foundation for rapid expansion of the private sector, whose role was officially recognized by Vietnam's 1992 constitution. The most important milestone was the Enterprise Law of January 2000, which represented a radical change in approach from the preceding Private Enterprise Law and the Company Law, both of which were approved in 1990. Private enterprises were allowed to operate prior to 2000, but were subjected to a series of government approvals and controls. With the introduction of the new Enterprise Law, citizens were allowed to establish and operate private businesses with limited intervention from government officials. The most important innovations introduced by the Enterprise Law were the simplification of registration procedures and the associated elimination of a large number of business licenses, which sharply reduced transaction costs for businesses and helped to instill greater business confidence. As a result of these reforms, the number of registered enterprises increased almost 15 times within only 10 years, from 31,000 in 2000 to 460,000 in 2009, according to Vietnam's Ministry of Planning and Investment.

External liberalization accelerated at all levels—unilateral, bilateral, regional, and multilateral—over the last two decades. Beginning in the late 1980s, tariffs were unilaterally reduced, and numerous quantitative restrictions on trade were abolished. Subsequently, Vietnam actively participated in bilateral and regional trade agreements. Membership in the Association of Southeast Asian Nations (ASEAN) in 1995 and its associated Asian Free Trade Area and the U.S.-Vietnam Bilateral Trade Agreement in 2001 were important steps in the integration process. Vietnam officially acceded to the WTO in January 2007. Becoming a WTO member has had important implications for Vietnam's development: major changes are taking place at the border (a reduction in import tariffs and removal of nontariff barriers to trade), beyond the border (greater access to overseas markets and to the WTO's dispute settlement mechanism), and behind the border (opening of service sectors and distribution systems and changes in legal and regulatory frameworks). Implementation of these agreements not only helped to promote exports and restructuring in the domestic economy, but also became key drivers of reform of the main institutional underpinnings of a market economy, including legal and judicial structures. The Common Investment Law of 2005, for example, helped to harmonize the treatment and regulation of all types of businesses, including domestic firms, foreign firms, and cooperatives.

Two decades of reform have helped to sustain high growth in the economy, transforming Vietnam in the process. Even with the marked slowdown in economic activity in the last few years, the Vietnamese economy has grown at an annual rate of more than 8 percent over the last decade. Today, the Vietnamese economy is four times larger than it was in the early 1990s, and the country now ranks as a lower-middle-income country. In 2010, per capita gross national income was more than US$3,000 in 2005 purchasing power parity (PPP).

This growth has been accompanied by pronounced structural changes at the aggregate level. Two decades ago, Vietnam was primarily rural, with nearly 80 percent of the population living in the countryside and only 20 percent residing in cities and towns. The urban sector was dominated by two major economic and political hubs: Hanoi in the north and Ho Chi Minh City in the south. In terms of GDP, slightly more than 40 percent of the economy was generated by agriculture, followed by services and then industry. The agriculture sector (cropping and farm sidelines) played an important role in the early years of Vietnam's development success. However, its share of GDP has fallen to half of what it was in the early 1990s, and in 2010 it contributed only 20 percent of GDP. Industry, which includes manufacturing, construction, and utilities, has been the most rapidly growing and dynamic sector and currently makes up 38 percent of GDP. Services contribute 42 percent, modestly higher than the level in the early 1990s.

These changes in the structure of the economy are largely mirrored in the composition of employment in Vietnam. In the early 1990s, three-quarters of the labor force cited agriculture as their primary source of employment, with only 10 and 15 percent, respectively, in industry and services. Rapid productivity growth in the farm sector has contributed to rising incomes in the countryside; equally important, it has enabled a growing share of labor to engage in even higher-value activities in industry and services. Today, the share of the labor force working in agriculture has fallen below 50 percent, while the share in both industry and services has doubled.

Accompanying this shift in the composition of employment has been a change in its type, most notably a reduction outside of agriculture in the role of self-employment (largely small, family-run businesses) relative to wage employment. The role of the state in wage employment has also declined. Overall, however, the state employs a slightly larger percentage (upward of 20 percent) of the labor force than it did in the early 1990s, reflecting the growth in wage employment in the state-owned enterprise sector. Urbanization, aided by migration from the countryside, has been increasing, but according to Vietnam's 2009 Housing and Population Census, only 30 percent of the population is classified as urban. This puts urbanization in Vietnam at levels observed elsewhere in Southeast Asia about a decade ago.

Thanks to external liberalization, Vietnam's foreign trade has grown at more than twice the rate of GDP, and in 2010 the foreign trade ratio (imports plus exports as a percentage of GDP) was an unprecedented 165 percent. By comparison, at its peak in China in 2006, it was only 70 percent. The composition of exports has slowly shifted. Exports of oil and agricultural products continue to remain important, but labor-intensive light manufacturing goods now represent the fastest-growing component of exports. Imports of capital machinery and intermediate goods dominate on the other side of the ledger. Export growth has been aided by the run-up in foreign direct investment in Vietnam, which rose from only US$0.5 billion in 1992 to around US$11.0 billion by 2010, with much of this growth occurring after WTO entry. Rapidly rising wages in China make Vietnam very appealing. Currently, foreign-invested firms are the source of half of Vietnam's non-oil exports. In terms of employment, however, these firms still employ less than 2 percent of the labor force.

In addition to productivity growth, rising rates of investment in the domestic economy have been an important source of growth. This works through two channels—on the demand side, as an important source of growth in expenditure, and on the supply side, through investment's role in expanding the country's productive capacities and introducing new technology and know-how into the economy. Between 1992 and 2010, gross capital formation rose from only 17.6 percent of GDP to 38.9 percent, comparable to levels observed in Japan, the Republic of Korea, and Taiwan, China, at their peaks. In 2010, the World Bank put domestic savings at 33.2 percent of gross national income. With the government sector typically running fiscal deficits and state-run firms being net borrowers, the substantial increase in savings is coming from a more than doubling in the saving rates of households and private enterprises.

Finally, reform and rising incomes have had a profound impact on household demographic behavior and population growth. In the early 1990s, average fertility rates of 3.4 births per woman translated into population growth rates of nearly 2 percent a year. By 2010, fertility had fallen to 1.8, below replacement levels, and population was growing at only 1 percent. Over the same period, average household size declined by nearly one person, from five to four. With the sharp drop in fertility, the percentage of the population of working age has increased, pushing labor force participation rates upward from 50 to 60 percent of the entire population. Vietnam's falling dependency ratio—that is, the ratio of those not working to those in the labor force—has had a direct impact on per capita incomes and an indirect effect through rising savings and investment rates and the demographic dividend.

Vietnam's remarkable progress in reducing poverty

Vietnam's dramatic decline in poverty is evident using a range of approaches to measure progress, whether assessed in terms of national or internationally comparable poverty lines based on data from household surveys or bottom-up community-based methods (box 1.1). The absolute number of poor people living in Vietnam has dropped sharply, and reductions in the poverty headcount have been accompanied by notable reductions in the depth and severity of poverty. However, progress has been uneven across regions and ethnic groups and has started to slow.

Measuring progress using Vietnamese and international poverty lines

The share of the population living below Vietnam's national poverty lines has declined dramatically. Figure 1.2 shows historical poverty trends based on GSO-WB estimates and official poverty lines and methods. The two separate systems for measuring and monitoring poverty produce widely different poverty estimates. Their continuing use has, at times, complicated the dialogue between the development community and local researchers (who typically use the GSO estimates) and the government (which tends to use the official MOLISA estimates). Although the use of different estimates sometimes has caused confusion, the ongoing development and use of rigorous approaches to measuring poverty have contributed to a better conceptualization of poverty on the part of government and the policy research community in Vietnam. Moreover, the higher poverty rates produced by the GSO methodology, particularly in the 1990s, helped to keep poverty high on the government's agenda.

Over time, as the poverty rate fell (narrowing the gap between MOLISA and GSO estimates) and as the poverty estimates produced through the VHLSS became increasingly recognized as valid and robust, MOLISA's poverty estimates have become more aligned with those produced by the GSO. As part of the work leading up to the 2011–16 SEDP, the government agreed formally to separate the two important tasks of (a) targeting poor households for social assistance and (b) measuring and monitoring

BOX 1.1 How does Vietnam monitor progress at reducing poverty?

Vietnam has used two very different approaches to measuring poverty and monitoring progress. Both were initiated in the early 1990s and have evolved over time.

The first approach was developed and led by the Ministry of Labor, Invalids, and Social Affairs (MOLISA), identified in the early 1990s as the primary government agency responsible for poverty reduction programs and policies. MOLISA is tasked with proposing official urban and rural poverty lines at the beginning of Vietnam's five-year Socio-Economic Development Plan (SEDP) and with setting the beginning-period poverty rate. MOLISA is also responsible for assessing changes in poverty and updating its list of poor households on an annual basis, using a "bottom-up" mix of local surveys and village-level consultations to count the number of poor at the local (commune) level. These local counts are then aggregated up to calculate annual provincial and national poverty rates. Progress is assessed against targets set in the SEDP. The MOLISA lines were initially based on rice equivalents, but since 2005 they have been calculated, with technical support from the General Statistics Office (GSO), using a cost-of-basic-needs (CBN) methodology similar to the approach led by the GSO, which is described next. Official lines are not adjusted annually for inflation, but they are revised in real terms every five years. MOLISA's primary objective is to determine budget allocations and define eligibility for several targeted poverty reduction programs (for example, the National Targeted Program for Sustainable Poverty Reduction).

The second approach, which is led by the GSO, measures poverty and monitors progress on the basis of nationally representative household surveys. GSO uses two different methods to measure poverty—one based on official poverty lines (adjusted for inflation) applied to per capita incomes and one using an approach developed by a joint GSO and World Bank (WB) team in the late 1990s and first used in the *Vietnam Development Report 2000: Attacking Poverty* (World Bank 1999). The GSO-WB poverty line is constructed using a standard CBN methodology, based on a reference food basket for poor households anchored in nutritional norms plus an additional allocation for essential nonfood needs. Unlike Vietnam's official poverty lines, the GSO-WB lines have been kept roughly constant in real purchasing power since the late 1990s and been applied to per capita consumer expenditures measured in successive rounds of the Vietnam Living Standards Survey (VLSS) and the Vietnam Household Living Standards Survey (VHLSS) to calculate poverty at the national, urban-rural, and regional levels.[a] The GSO-WB methodology has been used widely in Vietnam and in international forums to monitor changes in poverty since 1993. We use these poverty rates in figure 1.1.

---

a. In 1993 and 1998, the Vietnam Living Standards Survey was led and financed primarily by international partners. Starting in 2002, the GSO revised the VLSS questionnaire, scaled up the sample size, and changed the name to Vietnam Household Living Standards Survey. The VHLSS was conducted in 2002, 2004, 2006, 2008, 2010, and 2012 (thus far) under the leadership of the GSO and was financed primarily by the government.

FIGURE 1.2 Progress at reducing poverty in Vietnam according to GSO-WB and MOLISA monitoring systems, 1993–2011

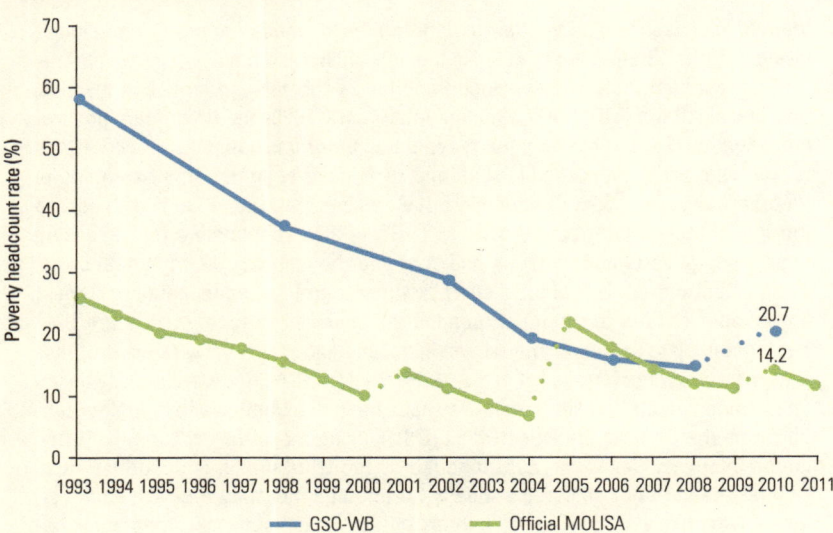

Sources: GSO-WB poverty headcount calculated using the 1993 and 1998 VLSS (World Bank 1995, 1999, 2003) and the 2004–10 VHLSS. MOLISA estimates taken from World Bank 2003; MOLISA 2014.
Note: The dots signify a break in the data because of a change in definition or methodology.

poverty over time.[1] The aim was to build on the strengths of both systems. As part of this agreement, the GSO was given formal responsibility for producing national and provincial poverty estimates, based on successive rounds of the VHLSS. MOLISA would identify which individual house-holds within provinces, districts, and communes should be included on its poverty list, and the GSO in consultation with MOLISA would propose a ceiling based on provincial poverty rates. The intention over the longer term was to align MOLISA and the GSO's poverty estimates at the national and provincial levels and to use the GSO's VHLSS-based measures of pov-erty to determine the aggregate number of households on the poverty list.

As part of this new arrangement, the GSO and MOLISA worked together to develop a common methodology for producing the national and provincial poverty estimates, including constructing new official urban and rural poverty lines for the period of the 2011–15 SEDP. The team developed three options for the new official lines, reflecting different requirements and living standards. The lower options were weighted more heavily toward food consumption and included a very limited allocation for nonfood spending. The higher option used the same food poverty line but allocated more for nonfood spending. Following intensive internal debate, the government chose the lowest of the three options. While the higher option was preferable on methodological grounds, the government operates under a constrained budget and was not willing to extend benefits under the National Target Program for Poverty Reduction and related programs to the large number of households expected to be eligible for support—the higher-option poverty lines implied national poverty rates of 18 to 20 percent. There is an inevitable tension between resource availability and needs. In light of this, Vietnam's official poverty lines are often referred to as "budgeting" or "planning" lines, and the process of agreeing on official poverty levels at the start of an SEDP as well as setting annual targets for poverty reduction over the course of its implementation involves a range of technical, financial, and political considerations. Other countries face similar challenges.

In September 2010, Vietnam announced a new official poverty rate of 14.2 percent (figure 1.2). The official poverty line for urban areas was raised from D 260,000 per person per month (US$1.34 person per day) to D 500,000 per person per month (US$1.61 per person per day; all figures in this paragraph are 2005 PPP). The official line for rural areas was raised from D 200,000 per person per month (US$1.03 per person per day) to D 400,000 per person per month (US$1.29 per person per day). A second, higher set of official "near-poor" lines was also approved, giving the government greater leeway in expanding eligibility criteria when deemed desirable, such as for determining eligibility of the "near-poor" for health insurance cards. The near-poor lines are 30 percent higher than the official poverty lines—D 650,000 per person per month (US$2.24 per person per day) for households living in urban areas and D 520,000 per person per month (US$1.83 per person per day) for households living in rural areas— and are similar in value (and implied national poverty rate) to the higher of the three poverty line options initially proposed.

The government set ambitious targets for poverty reduction in the 2011–15 SEDP; poverty at the national level is targeted to fall 2 percentage points each year between 2011 and 2015 and 4 percentage points in the poorest communities, including those with high proportions of ethnic minority households. Achieving these targets will require a substantially higher rate of progress than achieved under the previous SEDP and may be particularly challenging given the slowdown in economic growth and in the absence of substantially higher spending to support pro-poor policies. Progress is monitored closely down to the commune level, and there are strong incentives for local authorities to meet these targets.[2]

The GSO released the new poverty estimates for 2011 in the *2011 Vietnam Statistical Yearbook* based on an off-cycle 2011 VHLSS that covered nearly 47,000 households. Unlike earlier rounds of the VHLSS, the 2011 VHLSS was designated for internal use only, and the unit record data will not be released for public use. Based on 2011 survey results, poverty was reduced to 12.6 percent—a 1.6 percentage point reduction between

2010 and 2011. MOLISA released its own set of poverty estimates for 2011 in March 2012.[3] According to MOLISA, poverty was reduced to an estimated 11.8 percent—a 2.4 percentage point reduction between 2010 and 2011. MOLISA's estimates suggest that poverty fell most rapidly in Vietnam's high-poverty regions—the west northern mountains (6.4 percentage points), the north-central coast (5.7 percentage points), the central highlands (3.6 percentage points), and the east northern mountains (3.2 percentage points). Poverty fell only 1.2 percentage points in the Mekong Delta, well below targets set in the SEDP. MOLISA's latest round of poverty estimates were released in May 2013.[4] These show that poverty fell to 9.6 percent in 2012—an additional 2.2 percentage point reduction between 2011 and 2012. MOLISA is currently developing new average and minimum living standards that will provide a more scientific basis for benefit levels linked to future (new) social assistance programs. The methodology used to calculate minimum living standards is very similar to that used to calculate the 2010 GSO-WB poverty line.

For the present, given the differences in 2011 poverty estimates and pending stronger implementation of the assignment of responsibilities between MOLISA and the GSO, there is a strong rationale for continuing to use both the MOLISA approach (for targeting) and the GSO approach (for independent monitoring). We return to this issue in chapter 2.

In 2010–11, a team from the World Bank worked closely with the GSO and the Vietnam Academy of Social Sciences (VASS) to update the GSO-WB poverty line and related methodologies for monitoring poverty, with the aim of ensuring that the line and methods fully reflect current economic and social conditions. The resulting (new) GSO-WB poverty line is D 653,000 per person per month (US$2.24 per person per day, 2005 PPP), which yields a poverty rate of 20.7 percent in 2010 (figure 1.2). Chapter 2 describes proposed changes to the GSO-WB approach, including improvements to the VHLSS, updated welfare aggregates, and construction of a new 2010 GSO-WB poverty line. Poverty estimates using the new 2010 methodology are not strictly comparable to poverty estimates from earlier rounds of the VHLSS (2008 and earlier surveys) and are explicitly set apart in the tables and figures in the remainder of this chapter. The GSO began to use the new poverty line in 2010. The 2010 poverty line was recently updated to 2012 (adjusting only for inflation) and applied to the 2012 VHLSS. Despite a contraction in economic growth, poverty numbers continued to fall between 2010 and 2012—from 20.7 percent in 2010 to 17.2 percent in 2012.

The fraction of the population living below the international standards of US$1.25 and US$2.00 per person per day has also declined. Vietnam's own poverty line(s) are clearly better than international poverty lines for assessing progress and identifying remaining challenges within the country. However, PPP-adjusted international poverty lines are often used to compare progress

TABLE 1.1 **Number of poor people in Vietnam, 1993–2008**

Poverty standard	Number of poor (millions)			Change (millions)			Annual % point change 1993–2008
	1993	1998	2008	1993–1998	1998–2008	1993–2008	
Official GSO-WB poverty line:							
consumption	39.8	28.2	12.3	−11.5	−15.9	−27.4	−2.9
$1.25/day (2005 PPP):							
consumption	43.6	37.5	14.3	−6.2	−23.1	−29.3	−3.1
$2.00/day (2005 PPP):							
consumption	58.7	59.0	36.9	0.4	−22.1	−21.8	−2.8

Sources: VASS 2011a for 1993–2008 GSO-WB headcount estimates; POVCALNET for 1993–2008 US$1.25 and US$2.00 headcount estimates (http://iresearch.worldbank.org/PovcalNet/index.htm). Population statistics are from POVCALNET, except for 2010, which come from http://data.worldbank.org/country/vietnam.

across countries. Vietnam's progress at reducing poverty is equally impressive judged by international standards of US$1.25 and US$2.00 per person per day (poverty figures in this paragraph are 2005 PPP). Using US$1.25, the poverty headcount fell from 63.7 percent in 1993 to 16.7 percent by 2008, and using US$2.00 it fell from 85.7 percent in 1993 to 43.3 percent by 2008, the last year for which comparable poverty rates were published by the World Bank (table 1.1). Thus poverty fell an estimated 3 percentage points a year between 1993 and 2008, with faster progress in the 1990s and first half of the 2000s and slower progress in recent years.

Pace of poverty reduction

Nearly half of Vietnam's population has been lifted out of poverty in less than two decades. Measured by temporally comparable GSO-WB standards, more than 43 million people were lifted out of poverty between 1993 and 2008.

The depth and severity of poverty have also fallen sharply. The poverty headcount is a widely understood and widely reported measure of poverty. However, it ignores the fact that not all poor people are the same; some have incomes or consumption levels very close to the poverty line, while others live in much poorer conditions, well below standards captured in the poverty line. Two additional indicators are used to measure the depth and severity of poverty. The *poverty gap* (depth) measures the average, across all people, of the gap between the living standards of the poor and the poverty line. The *squared poverty gap* (severity) is calculated using a similar methodology, but gives greater weight to households whose living standards are farther from the poverty line.

According to table 1.2, Vietnam has made steady progress in reducing the depth and severity of poverty, whether measured by national or inter-

TABLE 1.2 Progress at reducing the incidence, depth, and severity of poverty in Vietnam, 1993–2010

	GSO-WB poverty line			$1.25/day poverty line, 2005 PPP			$2.00/day poverty line, 2005 PPP		
	Incidence	Depth	Severity	Incidence	Depth	Severity	Incidence	Depth	Severity
	Rate	Gap	Squared Gap	Rate	Gap	Squared Gap	Rate	Gap	Squared Gap
1993	58.1	18.5	7.9	63.7	23.6	11.0	85.7	43.5	25.7
1998	37.4	9.5	3.6	49.7	15.1	6.0	78.2	34.2	18.0
2002	28.9	7.0	2.4	40.1	11.2	4.1	68.7	28.0	14.1
2004	19.5	4.7	1.7	28.3	7.2	2.5	56.9	20.8	9.8
2006	15.9	3.8	1.4	21.4	5.3	1.9	48.0	16.3	7.3
2008	14.5	3.5	1.2	16.9	3.8	1.2	43.3	13.5	5.6
2010	20.7	5.9	2.4	n.a.	n.a.	n.a.	n.a.	n.a.	n.a.

Sources: VASS 2011a for 1993–2008 GSO-WB headcount estimates; POVCALNET for 1993–2008 US$1.25 and US$2.00 headcount estimates.
Note: Statistics for 2010 calculated by the World Bank using the comprehensive consumption aggregate. Poverty estimates using international poverty lines have not yet been published by the World Bank for Vietnam in 2010. n.a. = not applicable.

national standards. Living conditions have improved not only for households living near the poverty line, but also for many of Vietnam's poorest households.

But the pace of poverty reduction is slowing, linked to rising macro instability and slower growth. High and sustained rates of economic growth have been a key factor in Vietnam's success at reducing poverty. But the economy has slowed in recent years. Beginning in late 2007, Vietnam has struggled with economic turbulence and inflation, with sharp and persistent increases in the prices of many basic commodities. Many workers lost jobs, while others received lower wages and shorter working hours due to lower demand during the global economic crisis in late 2008 and early 2009. Farmers complain that the costs of agricultural inputs are rising, and profit margins are smaller. Food prices and the costs of electricity and fuel were rising in late 2011 and into 2012, putting additional pressure on household budgets. Households in urban and peri-urban areas have been particularly hard hit by high inflation, including rural-to-urban migrants who come to the city in ever-growing numbers in search of better jobs and higher pay. Migrants send money home to rural areas, and the impacts of higher urban prices are passed on to households living in rural areas in the form of declining remittances (see, for example, VASS 2011b). Urbanization is increasing rapidly, and the face of poverty and the sources of vulnerability in urban areas differ in important respects from more traditional poverty concerns in rural areas.

Progress on other dimensions of poverty

Vietnam has also made dramatic progress in improving the non-income dimensions of poverty and has met or is likely to meet most of the Millennium Development Goals (MDGs). Table 1.3 documents progress along other important dimensions of well-being. Vietnamese today are much better educated and arguably better prepared to get jobs in industry or services. In 1998, nearly a quarter of persons 15 to 24 years of age had not completed primary school. By 2010, only 12 years later, the percentage had fallen to only 4 percent, and upper-secondary enrollments had nearly doubled (to 60 percent for girls, 54 percent for boys). Moreover, by 2010, more girls than boys were enrolled in both levels of secondary school; Vietnam scores remarkably well on gender parity in education.

Vietnamese are also healthier and live longer today than they did in the 1990s; infant mortality (deaths per 1,000 live births) had fallen to 14 by 2010, which is impressive even by middle-income standards, and life expectancy had risen to 74.8 years. There was marked improvement in levels of nutrition, although stunting (low height for age) remains a concern in some regions of the country and among minority populations. While immunization coverage looks good on the surface—more than 90 percent of children begin the recommended series of childhood immunization (for example, for diphtheria, pertussis, and tetanus)—the 2010 Multiple Indicator Cluster Survey (MICS) documents immunization completion rates of only 60 percent (GSO 2011).

Access to infrastructure and local services has also improved; the number of households connected to the electricity grid increased from 77 percent in 1998 to nearly universal coverage (98 percent) by 2010. However, many households still do not have access to "improved" water sources, particularly in rural areas, or to sanitary latrines (table 1.3 defines "clean" and "improved" water sources). Although challenges in these areas remain, coverage has improved dramatically since 1998.

Improvements are also notable in housing and ownership of durable goods. By 2010, 89 percent of Vietnamese households owned a television (compared to 56 percent in 1998), 85 percent owned an electric fan (compared to 68 percent in 1998), 43 percent owned a refrigerator (compared to 9 percent in 1998), and a substantial 76 percent owned at least one motorbike (compared to 20 percent in 1998). If affluence and quality of life are reflected, at least in part, in the consumer durables that people own and use, then the improvements have been dramatic since the late 1990s.

According to the most recent Human Development Report for Vietnam (UNDP 2011), the country has achieved or is likely to achieve most of the MDG targets by 2015. However, concerns about clean water and sanitation remain (Goal 10), and Vietnam continues to make slow progress toward environmental goals (Goal 9).

TABLE 1.3 **Improvements in non-income dimensions of poverty in Vietnam, 1993–2010**

	1993	1998	2010
Education			
Share of population, age 15 or older, who have not completed primary school (%)	35.5	35.7	14.4
Share of population, ages 15–24, who have not completed primary school (%)	23.3	25.4	4.1
Primary enrollment rate (net)			
Female	87.1	90.7	92.8
Male	86.3	92.1	92.5
Lower secondary enrollment rate (net)			
Female	29.0	62.1	83.2
Male	31.2	61.3	80.2
Upper secondary enrollment rate (net)			
Female	6.1	27.4	60.1
Male	8.4	30.0	53.9
Health			
Immunization, DPT1: Share of children, ages 12–23 months (%)	91	94	93
Immunization, measles: Share of children, ages 12–23 months (%)	93	96	84
Infant mortality (per 1,000 live births)	34	29	14
Incidence of stunting (low height for age), children under age 5	51	34	23
Incidence of underweight (low weight for age), children under age 5	37	36	12
Life expectancy at birth (years)	68.1	71.0	74.8
Share of poor with health insurance (%)	n/a	7.8	71.6
Access to infrastructure and durables			
Share of population who use electricity as main source of lighting (%)	48	77	98
Share of population with access to an improved[a] water source (%)			
Rural	76	70	87
Urban	89	89	98
Share of population with access to clean[b] water (%)			
Rural	17	29	57
Urban	60	75	89
Share of population with sanitary latrines (%)	19	26	69
Rural	10	14	59
Urban	53	68	92
Share of households with durable goods (%)			
TV	22	56	89
Fan	31	68	85
Refrigerator	4	9	43
Car	0	0	1
Motorbike	11	20	76

[a] Improved water sources are defined as clean water sources plus hand-dug, reinforced wells and filtered spring sources.

[b] Clean water is defined as including piped water, bottled water, water from deep wells with pumps, and rainwater.

Sources: For 2010, statistics for immunization, malnutrition, and infant mortality come from various rounds of the MICS; for life expectancy, from World Bank World Development Indicators database; for all others, from World Bank 1999.

Progress on composite indicators of well-being

Progress is also apparent in composite indicators of well-being. Recent years have witnessed increasing interest in composite indicators of poverty, beginning with the human development index (HDI) in the early 1990s and more recently the multidimensional poverty index (MPI) launched in the 2010 Human Development Report for Vietnam (UNDP 2011). The MPI builds on earlier work done to measure nonmonetary poverty, such as the approach to measuring child poverty developed by the GSO and MOLISA with support from UNICEF, as well as a multidimensional poverty index that was presented in a recent study of urban poverty (Haughton, Nguyen, and Nguyen 2010).

Vietnam has seen steady improvement in human development, evidenced by increases in the HDI over time: the HDI value increased 19 percent between 1992 and 2008. With an HDI of 0.728, Vietnam is now comfortably placed in the mid-range of HDI (table 1.4).

The HDI is a composite index, and progress has been different for each of the subindexes. Strong economic growth between 1992 and 2008 increased the income index by 45 percent. The life expectancy index also saw significant gains, rising 19 percent between 1992 and 2008 on the basis of steady improvements in average life expectancy (from 65.2 years in 1992 to 72.7 years in 2008). The education index, which started from a relatively higher base in 1992, evidenced a slower rate of increase, rising only 7 percent by 2008. The contribution of the education index to overall growth in the HDI declined from around 25.9 percent in 1992–95 to 5.1 percent in 2004–08. Since 1992, rising GDP and longer life expectancy have been the main drivers of improvement in Vietnam's HDI. Slower gains in life expectancy are to be expected when years of life expectancy reach high levels. However, slowing gains in the education index may be cause for concern.

TABLE 1.4 Contribution of HDI components to HDI growth in Vietnam, 1992–2008

Year	HDI	Life expectancy index	Contribution of life expectancy index to HDI since previous period (%)	Education index	Contribution of education index to HDI growth since previous period (%)	Income index	Contribution of income index to growth since previous period (%)
1992	0.611	0.670	—	0.776	—	0.386	—
1995	0.639	0.690	18.8	0.808	25.9	0.420	55.3
1999	0.651	0.721	86.1	0.803	−13.9	0.430	27.8
2004	0.701	0.782	40.7	0.826	15.3	0.496	44.0
2008	0.728	0.794	15.2	0.830	5.1	0.559	79.7
Contribution to total change in HDI 1992–2008			35.2	n.a..	15.9	n.a.	48.95

Sources: UNDP 2001, 2011.

Note: HDI = human development index; — = not available; n.a. = not applicable.

There is a strong correlation between elements of good governance and higher levels of human development. Of the six dimensions of Vietnam's public administration performance index, public service delivery is most strongly correlated with the HDI, followed by transparency, participation at local levels, and vertical accountability. Control of corruption is also highly correlated with the HDI (CECODES et al. 2012).

Remaining challenges in poverty reduction

The task of poverty reduction is not finished, although Vietnam has made remarkable progress toward its long-standing goal of eradicating poverty. By the end of the 2006–10 SEDP, only 9.5 percent of households were estimated to live below Vietnam's official poverty lines, and poverty estimates based on the original GSO-WB basic-needs poverty line suggested similar results. Does this mean that the task of poverty reduction is largely finished, except for addressing a few remaining pockets of poverty and continuing to look after the poorest and most destitute?

The task may be finished in terms of meeting the most basic needs of Vietnamese citizens for food, shelter, and clothing. Vietnam rightly deserves to be recognized for this. But are these the right standards to apply in a rapidly growing, modernizing economy like Vietnam?

The task of eradicating poverty is not finished for two reasons:

- Standards have changed. By the end of the 2006–10 SEDP, Vietnam's system for measuring and monitoring poverty no longer adequately captured the living conditions of the population. The GSO-WB poverty lines were set in the mid-1990s and do not reflect the consumption patterns or broader aspirations of the population today.
- Many of the erstwhile poor remain vulnerable to slipping back into poverty. Weather shocks, health shocks, and income shocks are widespread and, in some areas, rising.

Moreover, Vietnam's rapid pace of development has bred its own challenges. The economy has experienced massive changes since the late 1990s. Workers who are now in their 40s and 50s made decisions regarding schooling and skills training in a much different economy, based on a different set of incentives. Many do not have the skills or training to compete for jobs in today's rapidly modernizing economy. Even young workers often leave school without adequate training for a modern skills-based economy.

The task of eradicating poverty has become more difficult in other important respects. Growth rates have fallen sharply compared to the first half of the 2000s, and growth is expected to remain sluggish in the foreseeable future. In addition, poverty reduction is becoming less responsive to economic growth. The remaining poor are harder to reach; the easy wins due, for example, to land reforms in the early 1990s, rapid expansion of rural areas into cash crop production, and agricultural diversification have, for the most part, been realized. The remaining poor are more concentrated in isolated regions and among ethnic minority groups, where structural issues linked to assets and location are binding constraints (for example, poorer-quality land, less education and training, and more limited infrastructure and public services). Poverty reduction policies and programs need to reflect these changing realities.

Vietnam's ongoing structural transformation to a market economy has given rise to trends that suggest new challenges for poverty reduction policies.

- Inequality is back on the agenda. Vietnamese citizens from all walks of life are concerned about rising inequality. Recent analysis suggests that income inequality increased between 2004 and 2010, driven predominantly by growing inequality within rural areas.
- Continuing disparities in human development contribute to income inequalities. While Vietnam has done a good job of improving the coverage of basic services, quality is uneven, and there are large perceived gaps between better-off and poorer households and regions. With the push toward "socialization" of health and education services, access has become more closely linked to incomes, and the burden of out-of-pocket spending for health and education is rising.
- Vietnam's cities and towns are growing rapidly, due in part to a massive influx of migrants from rural areas of the country. The urban cost of living is rising, due to rising food costs and rising demand, higher fuel prices, and higher water and electricity tariffs. The private sector accounts for an increasing share of the urban labor force, and many continue to work in the informal sector without social protection or employment benefits, as was revealed in recent studies such as the 2009 Urban Poverty Survey (Haughton, Nguyen, and Nguyen 2010), various rounds of the rapid impact monitoring (RIM) assessments of the global economic crisis conducted by the VASS (2009, 2011a), and the urban poverty monitoring studies of Oxfam GB and ActionAid (2008, 2011). New forms of vulnerability are developing, in particular among workers in the informal sector and rural migrants in cities like Hanoi and Ho Chi Minh City.

Revisions to Vietnam's poverty lines

The poverty lines used to monitor Vietnam's progress are low by international standards. When assessing Vietnam's performance in recent years, it is important to keep in mind that both official lines and the original GSO-WB poverty line are low by international standards, and, unlike in many other fast-growing economies, the GSO-WB line has not been revised since it was agreed in the mid-1990s. Using a constant standard to assess progress has many advantages. But most countries raise their standards—and their national poverty lines—as they become more affluent and as the aspirations and expectations of citizens change. Figure 1.3 shows the strongly positive relationship in developing and transition countries between national poverty lines (U.S. dollars per month) and average per capita expenditures (Chen and Ravallion 2008). The overall income elasticity of the national poverty line for countries in the sample is 0.66, with a substantially higher elasticity for the nonfood component of poverty lines (0.91) than the food component (0.47). Thus, assessed globally, the economic gradient in national poverty lines is driven more by the gradient in nonfood needs, which account for more than 60 percent of the overall elasticity. This is not surprising; food consumption becomes a much smaller share of total consumption as populations become more affluent. In countries like the United States, for example, even the poor spend only 20 to 25 percent of total expenditures on food.

The poverty statistics cited at the beginning of this chapter are based on the original GSO-WB poverty line of only US$1.10 per person per month, which is even lower than the US$1.25 per person per day poverty line used by the World Bank to measure global progress (all US dollar poverty figures in this paragraph are 2005 PPP). However, the US$1.25 poverty line sets a very low standard; it was constructed by averaging the

FIGURE 1.3 National poverty lines and average per capita consumption in developing and transition countries

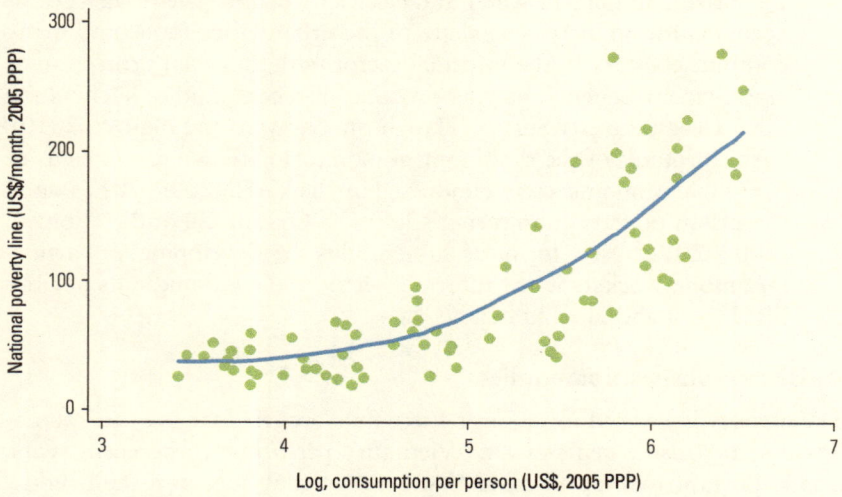

Source: Chen and Ravallion 2008.
Note: Fitted values are constructed using a locally weighted scatterplot smoothing (lowess) with band width = 0.8.

national poverty lines for the 15 poorest countries in the World Bank's database of comparator countries (Ravallion, Chen, and Sangraula 2008).[5] Most of these countries are in Sub-Saharan Africa. Much higher national and international poverty lines are typically used by rising middle-income countries. The median poverty line for all developing and transition countries is US$2.00 per person per day, and the median line for all countries excluding the poorest 15 countries is US$2.50 per person per day. An international poverty line of $4.00 per person per day is used by most countries in Latin America.

Vietnam's poverty lines are low relative to its rising prosperity and rising aspirations. Poverty lines typically increase with economic development because norms change; what was considered an acceptable level of deprivation in the 1990s is no longer acceptable today. Poverty lines also rise because governments have greater capacity and more resources to respond to changing norms.

Evidence of changing norms is reflected in the subjective poverty lines reported by households in the 2010 VHLSS, based on the perceived adequacy of their current level of consumption. Subjective lines suggest national poverty rates of 20 to 25 percent, which are substantially higher than current official poverty estimates (chapter 2).

Changing norms and higher aspirations are also captured in qualitative field studies and assessments carried out over the past decade. For example, in the 1999 and 2003 participatory poverty assessments (PPAs) led by the World Bank in collaboration with other donors, international nongovernmental organizations, and Vietnamese partners, poor respondents defined well-being in terms of adequate food, a stable endowment of assets (adequate land, labor, and housing), plus nonmaterial factors such as community respect and freedom from debt and anxiety (ADB 2003; World Bank 1999). Respondents in a more recent 2008 PPA did not refer to hunger or food security, but instead spoke about rising food prices, access to employment, and stable jobs—reflecting the emerging impacts of the global financial crisis.

New research on ethnic minority poverty was carried out for this book and is described briefly in annex 1A. Ethnic minority respondents in three regions of Vietnam (the Mekong Delta, central highlands, and northern mountains) were asked about indigenous definitions of success. The most common response was linked to the satisfaction of basic needs: enough food to eat year-round, clothes to wear, decent housing, and ability to participate in cultural festivals and customs. However, some respondents realized that standards of success were changing, pointing to increasing material prosperity and the importance of connections to the market economy. One minority official in Muong Khuong District, Lao Cai, said, "In the past it was considered enough to have a full stomach and dress warmly [an no, mac am]; now people want to eat well and dress beautifully [an *ngon, mac dep*]." Better-off respondents, including a group of traders, mentioned building a large, clean multistoried house as a key indicator of success. Among respondents who have transitioned out of agriculture and into trading or small-scale industry, the concept of success included having children who are well educated and have stable jobs, particularly in the state sector. Thus ideas of well-being, even among poorer Vietnamese, are shifting from satisfying basic needs to owning more material assets, combined with social status and non-income factors such as better health and education.

Vietnam raised its official poverty lines in late 2010, and a new GSO-WB line is described in chapter 2 of this book. Despite intense internal debate—many policy makers believe that Vietnam should set more ambitious goals in the fight against poverty, given its rapid economic growth and aspirations to become a modern industrial society—the new official poverty lines set in 2010 for the 2011–16 SEDP are still low by international standards. The new urban line is still well below US$2 per person per day (2005 PPP), and the new rural line is only a little above the US$1.25 per person per day standard applied in the world's poorest countries.

As noted earlier in the chapter, the World Bank has worked closely with the GSO and other local partners to update GSO's poverty monitoring system, including improved design and coverage of the VHLSS, more comprehensive welfare aggregates, and a new GSO-WB poverty line based on an updated food reference basket (from the 2010 VHLSS), a more comprehensive measure of nonfood spending that includes the flow of consumption from household assets (consumer durables and housing), and new spatial cost-of-living indexes. Details are provided in chapter 2, and a new poverty profile is presented in chapter 3.

Vulnerability to poverty

Despite progress, many households remain vulnerable to falling into poverty in Vietnam, and new sources of vulnerability are emerging as a result of external global events and internal instability. Although tens of millions of Vietnamese households have risen out of poverty over the last decade, many have incomes very near the poverty line and remain vulnerable to falling back into poverty as a result of idiosyncratic shocks (such as job loss, accidents, and death or illness of a household member) or economy-wide shocks (for example, effects of climate change on rainfall and temperatures, human and animal influenza pandemics, and impacts of the recent global financial crisis). The combination of large shocks and many small, often local shocks can be difficult to manage for poor, near-poor, and even nonpoor households. The strategies used by households to cope with unanticipated shocks, such as reducing spending on health care, selling off assets like land and livestock, and taking children out of school, can themselves have longer-term adverse consequences. At any point in time, apart from the households living below the poverty line, a substantial number of households may be at risk of falling back into poverty—that is, they remain vulnerable to poverty.

Some studies define the vulnerable in terms of the near-poor—households whose incomes lie above but still very close to the poverty line. MOLISA recently developed official near-poor poverty lines that are 1.3 times the official urban and rural poverty lines. If a similar approach to defining the near-poor is applied to the 2010 GSO-WB methodology, there would be 13 million near-poor households in 2010 in addition to 18 million poor households. A study led by the Vietnam Academy of Social Sciences uses a different approach to measure vulnerability to poverty (VASS 2011a). The study analyzes poverty dynamics using a panel data set from the 2002, 2004, and 2006 VHLSS and finds that one-fourth of those who were poor in 2002 were chronically poor (poor in all three periods), while the remaining three-fourths experienced temporary bouts of poverty and thus were labeled the transient or stochastic poor. The study identifies a great deal of churning—households moving above and below the poverty line—over the period, including many households that escaped poverty. Ethnic minority households were much more likely to be among the chronic poor.

Additional evidence is presented below, using a methodology initially developed and applied in a study for China (World Bank 2009), which measures vulnerability to poverty based on a panel of 1,800 households from the 2004, 2006, and 2008 VHLSS. It constructs an index of vulnerability to poverty, defined as the share of the population who were poor in at least one year (2004, 2006, or 2008) divided by the average poverty rate across all three years. The results, summarized in table 1.5, suggest that a considerable number of households that are not poor in a specific year nonetheless remain vulnerable to falling into poverty. At the national level, only 7 percent of panel households were among the chronic poor (poor in all three years), despite an end-period (2008) poverty rate of 13 percent. Vulnerability to poverty was particularly high in wealthier areas of the country such as the Red River Delta (where Hanoi is located) and the southeast (where Ho Chi Minh City is located). It was surprisingly high in provinces in the south-central coast and Mekong Delta. Consistent with VASS findings, upland regions with a high proportion of ethnic minorities evidenced higher rates of chronic (structural) poverty.

Vietnam's rich body of qualitative research on poverty documents widespread concerns about vulnerability. The groundbreaking PPAs carried out in 1999 identify some important sources of vulnerability such as crop failures (weather shocks, insects and other pests, landslides), human disasters (severe illness, death of a laborer, alcoholism, drug addiction), other economic shocks (job loss, death of animals, business failures), and material

TABLE 1.5 Vulnerability to poverty in Vietnam, 2004, 2006, and 2008
Percent

Subgroup	Poor in all 3 years (1)	Poor in 2 of 3 years (2)	Poor in 1 of 3 years (3)	Poor in at least 1 year (4) = (1)+(2)+(3)	Not poor in any year (5)	Consumption poverty (GSO-WB) Headcount, 2004 (6)	Headcount, 2006 (7)	Headcount, 2008 (8)	Average headcount, 2004–08 (9) = [(6)+(7)+(8)]/3	Vulnerability-to-poverty ratio (10) = (4)/(9)
National	7.0 (27)	6.7 (26)	12.3 (47)	26.0 (100)	74.0	20.0	13.7	13.0	15.6	1.7
Red River Delta	2.1 (13)	5.0 (32)	8.5 (54)	15.7 (100)	84.3	10.9	7.5	6.5	8.3	1.9
East northern mountains	10.4 (33)	10.3 (33)	10.8 (34)	31.5 (100)	68.5	26.3	17.3	19.0	20.9	1.5
West northern mountains	40.5 (56)	15.8 (22)	16.2 (22)	72.5 (100)	27.5	59.5	51.4	58.4	56.5	1.3
North-central coast	10.3 (25)	11.5 (28)	19.9 (48)	41.7 (100)	58.3	32.5	25.7	15.6	24.6	1.7
South-central coast	9.8 (35)	8.2 (29)	10.0 (36)	28.0 (100)	72.0	24.0	15.7	16.0	18.6	1.5
Central highlands	19.1 (57)	10.3 (31)	3.9 (12)	33.3 (100)	66.7	31.8	27.9	22.2	27.3	1.2
Southeast	3.1 (28)	1.6 (14)	6.3 (57)	11.0 (100)	89.0	8.2	6.2	4.5	6.3	1.8
Mekong Delta	2.2 (8)	4.2 (16)	20.0 (76)	26.4 (100)	73.6	16.9	6.7	11.5	11.7	2.3
Rural	8.8 (28)	8.2 (26)	14.3 (46)	31.3 (100)	68.7	24.4	16.6	16.0	19.0	1.6
Urban	0.7 (10)	1.6 (21)	5.3 (70)	7.5 (100)	92.5	4.4	3.6	2.5	3.5	2.1
Ethnic minority	34.0 (50)	19.4 (28)	15.3 (22)	68.7 (100)	31.3	59.7	49.0	47.5	52.1	1.3
Ethnic majority	2.6 (14)	4.6 (24)	11.8 (62)	19.1 (100)	80.9	13.6	8.0	7.4	9.7	2.0

Sources: VHLSS tabulations using 2004, 2006, and 2008 panels of households.

crisis (damage to homes, theft, violence). See Vietnam-Sweden Mountain Rural Development Program et al. (1999).

Respondents in additional PPAs carried out in 2003 and 2008 also discussed risks. The 2008 PPA highlights the fragile balance between opportunities and risks (VASS 2009); households must grasp new economic opportunities in order to move out of poverty, but doing so has inherent risks, and households may be pushed back temporarily into poverty as a result of setbacks, temporary loss of assets, or changes in family circumstances. Many households raised concerns about rising debt and being caught in a "debt spiral." There were widespread reports of health shocks pushing some households back into poverty; households reported selling assets and taking on extra debt in order to cope with health shocks.

Some new activities have been launched to monitor the impacts of recent shocks on poverty. Oxfam GB and ActionAid carried out an annual program of poverty monitoring in 12 sites in Vietnam (nine in rural areas, three in urban areas) between 2007 and 2011, and VASS (with active participation from development partners) carried out several rounds of a RIM study beginning in late 2008 (Oxfam GB and ActionAid 2008, 2011; VASS 2011b). Results highlight the effect on household living conditions of occasional and often severe individual risks (for example, health related) coupled with more common seasonal risks that are specific to the local context (for example, bad weather). They also document the emerging impacts of "macro" risks such as inflation and global economic crises. Even for the most affected groups, while macro risks worsened existing difficulties (for example, lower purchasing power), they rarely caused households to relapse into poverty. However, risks and vulnerability were important causal factors in chronic poverty and were linked to slow poverty reduction among ethnic minority households. Evidence from the RIM and related studies suggests that the 2009 global crisis had a negative but short-lived impact on the living standards of poor households, with particularly adverse effects on Vietnam's large pool of migrant workers—many of whom work in factories with foreign links (via export production or foreign employers)—and rural households whose livelihoods depend on migrant remittances.

Three new qualitative field studies were carried out as part of the research described in this book, with the aim of developing a deeper understanding of both old and new sources of poverty and vulnerability. Short summaries are provided in annex 1A. Low-income respondents in a field study designed to explore "perceptions of inequality" raised concerns that inflation could widen the gap between the poor and better-off and further reduce opportunities to access education, health care, and other services. Competition for jobs will increase as the economy continues to slow, and good jobs are likely to go to applicants who have the right connections or are willing to pay bribes to potential employers. Concerns about "land grabs" have been widely discussed in the press and were raised again in the perceptions of inequality study as well as a field study carried out jointly by the World Bank and Oxfam to identify the "long-run drivers of poverty reduction." Rural households living in or near urban centers felt increasingly vulnerable to having their land "acquired" by the government for industrial and other development purposes. Few felt that they would be properly compensated for the loss of land, and many said that losing their land would lead to an inevitable drop in living standards. A third study of "positive deviance" in poverty reduction analyzed a range of concerns specifically linked to poverty and progress among ethnic minorities. Minorities depend heavily on earnings from agriculture, both crops and animal products, and are particularly vulnerable to weather shocks and other natural disasters as well as commodity and input price volatility. Ethnic minority respondents were acutely aware of the substantial and persistent gap in living conditions between minority and majority households, which they attributed to various factors, including substantial gaps in opportunities and discriminatory attitudes and practices.

Growing concentration of poverty among ethnic minorities

Poverty is increasingly concentrated among Vietnam's ethnic minority populations, who constitute less than 15 percent of the population but nearly half of the remaining poor and two-thirds of the extreme poor. Vietnam has 54 officially recognized ethnic groups, of whom the Kinh (Viet) are by the far the most numerous, accounting for nearly 74 million people (85.7 percent of the population) according to the 2009 Population and Housing Census. In 2009, five other ethnic groups (the Tay, Thai, Muong, Khmer, and H'mong) had populations of more than 1 million each, and another three (the Nung, Dao, and Hoa) had populations of between 500,000 and 1 million each. At the other extreme, some ethnic groups had populations of less than 5,000 people. With the exception of the Hoa (Chinese), Khmer, and Cham, most ethnic minority groups live in highland or upland areas, away from the coastal plains and major cities. The largest minority populations are found in the northwest, northeast, and central highland regions, although there are also clusters of ethnic populations in the north-central, south-central, and Mekong regions.

Despite remarkable progress in reducing overall poverty, including a steady reduction in ethnic minority poverty, there remains a substantial and widening gap in living conditions and poverty rates between the Kinh majority and ethnic minorities. This is illustrated in figure 1.4, which graphs annual real rates of growth in per capita expenditures (from the 1998 VLSS and the 2010 VHLSS) between 1998 and 2010, by region and ethnicity. Since 1998, per capita expenditures have grown at an average annual rate of 9.4 percent for the Kinh and only 7.4 percent for ethnic minorities. Disparities are largest in some of the poorest and least accessible regions of Vietnam (the northern mountains) and the north-central

FIGURE 1.4 **Average annual rates of real growth in per capita expenditures among the Kinh and Hoa majority and ethnic minorities in Vietnam, by region, 1998–2010**

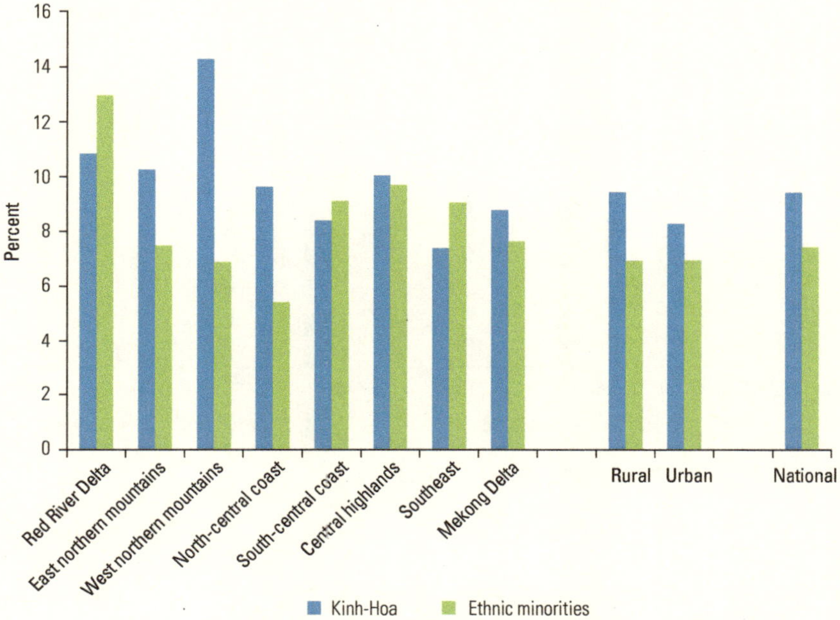

Sources: 1998 VLSS; 2010 VHLSS.

coast. As discussed in chapter 6, growth in income has been uneven across minority households, with higher rates of growth among the better-off. However, even these better-off ethnic minorities experience slower growth rates than the average Kinh.

Consistent with differential rates of growth, the concentration of minorities among the poor is rising; in 1993, poverty was widespread and minorities constituted only 20 percent of all poor households (figure 1.5). By 1998, the share of minorities among the poor had increased to 29 percent, and by 2010, minorities accounted for 47 percent of the total poor in Vietnam and a resounding two-thirds of individuals in the poorest 10 percent of the population. Using the new GSO-WB poverty line, 66.3 percent of minorities were poor in 2010 compared to only 12.9 percent of the Kinh majority.

The increasing concentration of minorities among the poor and extreme poor is a serious concern. But not all minorities are poor. There is encouraging evidence of recent improvements in welfare and livelihoods for many minority groups, and analysis of the 2010 VHLSS documents the presence of some better-off ethnic minority households among middle- and upper-

FIGURE 1.5 Poverty rates and changing composition of the poor among the Kinh and Hoa majority and ethnic minorities in Vietnam, 1993–2010

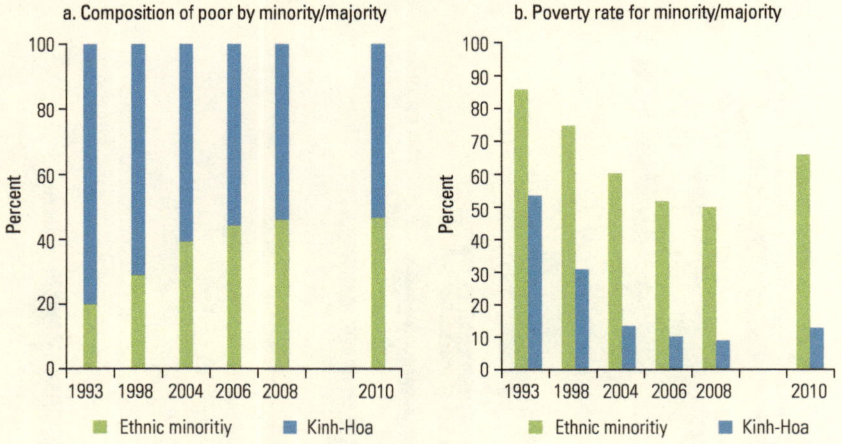

a. Composition of poor by minority/majority

b. Poverty rate for minority/majority

■ Ethnic minoritiy   ■ Kinh-Hoa

Sources: 1993, 1998 VLSS; 2004, 2006, 2008, 2010 VHLSS.

income deciles. These issues are explored in greater depth in chapter 5, which describes important signs of progress in some areas and among some groups (examples of "positive deviance") and identifies the key pathways out of poverty for ethnic minorities. The work suggests that these pathways are not fundamentally different from those of the Kinh majority in certain respects, including a shift out of semi-subsistence agriculture and into commercial agriculture, accompanied by diversification into non-agricultural activities and entry into broader market relations, including international markets. Concerns have been raised that economic progress will lead to additional pressures for cultural and linguistic assimilation of minorities. Although these pressures are real, especially for some of the smallest minority groups, new research on processes of poverty reduction and development show that some ethnic communities have indeed begun to prosper without losing their identity. In fact, cohesive communities of people who are not poor have a better chance of maintaining their language, religion, and other cultural traditions than communities who are struggling at the edge of subsistence.

Income inequality and access

In recent years, growth has favored the better-off, resulting in rising income inequality. Unlike other fast-growing economies in East Asia, past empirical work suggests that Vietnam's development trajectory has been one of growth without an appreciable rise in inequality. Standard measures of inequality increased during the early part of the 1990s and then stabilized. However, recent studies, including reports by the Vietnamese Academy of Social Sciences, note that the relatively modest changes in inequality based on household surveys stand in sharp contrast to widely shared perceptions among the Vietnamese people that inequality in incomes and wealth is rising (VASS 2011a). These perceptions are increasingly noted in the press as well as among policy makers and academics in Vietnam.

This book looks at inequality through two lenses: first, through a new qualitative study of "perceptions of inequality" and, second, through new empirical analysis of the VHLSS, which builds on lessons from the qualitative study. Taken together, they provide a rich and complex picture of the inequalities in outcomes, opportunities, and social and political capital among Vietnamese people. Inequality in outcomes refers to inequalities in income, consumption, and wealth, while inequality in opportunities refers to differences in human outcomes linked to differences in circumstances such as gender, ethnicity, location, or parental characteristics. Inequality in social and political capital refers to differences among individuals measured in terms of connections, voice, and power. Details of the work are included in chapter 6.

The perceptions study helps to identify which types of inequalities are seen as acceptable and which are seen as unacceptable by the Vietnamese people. It suggests that people from all backgrounds—rural and urban, rich and poor—perceive that inequality has risen substantially over the last five years. Participants rarely discussed income and wealth inequalities in isolation, but instead focused on their determinants—notably, inequalities in the quality of education, access to good employment opportunities, access to land, and access to connections, power, and influence. Inequality in access to good jobs was seen as a consequence of inequality in access to education, which then leads to inequalities in income, expenditures, and wealth. Those who lack power and connections were seen as having less access to good jobs and as being more exposed to predatory behavior on the part of local officials, including loss of land and inadequate compensation. Most respondents considered inequalities in income and wealth as acceptable—it was fine for some to get rich and live well—so long as wealth was the result of education, skills, luck, and hard work and not achieved through unfair or corrupt practices.

New empirical analysis based on recent rounds of the VHLSS suggests a modest rise in income inequality: the Gini index for per capita income has risen from 0.40 to 0.43. Figure 1.6 presents a growth incidence curve[6] showing growth rates in income ranked by per capita income deciles between 2004 and 2010. Real income growth rates over the period varied considerably for households at different points in the income distribution, ranging from around 4 percent for households at the bottom of the income distribution to 9 percent for households at the top. Growth was pro-poor,

FIGURE 1.6 **Growth in income per capita in Vietnam, by income group, 2004–10**

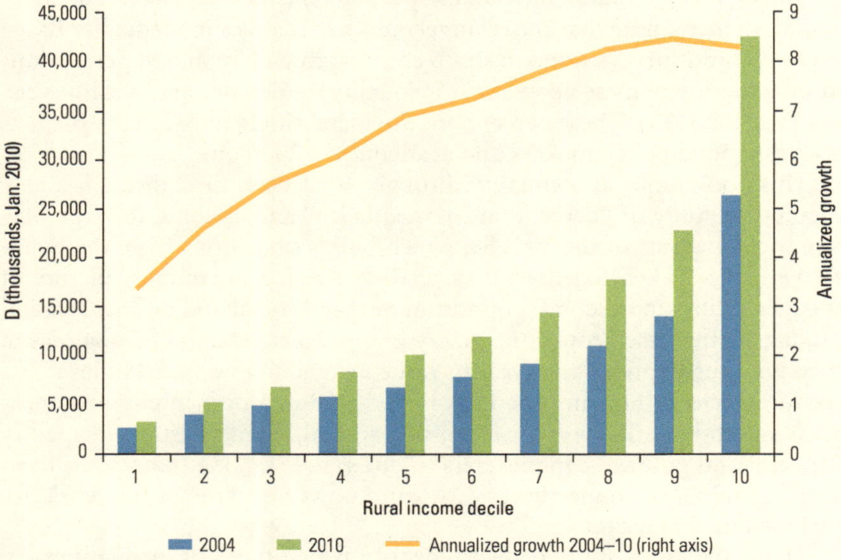

Sources: 2004, 2010 VHLSS.

inasmuch as it contributed to continued progress toward reducing poverty over the period. However, because growth favored better-off households, both the relative and the absolute gaps in incomes between the rich and the poor have risen over time.

The trend of rising inequality with economic growth is common across many countries in the East Asia and Pacific region. While rising income inequality may be a manifestation of growth processes that raise overall income and reduce poverty and thus be considered a natural consequence of an economic landscape favoring entrepreneurship, innovation, and economic progress, if left unchecked some types of inequalities can lead to rising social tensions and undermine social cohesion. The variation in growth across households in Vietnam reflects powerful and potentially opposing changes in the economic fabric: changes in returns to education and skills in labor markets, sectoral and occupational transitions, and rising geographic mobility as individuals leave rural areas in search of better opportunities in cities and towns. But these forces interact with inequalities in opportunities—inequalities in education, patterns of social exclusion between ethnic minorities and the majority population, access to good jobs, and geographic disparities—to increase income inequality and widen the income gaps between rich and poor households. As Vietnam continues to grow and basic-needs poverty becomes a thing of the past, poverty reduction policies will increasingly focus on monitoring and promoting equitable development processes to ensure that all Vietnamese share in the benefits of economic growth and transformation.

Disparities in human development

Disparities in key aspects of human development persist and in some cases appear to be widening. Vietnam has not only succeeded in raising incomes. Progress in human development has been equally impressive. But as in the case of income growth and poverty reduction, progress has been uneven. Inequalities may undermine growth processes if they are driven by disparities in circumstances—such as ethnicity, gender, and unequal opportunities for acquiring a good education—that ultimately prevent some groups from benefiting equally in the gains from high growth and development.

Consider the example of education. Figure 1.7 depicts the ratio of enrollment rates for Kinh majority children compared to enrollment rates for children from specific ethnic minority groups. A ratio of less than 1 indicates that minority children are participating in school at a lower rate than majority children. Although there has been considerable progress since 1998, ethnic minority populations continue to have lower enrollments than the majority, and these differences are substantial at the upper-secondary level.

FIGURE 1.7 **Ratio of ethnic minority to Kinh majority enrollment rates in public schools in Vietnam, by level of education, 1998 and 2010**

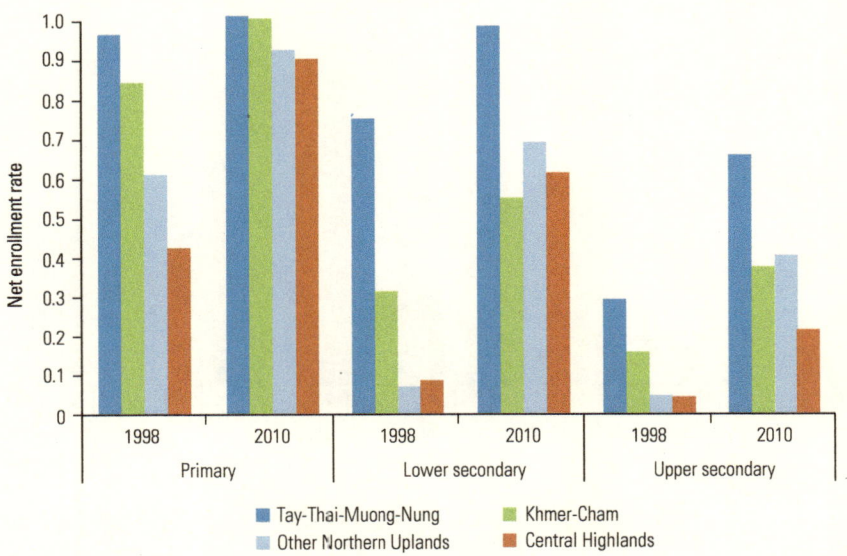

Sources: 1998 VLSS; 2010 VHLSS.

Incomes affect access to quality health and education services. The growing emphasis on "socialization" in the provision of health and education services in Vietnam—which stresses the sharing of social costs and responsibilities between individuals and the state and nonstate sectors—means that incomes are beginning to matter more for determining access to basic services. Rising disparities in income will contribute to rising social disparities, including disparities in school enrollment (particularly for secondary and higher education) and access to health services.

A direct consequence of this is that the burden of out-of-pocket health and education expenditures is substantial, particularly for less-well-off households. Analysis based on the VHLSS shows that spending on education rose in real terms between 2004 and 2010 across all levels, and out-of-pocket costs are higher as students move from primary to lower- and upper-secondary levels. Compared to the poor, better-off households spend substantially more on education in general and on extra courses and after-school tutoring in particular. Higher spending on the part of better-off households is evident even at upper secondary and university levels (figure 1.8). Given these advantages, it is not surprising that students from wealthier households perform better in the classroom and on standardized tests and are more likely to obtain higher degrees and training.

FIGURE 1.8 Out-of-pocket spending per student in Vietnam, by education and expenditure quintile, 2004 and 2010

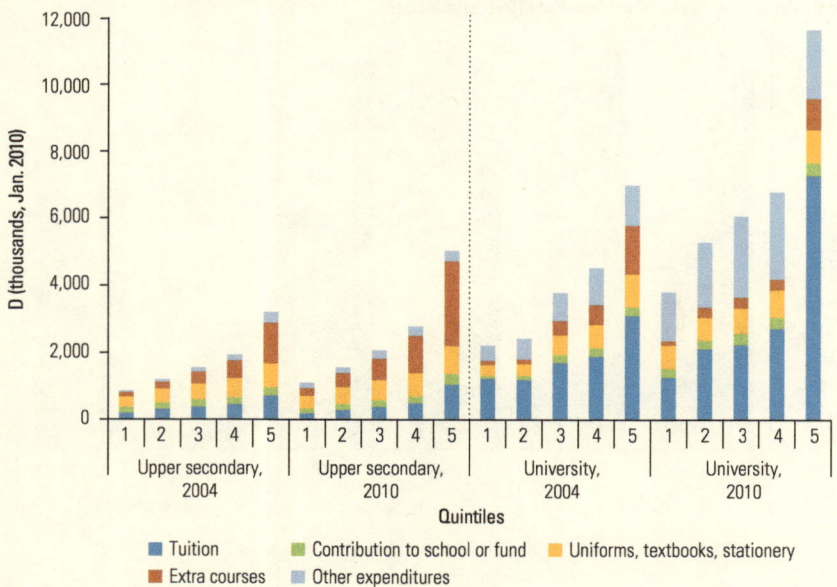

Sources: 2004, 2010 VHLSS.

Research suggests that while ill health is more concentrated among the poor, the poor are less likely than the better-off to use health services (World Bank 2012). Moreover, public spending on health decidedly favors the better-off; for example, spending on commune health centers, used by the rural poor, is lower than spending on government hospitals, used by the better-off. Concerns have been raised about the impoverishing effects of catastrophic health costs, including concerns that the poor will forgo care when faced with serious illnesses. A large and growing number of the poor have free health cards, which help to reduce the costs they pay for services, but the quality of care they receive is a concern. Various studies highlight Vietnam's high out-of-pocket health payments, which persist despite improved coverage of the National Health Insurance Scheme as a result of the 2008 Law on Health Insurance. The new law provides fully subsidized health insurance premiums for the poor and partially subsidized premiums for the near-poor. However, health insurance has had a modest impact on reducing out-of-pocket health payments, including catastrophic health costs (Lieberman and Wagstaff 2008; Wagstaff 2007). Households with young children and elderly members have higher exposure to health risks and report higher rates of catastrophic health spending (Hoang et al. 2012).

Rising vulnerability in urban areas

Urban residents face significant challenges of rising costs and economic instability. Vietnam weathered the global economic storm following the financial crisis of 2008–09 better than most countries. Growth hit a decade low of 5.4 percent in 2009, down from a decade high of 8.5 percent just two years before, but in 2010 it bounced back to 6.4 percent. Growth slipped again to 6.2 percent in 2011 and slipped further to a record low of 5.3 percent in 2012. While these growth rates are low for Vietnam, they remain more than 1 percentage point above the average for emerging and developing economies.

Behind Vietnam's resilience to external shocks, however, is a more complicated story of volatility and vulnerability that plays out in Vietnam's cities and towns. As export demand fell following the global financial crisis, so did demand for factory labor. Fortunately, the labor market bounced back quickly and strongly, with regard to both working hours and wage rates. However, urban residents were buffeted by inflationary shocks before and after the crisis. In 2008, the GSO reported a price increase of 23 percent overall as Vietnam felt the effects of the global food crisis—with food price inflation registering at 34 percent. Inflation moderated in 2010, but rose again in late 2011 to around 18 percent nationally, in both urban and rural areas, with a steeper rise in the price of food and foodstuffs and electricity and fuel.

These events have brought considerable challenges for urban residents, which have been documented in various studies and rapid assessments, including Oxfam GB and ActionAid (2008, 2011), VASS (2009, 2011b), and Haughton, Nguyen, and Nguyen (2010). For example, 65 percent of households surveyed in the 2009 Urban Poverty Survey reported higher prices for food and essential items as a source of difficulty, making inflation by far the most common factor among job loss, business slowdowns, natural disasters, health shocks, and others (16 percent of households reported job loss or business slowdown as a source of difficulty). On a positive note, a price impact survey carried out by Oxfam GB and ActionAid in May 2011 found that inflation has not caused families to go hungry or children to drop out of school (which may be due to parents giving top priority to their children's education). Still, serious issues remain. Those living off of savings or on fixed incomes that are not indexed to inflation, such as pensioners, beneficiaries of social protection, and those unable to work due to health issues, are vulnerable to the effects of inflation in obvious ways. The year 2012 has been another difficult one for urban households; preliminary estimates from the 2012 VHLSS suggest no measurable reduction in urban poverty between 2010 and 2012.

Combined with employment instability like that introduced by the global recession, inflation poses especially acute issues for urban migrants, who often face higher prices for accommodation, electricity, and water than local residents and have difficulty accessing social services; they are especially endangered by instability in their livelihoods. Urban migrants surveyed in Oxfam GB and ActionAid's participatory monitoring of urban poverty (Oxfam GB and ActionAid 2011) reported that wage increases have failed to keep pace with price increases; average monthly expenditures net of savings and remittances increased 87 percent between 2008 and 2011, while monthly income increased only 66 percent. There have been signs of rising labor tensions as a result of this dynamic and lower remittances to rural areas. Instability in urban livelihoods exacerbates poverty not just in urban areas, but, via this remittance mechanism, in rural areas as well.

Overview of the book: Addressing Vietnam's old and new poverty reduction challenges

This book takes the view that despite remarkable progress, the task of poverty reduction in Vietnam is not complete. It has three aims.

First, it documents recent revisions to Vietnam's poverty monitoring system, including improvements in the VHLSS, more comprehensive welfare aggregates, and a new poverty line, with the aim of bringing these more in line with economic and social conditions in present-day Vietnam.

Second, it uses the new methodology to revisit the stylized facts about deprivation and poverty in Vietnam and develops an updated profile of poverty based on data from the 2010 VHLSS and new qualitative field studies.

Third, it selectively analyzes some of the key challenges for reducing extreme poverty and promoting shared prosperity in the next decade. Chapter 4 presents new poverty maps based on the 2009 Population and Housing Census and 2010 VHLSS and compares these to earlier poverty maps from the 1999 census. Chapter 5 focuses on ethnic minority poverty, with the aim of identifying current constraints faced by minority populations as well as important signs of progress. Chapter 6 takes a fresh look at inequality of outcomes and opportunities, combining analytic work using the VHLSS with findings from a new qualitative field study of perceptions of inequality.

Annex 1A New qualitative research carried out for the 2012 Vietnam poverty assessment

This annex describes three new qualitative field studies that were carried out to develop a deeper understanding of both old and new sources of poverty and vulnerability.

Identifying factors leading to poverty reduction and income growth: "Positive deviance" study on ethnic minority poverty

Carried out from November 2011 to February 2012, this field study aimed to identify ethnic minority communities that show unusually strong poverty reduction and income growth and to identify factors contributing to these positive results. Positive deviance is a methodology that originates in Vietnam, from a 1990s nutrition program led by Save the Children; it has since been applied worldwide by nongovernmental organizations and researchers (Marsh et al. 2004; Ramalingam 2011). Successful families and communities are "positive" because they escape poverty despite facing the same challenges and obstacles as their neighbors and are "deviants" (or outliers) because they practice different behaviors from others.

The researchers visited ethnic minority communities in Dak Lak Province (Ea H'leo District), Tra Vinh Province (Chau Thanh and Tra Cu districts), and Lao Cai Province (Muong Khuong and Bac Ha districts), conducting semi-structured interviews with more than 100 ethnic minority residents and local government officials. Sites were selected using a combination of quantitative analysis and a snowball sample based on expert recommendations and secondary literature. Data from census samples were analyzed to determine rates of poverty reduction (or increase) among ethnic minority respondents in each province and district over the periods 1999–2006 and 2006–09. Census data were also processed to calculate the mean reported expenditures of ethnic minority respondents (as a proxy for income) by province and district and the percentage of the ethnic minority sample in the top 15 percent of expenditures in each location. Qualitative hypotheses were then developed of possible factors leading to poverty reduction and income growth, outlining "provocative propositions" for collecting qualitative data that were explored through interviews and field observations.

Identifying long-run drivers of poverty reduction: The Q-square pilot

Oxfam and the World Bank carried out a qualitative pilot study in August 2011 to identify the key long-run drivers of poverty reduction over the past two decades in Vietnam. (Nguyen and Hoang 2012). The study was framed around the complementary concepts of opportunities and constraints in assessing income and welfare dynamics at the household and community levels. The longer-run aim was to develop a panel data set of households and communities spanning 20 years, drawing on the initial set of communities and households surveyed in the 1992–93 and 1997–98 VLSS.

Sites were selected from the 1997–98 VLSS list of districts and communes based on district-level poverty rates and the district-level population of ethnic minorities and Kinh and Hoa. Efforts were made to visit a range of locations, roughly representative of Vietnam's different regions. In total, the team interviewed 220 households that had been initially surveyed in the VLSS panel, updated household rosters for these households, and held group discussions with nearly 250 respondents at both village and commune levels.

Qualitative exercises were carried out including (a) wealth ranking, (b) time-line exercises to explore commune and village histories since 1992, and (c) card-sorting exercises and mobility diagrams to list and rank opportunities and constraints in communities over the two decades. Village officials were also asked to discuss their perceptions of how life had changed and what had happened to poverty levels since the early 1990s. Additional life history interviews and diagrams were conducted with representatives from selected households, focusing on households that had done exceptionally well (and why) or done very poorly (and why). The team also interviewed important "change agents" such as local businesses, cooperatives, shops, and projects or programs.

Exploring perceptions of inequality in Vietnam

A field study was carried out in March and April 2012 to collect and analyze information on perceptions of inequality held by diverse elements of Vietnamese society. The work explored three key areas: (a) the perceptions of social and economic disparities within and between different reference groups, (b) the factors that determine these perceptions, and (c) the extent to which disparities have changed over time. Discussions were organized around reference focus groups—that is, better-off households, poor households, senior citizens, groups of students as well as working young people, and (in the case of urban areas) rural to urban migrants. Three sentinel groups of sites were selected—six locations in metropolitan cities, two locations in smaller cities, and seven locations in rural areas.

Four overlapping aspects of inequality were highlighted by all groups—inequalities in economic outcomes (incomes, wealth) as well as inequalities in access to education, jobs, and land. Causes of inequality were seen as overlapping and complementary—for example, some rural respondents raised concerns about the poor quality of education in their area, which contributed to poor skills and unequal access to good jobs. There was strong support for policy measures to ensure equality of opportunities. Many respondents, particularly young, educated people living in urban areas, were tolerant of inequalities in outcomes—for example, ownership of fancy cars, big houses, and the lastest technology—so long as these gains were earned through hard work and legitimate means. Many groups raised concerns about ill-gotten gains, bribery, and misuse of power leading to rising inequalities. And there were widespread concerns about "procedural" inequalites—the gaps in how systems were supposed to work in principle and how they worked in practice (for example, implementation of land compensation policies).

Notes

1. Prime Minister's Decision 60/2010, On the Issuance of Principles, Criteria, and Norms for the Allocation of Development Investment Funding in the State Budget 2011–2015.
2. Detailed work, including field studies carried out as part of the poverty assessment, indicates considerable variation in how resources for poverty reduction are used at the local level. There are incentives to show progress, and in some cases these incentives may cause officials to focus resources on households just below the poverty line (because progress is judged in terms of crossing the poverty line) rather than on households that are categorized as the chronic or extreme poor.
3. MOLISA Decision 375/QD-LDTBXH, issued on March 28, 2012.
4. MOLISA Decision 749/QD-LDTBXH, issued on May 13, 2013.
5. Chad, Ethiopia, The Gambia, Ghana, Guinea-Bissau, Malawi, Mali, Mozambique, Nepal, Niger, Rwanda, Sierra Leone, Tajikistan, Tanzania, and Uganda.
6. A growth incidence curve plots the annualized rate of growth between two points in time for specific percentiles of the income distribution.

References

ADB (Asian Development Bank). 2003. "Participatory Poverty and Governance Assessment: Central Coast and Highlands Region." ADB, Hanoi.

CECODES (Centre for Community Support and Development Studies), FR (Central Committee for the Viet Nam Fatherland Front), CPP (Commission on People's Petitions of the Standing Committee for the National Assembly of Viet Nam), and UNDP (United Nations Development Programme). 2012. *The Viet Nam Governance and Public Administration Performance Index (PAPI) 2011: Measuring Citizen's Experiences.* Hanoi: CECODES, FR, CPP, and UNDP.

Chen, Shaohua, and Martin Ravallion. 2008. "New Global Poverty Estimates." *World Bank Research Digest* 3 (1, Fall): 4.

GSO (General Statistics Office). 2011. *Vietnam Statistical Handbook.* Hanoi: GSO.

———. 2012. *Vietnam Statistical Handbook.* Hanoi: GSO.

Haughton, Jonathan, Thanh Loan Thi Nguyen, and Bui Linh Nguyen. 2010. "Urban Poverty Assessment in Hanoi and HCMC." UNDP and GSO, Hanoi.

Hoang, Van Minh, Kim Phuong Thi Nguyen, Priyanka Saksena, Chris D. James, and Ke Xu. 2012. "Financial Burden of Household Out-of-Pocket Health Expenditure in Vietnam: Findings from the National Living Standards Survey 2002–2010." *Social Science and Medicine* 96 (November): 258–63.

Iyer, Lakshmi, and Quy-Toan Do. 2008. "Land Titling and Rural Transition in Vietnam." *Economic Development and Cultural Change* 56 (3): 531–79.

Lieberman, Samuel, and Adam Wagstaff. 2008. *Health Financing and Delivery in Vietnam: The Short and Medium Term Policy Agenda*. Hanoi: World Bank.

Marsh, David, Dirk Schroeder, Kirk Dearden, Jerry Sternin, and Monique Sternin. 2004. "The Power of Positive Deviance." *British Medical Journal* 329 (7475): 1177–79.

Nguyen, Giang Tam, and Thanh Xuan Hoang. 2012. "Long-Run Drivers of Poverty Reduction in Vietnam between 1992 and 2011." Background paper prepared for the 2012 Poverty Assessment, Hanoi.

MOLISA (Ministry of Labor, Invalids, and Social Affairs). 2014. "The Government Report on the Implementation of Policies and Laws on Poverty Reduction between 2005 and 2012." Report 63/BC-CP, MOLISA, Hanoi.

Oxfam GB and ActionAid. 2008. "Participatory Monitoring of Urban Poverty in Vietnam: Synthesis Report 2008." Oxfam GB and ActionAid, Hanoi.

———. 2011. "Participatory Monitoring of Urban Poverty in Vietnam: Fourth Round Synthesis Report 2011." Oxfam GB and ActionAid, Hanoi.

Ramalingam, Ben. 2011. "A Q&A on Positive Deviance, Innovation, and Complexity." Aid on the Edge of Chaos, February 8. http://aidontheedge. info/2011/02/08/a-qa-on-positive-deviance-innovation-and-complexity/.

Ravallion, Martin, Shoahua Chen, and Prem Sangraula. 2008. "Dollar a Day Revisited." *World Bank Research Digest* 2 (4, Summer): 1–16.

UNDP (United Nations Development Programme). 2001. *Doi Moi Processes and Human Development: Vietnam Human Development Report 2001*. Hanoi: UNDP.

———. 2011. *Social Services for Human Development: Vietnam Human Development Report 2011*. Hanoi.

VASS (Vietnam Academy of Social Sciences). 2009. "Participatory Poverty Assessment: 2008 Synthesis Report." VASS, Hanoi.

———. 2011a. *Poverty Reduction in Vietnam: Achievements and Challenges*. Hanoi: VASS.

———. 2011b. "Rapid Impact Assessment: Vietnam in 2011; Synthesis Report." VASS, Hanoi.

Vietnam-Sweden Mountain Rural Development Programme, ActionAid, Save the Children UK, and Oxfam GB. 1999. *A Synthesis of Participatory Poverty Assessments from Four Sites in Vietnam: Lao Cai, Ha Tinh, Tra Vinh, and Ho Chi Minh City*. Hanoi: World Bank.

Wagstaff, Adam. 2007. "Health Insurance for the Poor: Initial Impacts of Vietnam's Health Care Fund for the Poor." Policy Research Paper WEPS 4134, World Bank, Washington DC.

World Bank. 1995. *Vietnam: Poverty Assessment and Strategy*. Report 13442-VN. Washington, DC: World Bank.

———. 1999. *Vietnam Development Report 2000: Attacking Poverty*. Washington, DC: World Bank.

———. 2003. *Vietnam Development Report 2003: Poverty*. Hanoi: World Bank.

———. 2009. *From Poor Areas to Poor People: China's Evolving Poverty Reduction Agenda: An Assessment of Inequality and Poverty*. Washington, DC: World Bank.

———. 2012. *Health Equity and Financial Protection Report: Vietnam*. Washington, DC: World Bank.

CHAPTER 2

Updating Vietnam's Poverty Monitoring System

Vietnam's poverty monitoring system was updated to reflect changing economic conditions since the first Vietnam Living Standards Survey was conducted in 1993. New, comprehensive consumption aggregates were created using data from the 2010 Vietnam Household Living Standards Survey and adjusted for spatial cost-of-living differences using updated regional price indexes. The GSO-WB poverty line was also updated, yielding a national poverty rate of 20.7 percent in 2010.

Vietnam has a robust system for monitoring changes in poverty, based on a long-running system of nationally representative, comparable surveys—the Vietnam Living Standards Survey (VLSS) and the subsequent Vietnam Household Living Standards Surveys (VHLSS)—consistent estimates of household welfare, and a poverty line that was kept constant in real purchasing power since the mid-1990s, when it was agreed between the General Statistics Office (GSO), the World Bank (WB), and other development partners.[1] Consistency in methodology and comparability over time are two of the great strengths of Vietnam's poverty monitoring system. However, by 2009, it had become clear that key aspects of the system were outdated. The methods used to measure household welfare and construct the original GSO-WB poverty line were based on economic conditions and consumption patterns of poor households in the early 1990s. Conditions have changed: Vietnam today is very different from Vietnam in the 1990s. The economy is more diversified and better integrated in the global economy. Connectivity and access to markets have improved, even for households living in more remote rural areas. In addition, the production structure of households has changed: households have access to a much wider array of consumer goods, and they purchase more food from the market and produce less food at home than before. Incomes are more diversified, and there has been a rapid shift out of agriculture and into industry and services. These changes affect households across the income distribution. Especially important for defining the poverty line, the consumption patterns of poor households today are substantially different from those of the 1990s.

This chapter describes revisions and updates to Vietnam's poverty monitoring system, including (a) improvements to the 2010 VHLSS (and subsequent rounds), (b) revisions to the definition of household welfare to make it a more comprehensive measure of well-being, (c) new indexes to adjust for spatial cost-of-living differences, and (d) an update to the original GSO-WB poverty line. The methodology used to construct the new poverty line is consistent with the original GSO-WB methodology, but it is based on new information from the 2010 VHLSS.[2] The revisions described in this chapter result in higher estimated poverty for 2010 than the original GSO-WB poverty line would have yielded and higher estimated poverty, particularly for rural areas and areas with high numbers of ethnic minority households, than those of the Ministry of Labor, Invalids, and Social Affairs (MOLISA) using official poverty lines. Reasons for these differences are also discussed.

The chapter also describes a new methodology for estimating "subjective" poverty lines for Vietnam, drawing on experimental questions introduced in the 2010 VHLSS. Poverty estimates based on the subjective poverty line are very similar to those using the updated GSO-WB poverty line.

Due to the design of the survey and size of the sample, the 2010 VHLSS can only produce reliable estimates of poverty at the national level, for urban and rural areas, and by region. Chapter 3 describes a small-area (poverty mapping) methodology that is used to estimate poverty at lower levels of spatial disaggregation—in Vietnam's case, for provinces and districts—and presents new district- and provincial-level poverty maps based on the 2009 Housing and Population Census and the 2010 VHLSS.

Rethinking poverty in Vietnam

Poverty is defined as *unacceptable deprivation in well-being*. But well-being can encompass a multitude of dimensions, and there are many different views about what constitutes an acceptable (or unacceptable) standard of living. In many countries, setting (or revising) the poverty line involves active public debate and a careful balancing of political and scientific considerations. The enormous public response, in India and internationally, to the Indian Planning Commission's announcement of new poverty estimates and revised urban and rural poverty lines provides a recent example of the challenges inherent in updating poverty lines, with some interesting parallels to current discussions in Vietnam (box 2.1).

The official poverty lines developed for the 2011–15 Socio-Economic Development Plan (SEDP) are more akin to Abhijit Banerjee's concept of an administrative poverty line: they aim to help the government to target limited public resources to those most in need and should be assessed

BOX 2.1 **Do India's new official poverty lines measure up?**

The Indian Planning Commission released a new set of poverty estimates and new poverty lines in March 2012. Many observers believe that the new poverty lines are much too low—Rs 29 per person per day for rural households (just under US$1.25, 2005 purchasing power parity [PPP]) and Rs 32 per person per day for urban households (US$1.65, 2005 PPP). The Planning Commission's new estimates showed a 7-percentage-point drop in poverty, the largest drop since the official poverty rate was first calculated in 1962. The announcement caused a furor in the Indian and international press: Indian poverty lines have always been low by international standards, and the new lines were seen as a missed opportunity to rectify this.

One important criticism is that the nutrition standards embedded in India's new lines continue to be based on the sparse diet that the poor consumed per the 1973–74 National Sample Survey. Like in Vietnam, consumption patterns in India have changed substantially since these standards were set. Another criticism is that India's new poverty lines do not "constitute an adequate definition of poverty because they do not take into account malnutrition, sanitation, drinking water, housing, and health needs" (Gill 2012). Similar criticisms were leveled at Vietnam's long-standing GSO-WB poverty line. The new 2010 poverty line takes full account of housing, durables, nutrition, clean water and sanitation, and health needs.

If India is using the same methodology it used in the past, why the big controversy now? Over time, the Indian poverty line has increasingly been used as a cutoff to determine eligibility for India's social welfare schemes and targeted poverty reduction programs. People who fall below the poverty line are eligible for a range of social benefits; states receive funds for some poverty reduction programs (for example, the Public Distribution System, which distributes subsidized rice to poor households) according to the number of residents who fall below the official poverty line. So where the poverty line is set is not just a statistical artifact, but an important policy decision that determines the eligibility of millions of families for public support. The Indian government cannot afford a poverty cutoff that is too high, and—as the controversy continues—it appears that the people of India will not accept a poverty cutoff that is too low.

In a recent article in the *Hindustan Times,* Abhijit Banerjee, Ford Foundation International Professor of Economics at the Massachusetts Institute of Technology, suggested that the way out of the current muddle is to have "two different poverty lines: an ethical poverty line to describe the standard we should aspire to . . . and an administrative poverty line which tells us how to best target our limited resources. As [India] gets richer, perhaps the latter will be raised till it is effectively the same as the former. But right now we don't want to hurt the poorest [by spreading resources too thinly] in the name of being more aggressive about poverty" (Banerjee 2011).

against this objective. The updated GSO-WB poverty line better captures what Banerjee refers to as an ethical poverty line; it reflects what Vietnam should aspire to achieve. The good news is that compared to the situation in the 1990s, the gap between Vietnam's administrative poverty lines and the monitoring poverty line has become much smaller. Moreover, the official poverty lines do indeed help to target poverty reduction policies and programs to those most in need and thus help Vietnam to achieve its poverty reduction goals.

Capturing different dimensions of poverty

Measuring poverty is a challenging and complicated task, because poverty itself is complex and multidimensional. This chapter focuses primarily on conventional approaches to measuring poverty, including absolute poverty lines and consumption-based measures of welfare. While familiar to the public and policy makers in Vietnam, the standard methodology may not fully capture other important dimensions of well-being. For example, households living in large, prosperous cities like Hanoi or Ho Chi Minh City may have access to better-quality schools and health facilities than households in other regions. But students attending higher-quality schools do not necessarily face higher school fees; in fact, households living in areas with poor schools may have to pay more—for instance, for extra tutoring to compensate for quality differences. Poor households that live in areas with low-quality schools but cannot afford to pay more may be at an additional disadvantage not captured in standard poverty analysis. Similarly, two households that look the same in terms of schooling and skills endowments may not earn the same income if one of the households faces discrimination in hiring—due to ethnicity or gender—that limits its future prospects.

A variety of economic and social factors—some subtle and difficult to capture in standard poverty analysis—must be examined to get a full picture of poverty. Conventional poverty measures provide an important starting point for analyzing other dimensions of poverty. The profile of poverty presented in chapter 3 looks explicitly at other dimensions of poverty—for example, deprivations in education and skills, poor health status, and deprivations in access to basic services such as clean water and sanitation. The aim of multiple-topic surveys of living conditions (like the VHLSS) is to facilitate the measurement and analysis of poverty in multiple dimensions. The human development index (HDI) described in chapter 1 is a composite measure of well-being, as is the child poverty index (described in chapter 3) and the broader multidimensional poverty index proposed by several United Nations organizations.

Additional information on other dimensions of deprivation experienced by the poor can be identified by soliciting their perceptions and insights through discussions and open-ended interviews. Many participatory poverty assessments (PPAs) have been carried out over the years in Vietnam, including three new field studies carried out as input for this book (see chapter 1). Findings from these studies are referred to throughout the book. These studies let the poor themselves give voice and context to the story that emerges from more conventional statistical analyses—poor men and women in Vietnam highlight concerns about lack of skills and education, access to good jobs and stable employment, and access to land and job security. They also speak about poverty in terms of risks—linked to health shocks, aging, and disability; job loss and uncertain wages; and weather shocks that destroy crops and affect rural incomes. Many of the poor are highly indebted, and risk can undermine new economic initiatives. The importance of social identity is also evident; in rural areas, minority status is often equated with being poor.

Updating methods for measuring poverty

Two important decisions are required in order to measure poverty: first, how should welfare be measured—in income or expenditure terms—and second, what poverty threshold or line should be used. Both issues have been the subject of debate in Vietnam, as discussed in box 2.2.

The GSO-WB approach uses per capita expenditures from the VHLSS as a measure of individual welfare. The poverty line is constructed using a standard cost-of-basic-needs (CBN) approach, based on the observed consumption behavior of the poor, as reported in the VHLSS. It includes an allowance for food and nonfood spending. The food allowance (or food poverty line) is based on a single reference food basket for poor households, scaled up or down as needed to meet caloric norms and priced using a vector of national food prices. An additional allowance is added for essential nonfood spending, for example, on fuel, housing, schooling, health care, and clothing based on nonfood spending of households whose food spending is equal to the food poverty line (World Bank 1999).

Vietnam carried out two living standards surveys in the 1990s—the 1992–93 and the 1997–98 VLSS—with extensive technical support from international partners. Vietnam then carried out a series of government-led living standards surveys—the VHLSS—in 2002, 2004, 2006, and 2008, using a similar approach to the earlier VLSS. The design of the core expenditure and income modules of the VHLSS questionnaires were kept broadly consistent with similar modules of the VLSS, with the specific and laudable aim of maintaining comparability over time. As noted, comparability has been one of the great strengths of Vietnam's poverty monitoring system.

But by 2010, strict comparability was coming at too high a cost. The 2010 VHLSS and related welfare aggregates represent a break with the 2002–08 VHLSS series in three important respects: first, the 2010 VHLSS was based on a new master sample based on the 2009 Housing and Population Census, including a new set of communes and enumeration areas; second, the VHLSS household questionnaire was substantially revised (including revisions to the core consumption module) and shortened; and

BOX 2.2 How is poverty measured?

The poverty rate (or headcount index) is defined as the proportion of the population in a specific period whose welfare (consumption per capita) falls below the poverty line (figure B2.2.1).

FIGURE B2.2.1 Conventional poverty measurement methodology

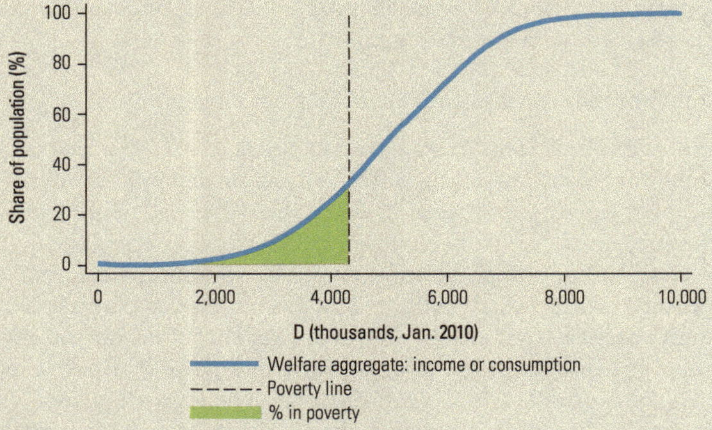
Share of population (%)
100
80
60
40
20
0
0
2,000
4,000
6,000
8,000
10,000
D (thousands, Jan. 2010)
Welfare aggregate: income or consumption
Poverty line
% in poverty

Choice of welfare indicator

Welfare is typically measured in terms of per capita consumer expenditures or per capita incomes. On a conceptual level, income is a measure of welfare opportunity—the level of well-being a household can afford to purchase at a particular point in time. Consumption can be thought of as a measure of welfare achievement—the level of well-being that a household actually achieves at a point in time. However, incomes are often more variable than expenditures: for example, farmers produce more in years when the weather is good than in years with unseasonable temperatures, droughts, and flooding. Households smooth income variations by saving in good years and not saving in bad years. Annual expenditures typically reflect a longer-run concept of income—that is, permanent income—rather than a shorter-run concept of annual income. It is therefore not surprising that income-based poverty statistics can be very different from consumption-based statistics. In the United States, for example, 30 percent of the income-poor own their own home compared to only 15 percent of the consumption-poor, and the food share is only 24 percent for the income-poor compared to 32 percent for the consumption-poor. It is generally assumed that poor households are less likely to own their own home (at least in high-income countries like the United States) and, according to Engel's law, spend a higher proportion of expenditures on food.

(Box continues next page)

BOX 2.2 (continued)

Defining the poverty line

The most commonly used approach to setting poverty lines is the cost-of-basic-needs (CBN) approach, which is widely applied in countries throughout the world and described in Ravallion (1998) and Ravallion and Bidani (1994). The CBN approach consists of first defining a basket of food and nonfood items that are adequate for satisfying the basic consumption needs of a household and then calculating the cost of this basket. Conceptually, a CBN poverty line measures the minimum income necessary for households to purchase a basic-needs basket of food and other commodities so that members have sufficient food to remain healthy and productive and have the means to participate fully in society. In practical terms, the poverty line is constructed by first defining a reference food basket (reflecting consumption patterns of the poor), anchoring it in an agreed nutrition norm (for example, 2,100 calories per person per day), and then adding an allowance for nonfood spending on essential goods (health care, education, housing, and durable goods) that is consistent with spending patterns of the poor.

third, an updated methodology was used to construct a more comprehensive consumption (welfare) aggregate. These improvements are summarized here and described in greater detail in Kozel, Hinsdale, and Nguyen (2013).

The VHLSS: Improved and shortened in 2010

Many improvements were made to the VHLSS in 2010, building on lessons from global best practices. The master sample for the VHLSS was updated using results from the 2009 Housing and Population Census, the household questionnaire was improved and shortened, and the survey period was adjusted to cover a full year.

Sampling

The 2002–08 rounds of the VHLSS used a master sample of communes and urban wards drawn from the 1999 Housing and Population Census. In each round of the VHLSS, half of the enumeration areas (villages) and households within the communes were kept and half were replaced, with the aim of ensuring stability in poverty measurement. While the approach helped to maintain stability, the 1999 master sample was substantially out of date by 2008. For example, it did not include large tracts of empty land in peri-urban areas, local towns, and villages that have since been turned into residential land to house Vietnam's burgeoning urban population. It is very important to maintain and update master samples in rapidly growing countries like Vietnam.

A new master sample of communes and wards was developed for the
2010 VHLSS and subsequent surveys using the 15 percent sample of the
2009 Housing and Population Census. The new master sample provides
better coverage of smaller households in urban areas and somewhat better
coverage of migrant households, many of whom come to work in urban
areas for extended periods. Individuals who reside in an urban area for
more than six months are supposed to be included in the VHLSS. Previous rounds of the VHLSS have been criticized for poor coverage of urban
migrants, who in the past were assumed by local officials to be members
of their rural "sending" households (Pincus and Sender 2008). A recent
study of poverty in Hanoi and Ho Chi Minh City (Haughton, Nguyen,
and Nguyen 2010) indicates that some unregistered short-term urban
migrants—those most likely to be undersampled in the VHLSS—may be
more vulnerable to income shocks and have lower living standards than
longer-term residents. These issues will be explored more systematically in
the future. The 2012 VHLSS includes a special module on migrants, focusing, in particular, on long- and short-term migration for work purposes.

The sample of households for the 2012 VHLSS will be drawn from the
same communes as the 2010 VHLSS, similar to the design of the 2002–08
sample. For 2014 and subsequent years, the GSO is advised (a) to update
the master sample through careful relisting of enumeration areas on a regular basis and (b) to refresh the sample by adding new communes to the
VHLSS master sample over time, paying particular attention to good coverage in peri-urban areas where the population is growing. The GSO is also
advised to explore alternative approaches to improve coverage of urban
migrants, either through more comprehensive sampling approaches (which
may be difficult) or through regular in-depth surveys of migrant populations. Given the high mobility of labor in Vietnam, the latter approach
may be more effective.

Questionnaire design

The VHLSS was heavily criticized for taking too long to administer in
the field, with related concerns about the quality and accuracy of data. In
response to these criticisms, many sections of the 2010 questionnaire were
shortened. The consumption modules were redesigned to collect information on food and frequent nonfood spending using a fixed reference period
(30 days) rather than a "typical month" (used in 2002–08), and beginning
in 2010 the VHLSS was administered in four rounds during each survey
year.[3] Additional sections were added to capture Vietnam's expanding
array of social insurance and social assistance programs, including more
detailed measures of remittances and transfers. Improvements were made
to the module on access to poverty programs, including targeting and coverage of benefits from targeted poverty reduction programs.

New, more comprehensive consumption aggregates

The first step in estimating a poverty line is to decide on the definition of the welfare aggregate. The consumption aggregates constructed from the VHLSS follow well-established practices (Deaton 1997; Deaton and Zaidi 2002). They include (a) food consumption, (b) frequent and infrequent nonfood items (personal care and hygiene, clothing, fuel, and household goods), (c) education (tuition, books and uniforms, tutoring, other fees), (d) health (curative and preventive care, health insurance), and (e) utilities (water, electricity, sanitation, trash collection). Two standard imputations are made in constructing the consumption aggregates: an annual flow of services from durables and an annual value of housing services and imputed rents.

The poverty line must be defined in the same terms as the welfare aggregate. Changes in the definition of the welfare aggregate will thus require revisions to the poverty line. Different countries use different welfare aggregates for measuring poverty; some countries use income, while others use household consumption. Within the set of countries using household consumption, there are substantial differences in how the measures are defined. For example, although many countries include health or education expenditures in the consumption aggregate, an increasing number of low-income countries in Sub-Saharan Africa do not. Moreover, if basic health services and primary education services are provided free of charge, they will not be reflected in household expenditures, however defined, unless imputations are made to value (nonpriced) publicly provided services. Instead of trying to value these directly—which can be complicated and controversial—researchers typically carry out additional analysis to measure deprivations in human development, as a complement to income- or expenditure-based measures of deprivation.

All countries include food in the consumption aggregate, including food purchased in the market, gifts and payments in-kind, and food produced at home. In the 1980s and 1990s, lack of food (basic calories) was a major cause of poverty throughout the world, and substantial effort went into obtaining good measures of food in poverty surveys and analysis. However, as countries become more affluent, the way we think about well-being and poverty is changing. Nonfood spending is becoming an increasingly important component of household welfare—including spending on local infrastructure, on amenities such as housing, electricity, and water, and on durable goods including furniture, small appliances, cell phones, and motorcycles. Spending on housing and durables needs to be handled in a different way than short-term spending on goods and daily needs. However, although broad measurement concepts may be similar—welfare is measured through a household-level expenditure aggregate—the great diversity in actual practice makes it difficult to compare national poverty lines and poverty rates across countries, even when converted into "internationally" comparable 2005 PPP measures. One reason India's national poverty line is low in PPP terms is because it is based on a very parsimonious consumption aggregate (box 2.1).

Two sets of consumption aggregates have been used to analyze poverty in Vietnam. One set of aggregates (referred to as "temporally comparable") was designed, as the name suggests, to be strictly comparable with the consumption aggregates initially developed using the 1992–93 VLSS. For example, although new durable goods were added to later rounds of the VHLSS (for example, cell phones and computers), only items available in the 1992–93 VLSS are included in the comparable aggregate. Similarly, estimates of the value of housing services are also based on spending patterns in the 1992–93 VLSS. Because Vietnam's housing market was very underdeveloped in the 1990s, imputed rents were calculated as a fixed percentage of total nonfood consumption rather than derived using conventional hedonic methods. This same fixed percentage (from 1993) was used to calculate the housing component of the consumption aggregate in all subsequent rounds of the VHLSS through 2008.

The vast majority of research and analytic work using VHLSS data has used the comparable consumption aggregate. The original GSO-WB poverty line, used extensively in the poverty literature for Vietnam, was constructed using the comparable aggregate. It is based on a reference food basket from the 1992–93 VLSS and related spending on a minimum basket of nonfood items.

Vietnam today is different from Vietnam in the 1990s, and expenditures, including the expenditures of low-income households, are far more diversified. Real estate markets are more developed, particularly in urban areas, and many households put considerable investment into housing and land. Vietnam is similar to other fast-growing economies in this respect. Housing values reported in recent rounds of the VHLSS are more reliable than those collected in earlier rounds.

A second set of "comprehensive" consumption aggregates was constructed using the 2004, 2006, 2008, and 2010 rounds of the VHLSS; these aim to make optimal use of all the expenditure information in a given year, unencumbered by considerations of strict comparability over time. There are some minor and major differences between "comparable" and "comprehensive" aggregates (see table 2A.1 for a detailed description). The comprehensive aggregate includes the imputed value for all durables owned by the household and an updated imputed flow of services from housing. The latter is a particularly important addition (box 2.3).

Comparable and comprehensive consumption aggregates for the last four rounds of the VHLSS are described in tables 2.1 and 2.2.[4] Comparing the numbers in these tables, it is clear that by 2010 the benefits of maintaining procedural consistency with 1993 consumption aggregates were sub-

BOX 2.3 How to value housing services in the VHLSS

Housing is an important component of household welfare, particularly as countries grow and prosper. Investments in housing are rising rapidly in Vietnam—families purchase new houses and build or add onto existing dwelling units. Housing expenditures—either actual or imputed—should be fully reflected in the consumption aggregate. In countries where housing markets function well, annual rental payments provide a good measure of the value of housing services. Using information on reported rents, a hedonic for housing can be used to impute the value of housing services (based on characteristics of the dwelling unit and neighborhood characteristics) in cases where information on rents is missing (for example, owner-occupied housing or housing supplied by employers).

However, Vietnam is an unusual case. Rental markets are still thin and there are not enough renters either in early or in more recent rounds of the VHLSS to estimate robust hedonic rent equations. Even the 2010 VHLSS includes only 243 households (out of 9,399) that report spending on rent—around 2.6 percent of total households in the sample. In contrast, the 2009 Housing and Population Census reports that 6.4 percent of all households in Vietnam rent their dwelling unit, including 13.2 percent of households living in urban areas.

Prior to 2010, the value of housing services was assumed to be a fixed percentage of nonfood consumption expenditures. Based on shares in 1992–93, the value of housing was set equal to 11.8 percent of nonfood consumption for rural households and 21.4 percent for urban households.

In constructing comprehensive aggregates, each household's annual consumption of housing services is calculated as a fixed share of the reported sales value of the dwelling unit. This fixed share is the same for all households and equals 2.88 percent, which is the median ratio of reported annual rent payments to reported sales value of the dwelling, among the subsample of households who report renting their dwelling. In essence, this method uses the information collected in the 2010 VHLSS about Vietnam's rental market to approximate the relationship that prevails in Vietnam between rental and ownership values in housing and then imputes annual consumption of housing services for all households using this relationship. While this method would not be preferable to hedonic estimation if a more comprehensive survey of Vietnam's renters were available, it has the virtue of not assuming that a household's consumption of housing remains a constant proportion of other nonfood consumption over time, an assumption made in the temporally comparable set of aggregates from 1993 to 2008. Derived directly from the reported value of each household's dwelling, the measure of housing consumption in the comprehensive aggregates is more sensitive to what each household reports about its living situation. The result is that, in 2010, housing averaged 15 percent of total consumption in the comprehensive aggregates compared to 6 percent in the temporally comparable aggregates. However, the share of housing is much lower for households in the poorest quintile (7.5 percent) and thus does not have a large impact on 2010 poverty rates.

TABLE 2.1 Comprehensive consumption aggregates for the VHLSS, 2004–10

Expenditure component	Mean consumption				Average share of total consumption			
	2004	2006	2008	2010	2004	2006	2008	2010
Food expenditure	1,753	2,378	2,993	6,515	42	42	38	46
Nonfood expenditure	1,050	1,449	2,142	3,220	21	21	22	20
Durables consumption	592	767	1,301	1,972	10	10	12	10
Education expenditure	261	334	461	769	5	5	5	4
Health expenditure	297	339	494	722	6	5	5	4
Utilities and electricity	140	183	233	373	3	3	2	2
Housing consumption	1,120	1,390	2,070	3,558	15	15	16	15
Total expenditure	5,212	6,840	9,694	17,129	100	100	100	100

Sources: 2004, 2006, 2008, 2010 VHLSS.

TABLE 2.2 Temporally comparable consumption aggregates for the VHLSS, 2004–10

Expenditure component	Mean consumption				Average share of total consumption			
	2004	2006	2008	2010	2004	2006	2008	2010
Food expenditure	1,857	2,502	3,153	6,401	49	49	47	54
Nonfood expenditure	986	1,396	1,987	2,975	20	21	23	21
Durables consumption	518	638	801	1,268	10	9	9	7
Education expenditure	246	330	423	732	5	5	5	5
Health expenditure	290	332	465	680	6	5	6	5
Utilities and electricity	147	191	233	378	3	3	3	3
Housing consumption	351	466	622	988	6	6	7	6
Total expenditure	4,394	5,855	7,683	13,422	100	100	100	100

Sources: 2004, 2006, 2008, 2010 VHLSS.

stantially outweighed by the resulting loss of information; there is a large and growing gap between the temporally comparable and comprehensive aggregates over time. Going forward, it is important to update the methodology for calculating consumption aggregates and poverty lines on a more frequent basis. How frequently will depend on Vietnam's rate of economic progress and how quickly consumption patterns change, particularly for households at the lower end of the income distribution. In deciding this, it is important to balance the benefits of stability and consistency over time with the ability of both the consumption aggregate and the poverty line to reflect contemporary living conditions. Given how quickly conditions are changing globally and in Vietnam, it is suggested that the methodology be revisited in five (or six) years to assess whether it is providing accurate estimates. However, despite efforts to ensure procedural consistency, comparisons between the 2010 VHLSS and earlier years using *either* comparable *or* comprehensive consumption aggregates must be interpreted with care.

FIGURE 2.1 **Composition of per capita expenditures in Vietnam, 2010**

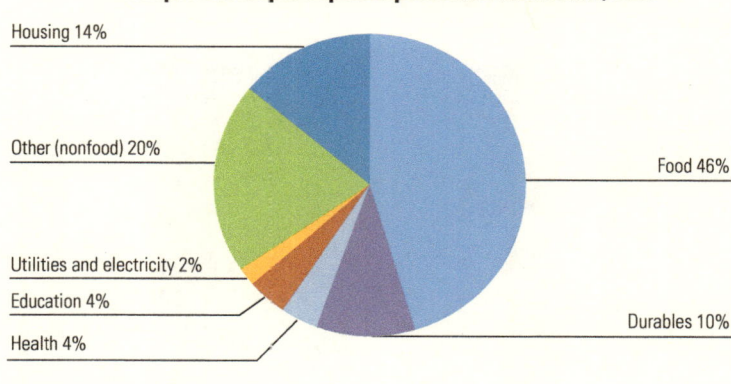

Housing 14%

Other (nonfood) 20%

Utilities and electricity 2%

Education 4%

Health 4%

Food 46%

Durables 10%

Source: 2010 VHLSS.

As described above, some important changes were introduced in the 2010 VHLSS—such as an updated sample frame, a shift to a fixed reference period in the expenditure module, and a revised definition of welfare— that make temporal comparisons difficult. The 2010 VHLSS and the new GSO-WB poverty lines provide a baseline for consistent poverty monitoring going forward—that is, for the 2012 and future rounds of the VHLSS.

Figure 2.1 shows the overall composition of per capita expenditures in the 2010 VHLSS. Spending on food now constitutes less than half of per capita expenditures compared to 57 percent in 1998, and durable goods and housing make up nearly a quarter of aggregate welfare.

Figure 2.2 shows the composition of expenditures, categorized by food, nonfood, durable goods, housing, and other spending—broken down by quintile of per capita expenditure. The share of food falls from 58 percent (in the poorest quintile) to only 32 percent (in the wealthiest quintile). In contrast, individuals in the bottom quintile spend only 7 percent of total expenditures on housing and another 7 percent on durables compared to 27 and 12 percent, respectively, for the wealthiest quintile. These gradients are consistent with those of other countries at similar levels of development.

Consumption adjusted for household size

Our objective is to calculate a measure of individual welfare and estimate the number of people who live below the poverty line. But in households, individuals live together, eat together, and often pool their resources. Household surveys like the VHLSS measure expenditures at the household rather than the individual level. Different approaches can be used to move from the household to the individual level. One approach is to use equivalence scales and to adjust for household-level economies of scale. In the absence of a well-defined equivalence scale for Vietnam and building on

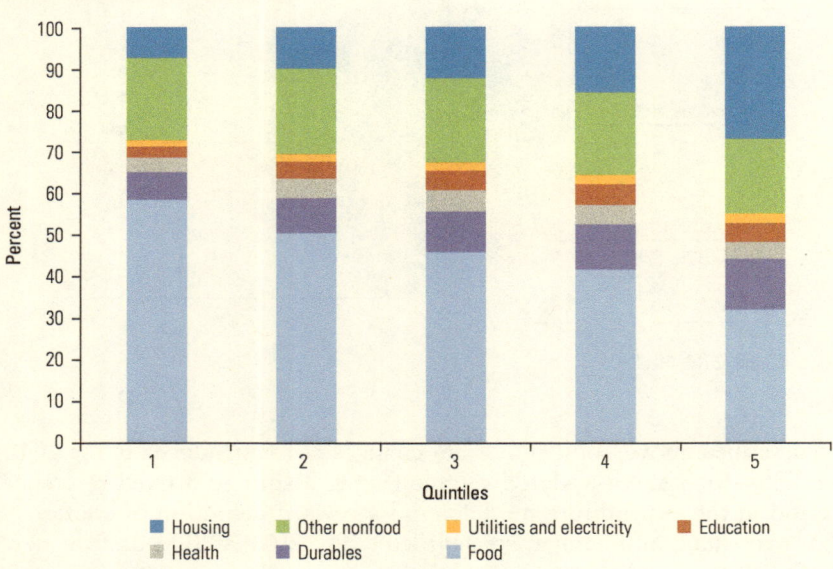

FIGURE 2.2 Composition of per capita expenditures in Vietnam, by per capita expenditure quintile, 2010

Legend:
■ Housing   ■ Other nonfood   ■ Utilities and electricity   ■ Education
■ Health   ■ Durables   ■ Food

Source: 2010 VHLSS.

past practices, household expenditure is converted into per capita terms by simply dividing by household size. The implications for the poverty profile of using alternative measures, such as adjusting for adult equivalencies and household economies of scale, are discussed in chapter 3.

Consumption adjusted for temporal and spatial cost of living

One of the advantages of the CBN methodology is that it anchors the poverty line at a fixed level of well-being and consequently allows for consistent poverty comparisons over time. However, households living in different regions of the country may face different prices for similar goods due to differences in transport, storage, and marketing costs. For example, consumers pay more per kilogram to purchase rice in a market in Ho Chi Minh City than they pay to purchase the same quality of rice in a rural district in the Mekong Delta, where the rice is grown. In contrast, laundry soap may cost more in rural areas than in cities, where it is produced and packaged. Prices also change over time due to inflation and other factors. Housing costs, in particular, vary substantially between urban and rural areas and across regions of the country.

Some countries (for example, Indonesia, Mozambique, and the Philippines) account for inflation and spatial cost-of-living differences by constructing different poverty lines for each region, based on region-specific prices and (sometimes) region-specific consumption baskets. In keeping with past practice in Vietnam, a single national GSO-WB poverty line was constructed using information from the 2010 VHLSS. The new GSO-WB poverty line is applied to spatially and temporally adjusted (that is, real) per capita expenditures to calculate poverty rates.

Temporal adjustments are straightforward; the consumption aggregates described in table 2.1 have been deflated to January of each survey year (for example, 2004, 2006, 2008, 2010) using the GSO's official consumer price index (CPI) deflators for rice, other foods, and nonfoods. Before 2010, spatial adjustments were made using regional CPI deflators provided by the GSO. For 2010, new spatial cost-of-living indexes (SCOLIs) were estimated and are used instead of regional CPI deflators to calculate poverty rates.

Rationale for the SCOLI

There are three reasons why prices collected for the CPI are poorly suited to measuring spatial differences in the cost of living. First, CPI prices are collected on a frequent basis in outlets where a wide range of consumer goods are available and shopping volumes are high. These are typically located in urban and peri-urban areas. But many of the rural population (including poor households) shop in local markets near where they live. Second, the specification of items whose prices are collected for the CPI is not the same across provinces. Vietnam's CPI price collection system maintains temporal consistency (prices for the same items are collected over time in each location) but not spatial consistency (items in the basket may be slightly different in each location). For example, prices of higher-end cotton shirts may be surveyed in large urban areas, while prices for lower-cost polyester shirts are surveyed in smaller towns or rural areas. Regional variations in the specification of items may reflect quality differences rather than capture only price differences for an identical good. Third, a CPI and SCOLI have different objectives, and the differences make it difficult for the two indexes to rely on the same set of price data. A CPI aims to give equal weight to every Vietnamese dong spent; it is used as a deflator to ensure that the real value of currency remains unchanged. Consequently, the expenditure patterns of wealthier households have more weight in a CPI because they spend more money, and a CPI price collection system targets outlets with a high volume of purchases. In contrast, a SCOLI is population weighted rather dong weighted; it is estimated using the prices paid by the average individual from each area, and prices are aggregated into a population-weighted index that treats everyone equally. In short, compared to the CPI, a SCOLI requires different budget shares for aggregating items into an index, a different set of outlets for collecting prices, and different weights for aggregating information on individuals to form regional averages.

TABLE 2.3 Spatial cost-of-living index (SCOLI) in Vietnam, by region and sector, 2010

Region	Urban households	Rural households
Red River Delta	1.00	0.79
Midlands and northern mountains	0.81	0.79
North-central coast	0.78	0.71
Central highlands	0.83	0.78
Southeast	0.97	0.77
Mekong Delta	0.74	0.7

Source: 2010 VHLSS.
Note: Calculations are based on a Törnqvist index applied to regional average prices that are pooled over the two rounds of SCOLI data collection and using person-weighted average budget shares, with housing values based on the hypothetical values reported by all survey respondents.

Regional adjustments were based on regional CPIs in earlier rounds of the VHLSS. However, for 2010, adjustments were made for regional cost-of-living differences using market price data from a SCOLI fielded in conjunction with the second and third rounds of the 2010 VHLSS. The approach is described in annex 2B.

The 2010 SCOLI ranges between 0.7 and 1.0 (table 2.3). The Mekong Delta has the lowest overall cost of living and the Red River Delta (which is also the base region) has the highest cost of living. In all but two of the six regions, the SCOLI shows only a small difference in the cost of living between urban and rural sectors. The two exceptions are the Red River and southeast regions, where the urban cost of living is approximately 20 percent higher than the rural cost of living, largely reflecting the higher estimated cost of housing and local amenities in the metropolitan areas of Hanoi and Ho Chi Minh City. Apart from these two exceptions, the variation in the cost of living is greater across regions than it is between the urban and rural sectors within a region.

Constructing a new GSO-WB poverty line

The poverty line consists of two components—a food poverty line and an additional allocation for essential nonfood needs. The food poverty line is estimated in three steps. First, a reference food basket is defined that reflects the consumption patterns of the poor; second, quantities are adjusted to reach an agreed nutrition norm; and third, the cost of purchasing the adjusted reference basket is calculated. An allowance for essential nonfood needs is estimated using an Engel's curve regression and is then added to the food poverty line in order to construct the total poverty line.

Defining the Reference Food Basket

The reference food basket used to construct the original GSO-WB poverty line is anchored in the food consumption patterns of poor households in the 1993 VLSS.[5] The reference food basket for the updated GSO-WB poverty line is anchored in the food consumption patterns of poor households in the 2010 VHLSS.

Defining the reference basket is an iterative process; we do not know in advance which households are poor so we begin with an initial reference group and adjust iteratively (see Pradhan et al. 2001). Households are ranked according to SCOLI-adjusted and temporally adjusted per capita expenditures (henceforth referred to as real per capita expenditures) from least well-off to most well-off, and the poor are initially defined as those in the bottom 2.5–20 percent of the distribution of real per capita expenditure.[6] The initial reference group ultimately became the final reference group; the 2010 poverty rate, based on an updated GSO-WB poverty line, was close to 20 percent.

Analyses were carried out to assess the stability of the poverty line food basket across different reference groups; food consumption patterns of the bottom 2.5–20 percent (bottom quintile) of individuals were compared with the bottom 2.5–10 percent (bottom decile). The initial 2.5–20 percent reference group was divided further to compare (a) food baskets for bottom-quintile ethnic minorities and bottom-quintile majorities and (b) food baskets for bottom-quintile urban and bottom-quintile rural households. Details are presented in table 2A.2.

Food consumption patterns are very similar for the poorest 10 percent and the poorest 20 percent of the population. Similarly, the consumption patterns of poor minority households are, on average, very similar to consumption patterns of poor Kinh households. Dietary patterns, however, are different for urban and rural households in the reference group: urban poor households consume less rice and more higher-priced calories (meats, oils) and are more likely to consume food and drinks outside the home than rural households.

Although the GSO-WB poverty line is based on a single national reference basket for poor households, Vietnam's official poverty lines use different reference baskets for urban and rural households. Other countries, including, for example, Indonesia, Mozambique, Papua New Guinea, and the Russian Federation, define regional reference baskets that reflect local preferences and tastes. The problem with using different reference baskets, particularly for urban and rural areas, is that the different baskets often reflect diets of different quality, so the poverty line for urban areas (based on the consumption patterns of urban households) may reflect a superior standard of living than the poverty line for rural areas (based on the consumption patterns of rural households). In 2010, only a small fraction (9 percent) of the nationally defined reference group actually lived in urban areas. Given this, coupled with concerns about avoiding quality differences (that is, setting a higher standard of living for urban households), a single national reference food basket was used to construct the new GSO-WB poverty line.

FIGURE 2.3 **Nutrition norms used to anchor poverty lines in different countries**

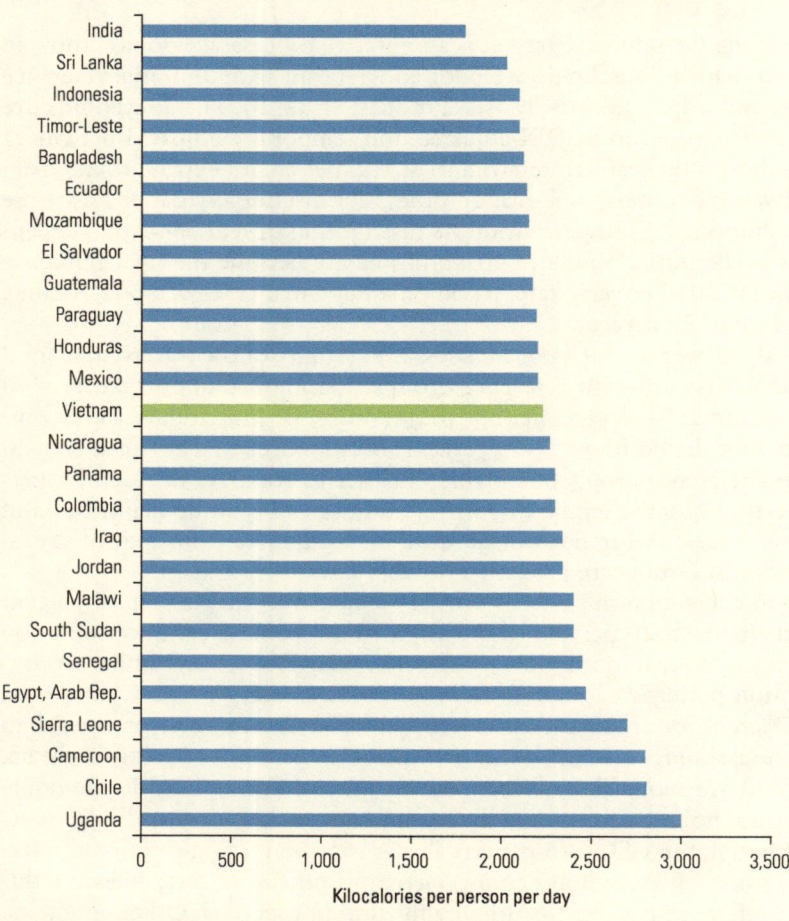

Sources: United Nations Statistics Division 2005; World Bank staff estimates.

In line with standard CBN practice, food quantities in the reference basket are scaled up to an "acceptable" nutritional norm, holding constant the relative composition of the reference basket (that is, all quantities are scaled up by the same factor). But what constitutes an acceptable norm? International experience shows that countries anchor their poverty lines in very different caloric norms, ranging from a low of 1,800 kilocalories per person per day for India (India, Planning Commission 2009) to 3,000 or more kilocalories for some countries in Africa (figure 2.3).

The original GSO-WB poverty line was anchored in a caloric norm of 2,100 kilocalories per person per day. However, the composition of the Vietnamese population has changed since the early 1990s, when the 2,100 kilocalories norm was set. The share of young children in the population (who consume less food) has decreased, and the share of adults (who consume more) has increased. A new caloric norm of 2,230 kilocalories per person per day was estimated using age- and gender-specific caloric requirements for the Vietnamese population developed by the Nutrition Institute in the Ministry of Health (MOH 2006) and weighted by the relevant age-gender composition of the national population in the 2010 VHLSS. These new norms compare well with international practice

Table 2.4 compares the calorie and expenditure composition of the 1993 reference food basket used to estimate the original GSO-WB poverty line with the new reference food basket used to construct the 2010 GSO-WB poverty line. The 1993 reference basket was heavily dominated by rice (79 percent of calories, 46 percent of food spending). The 2010 basket is more diversified; although rice continues to be an important source of food for the poor (66 percent of calories, 30 percent of food spending), the poor's consumption patterns have become more diversified to include, for instance, pork and other meats and seafood, vegetables and fruits, more oils, and more calories from meals eaten outside the household. Rice calories are very cheap; calories from pork, oils, and seafood are more expensive. The cost of the 2010 reference basket is therefore higher than the original 1993 reference basket. In addition, there has been a substantial increase in the nonquantified share of consumption—that is, food reported under "other" categories and meals eaten outside the household. More than 95 percent of food consumption was recorded under quantified items in the 1998 VLSS compared to less than 80 percent in the 2010 VHLSS. An extended list of food items was included in the 2012 VHLSS, with the aim of getting better (more quantified) measures of food consumption.

Calculating the food poverty line

The food poverty line is defined as the cost of purchasing the (scaled) reference food basket. Three sources for food prices could be used to estimate the food portion of the poverty line: (a) unit values (reported value of food consumption divided by reported quantities) calculated from the 2010 VHLSS survey, (b) food prices collected by the GSO Price Department for the CPI, and (c) food prices collected through the SCOLI survey.

The original GSO-WB food poverty line was based on CPI food prices provided by the Price Department. However, Vietnam's new official poverty lines are calculated using unit values from the 2006 VHLSS and adjusted for inflation. Both the SCOLI and CPI prices cover only a subset of food items in the 2010 VHLSS. Unit values (real or imputed in the case of non-quantified consumption) are available for all food items in the VHLSS and, moreover, can be estimated specifically for low-income households, thus reflecting what the poor actually purchase (quality, brand) and what they pay. There are mixed views in the literature (Deaton 1988, 1997; Deaton

TABLE 2.4 Composition of the reference food basket for Vietnam, 1993 and 2010

Food item	1993		2010	
	Average share of total calories	Average share of total food expenditure	Average share of total calories	Average share of total food expenditure
Plain rice (including fragrant and specialty rice)	78.9	46.5	66.4	30.5
Sticky rice	2.7	2.3	4.2	2.5
Maize (in seed equivalent)	1.0	0.4	1.6	0.4
Cassava (in fresh-type equivalent)	1.9	0.9	1.0	0.3
Potatoes of various kinds (in fresh-type equivalent)	1.6	2.5	0.3	0.3
Wheat grains, bread, wheat powder	0.3	0.4	0.3	0.3
Flour noodles, instant rice noodle/ porridge	0.3	0.7	1.3	1.6
Fresh rice noodles, dried rice noodles			0.4	0.5
Vermicelli			0.1	0.2
Pork (in equivalent of the pork type with removed fat)	2.4	9.3	4.0	11.1
Beef			0.1	0.8
Buffalo meat	0.0	0.5	0.0	0.2
Chicken meat	0.7	5.1	0.9	5.1
Duck and other poultry meat	0.1	0.7	0.2	1.0
Other types of meat			0.0	0.3
Processed meat			0.1	0.6
Lard, cooking oil	1.8	1.5	4.2	2.5
Fresh shrimp, fish	1.3	8.3	1.4	6.9
Dried and processed shrimp, fish			0.3	1.2
Other aquatic products and sea-food (crabs, snails, . . .)			0.1	0.5
Eggs of chickens, ducks, Muscovy ducks, geese	0.0	0.3	0.7	1.7
Tofu	0.4	0.9	0.6	1.3
Peanuts, sesame	0.7	0.8	0.5	0.4
Beans of various kinds	0.4	0.6	0.3	0.3
Fresh peas of various kinds			0.1	0.4
Morning glory vegetables	0.6	2.2	0.5	1.1
Kohlrabi	0.3	1.0	0.1	0.2
Cabbage	0.2	1.0	0.1	0.4
Tomato	0.1	0.7	0.0	0.4
Other vegetables			0.7	3.3
Orange	0.0	0.2	0.0	0.2
Banana	0.7	1.2	0.6	0.6
Mango	0.0	0.3	0.0	0.2
Other fruits			0.4	1.5
Fish sauce	0.3	2.0	0.2	1.1
Salt	0.0	0.5	0.0	0.3

(Table continues next page)

TABLE 2.4 (continued)

Food item	1993		2010	
	Average share of total calories	Average share of total food expenditure	Average share of total calories	Average share of total food expenditure
MSG	0.0	0.8	0.0	0.3
Glutamate			0.0	1.3
Sugar, molasses	1.3	1.3	1.3	1.2
Confectionery			0.6	1.0
Condensed milk, milk powder	0.0	0.1	0.2	0.7
Ice cream, yoghurt			0.0	0.2
Fresh milk	0.8	0.9	0.1	0.5
Alcohol of various kinds	0	0	1.3	1.8
Beer of various kinds			0.1	0.3
Bottled, canned, boxed beverages			0.1	0.2
Instant coffee			0.0	0.2
Coffee powder			0.0	0.1
Instant tea powder			0.0	0.1
Other dried tea	1.0	6.3	0.4	1.1
Tobacco			0.0	2.3
Betel leaves, areca nuts, lime, betel pieces			0.0	0.1
Outdoor meals and drinks			3.3	5.9
Other food and drinks			1.0	2.6

Sources: For 1993, World Bank 1999; for 2010, 2010 VHLSS.

Note: The 1993 food basket includes only a subset of the food categories in the 1993 VLSS. In particular, it does not include non-quantified food categories (for example, other vegetables) or categories with negligible levels of reported consumption. The share of consumption reported in non-quantified categories increased substantially between 1993 and 2010, and special methods were used to impute prices and estimate calories for non-quantified consumption in the 2010 VHLSS.

and Tarozzi 2005) about whether unit values are adequately well specified to be used as prices. Even well-defined items in the household consumption module, such as rice, are available in a range of qualities, and prices vary between urban and rural areas and among regions. Limiting unit values to a group of poor households will help to control for quality differences, which are usually linked to income levels (for example, wealthier households tend to purchase higher-quality, more expensive rice).

Consistent with the methodology used by the government to estimate Vietnam's official poverty lines, the new GSO-WB food poverty line is calculated using mean unit values for food purchases by poorer households (bottom 2.5–20 percent) reported in the 2010 VHLSS. National food poverty lines are estimated for each round of the 2010 VHLSS (June, October, December) using the national reference food basket and unit values from each round, adjusted for inflation, and then averaged to construct a national food poverty line in January 2010 dong.

The new GSO-WB food poverty line for 2010 is D 343,000 per person per month (D 4,116,000 per person per year).

Calculating the total poverty line, including food and essential nonfood spending

In addition to food, an allowance is added for essential nonfood spending such as for fuel, housing, schooling, health care, clothing, and other daily needs. However, estimating the nonfood component of the poverty line is not as straightforward as estimating the food poverty line because there is no easily defined "norm" for nonfood expenditures in the way that caloric norms can be used to define food needs.

The CBN approach looks at the actual expenditure patterns of the poor in the 2010 VHLSS with the aim of estimating (a) an "austere" allowance for nonfood needs, based on the typical value of nonfood spending by households whose total expenditure just equals the cost of the food poverty line and (b) a "minimal but adequate" allowance for nonfood needs, based on the typical value of nonfood spending by households whose food spending is equal to the cost of the food poverty line, so that basic food needs are fully met.

The relationship between the share of spending on food and total per capita expenditures is measured by an Engel's curve. Engel's law states that the food share decreases as expenditure (welfare) rises. The average food share for each group of households is calculated using the following Engel's curve regression (Ravallion and Bidani 1994):

$$\frac{f(y_i)}{y_i} = \alpha + \beta_1 \log\left(\frac{y_i}{b^f}\right) + \gamma'(d_t - \overline{d}) + residual_i, \tag{2.1}$$

where $\frac{f(y_i)}{y_i}$ is the food budget share, α is a national intercept, $\left(\frac{y_i}{b^f}\right)$ is total (nominal) expenditure divided by the food poverty line, and d_t is a vector of demographics with mean $\overline{d}$.

In keeping with international practice, we propose using the upper-bound poverty line (that is, with "minimal but adequate" allowance for nonfood) as the new GSO-WB poverty line, which is defined as the food poverty line divided by Engel's coefficient estimated from the following regression (0.525):[7]

$$\frac{b^f}{\alpha^*}. \tag{2.2}$$

The new poverty line is based on the nonfood spending of a typical household at the point on the Engel's curve where actual food expenditure is equal to the food poverty line.

The new GSO-WB poverty line is therefore defined as D 653,000 per person per month, which is calculated as D 343,000 (food poverty line) / 0.525.

New poverty estimates for 2010: GSO-WB and official poverty methodologies

New poverty estimates were calculated using the new GSO-WB poverty line and consumption aggregates described in this chapter; they are presented in table 2.5. For purposes of comparison, the table also presents Vietnam's official household-level poverty estimates for 2010,[8] based on current official poverty lines of D 400,000 per person per month (rural) and D 500,000 per person per month (urban). National poverty rates based on the GSO-WB methodology are higher overall—20.7 percent compared to 14.2 percent—which is not surprising given that the GSO-WB poverty line (D 653,000 per person per month) is higher than the official poverty lines. Comparing the two estimates for 2010, official estimates suggest higher rates of poverty in the north-central and south-central coastal regions compared to GSO-WB estimates and slightly lower rates in the central highlands and southeast regions. Differences in poverty estimates for the southeast primarily reflect the fact that the SCOLI methodology estimates a higher cost of living in the southeast compared to the CPI-based regional deflator. Overall, the GSO-WB methodology suggests lower poverty rates in urban areas than official estimates.

Although the methodologies are broadly similar (both use a CBN approach based on spending behavior of the poor in the VHLSS), the new GSO-WB poverty line is higher than official lines for the following reasons:

- Official lines were finalized in late 2010, before the 2010 VHLSS data were available and are thus based on a food reference basket and consumption behavior of poor households in the 2006 VHLSS. As noted, the 2010 VHLSS is different from the 2006 VHLSS in several important respects, including sampling and design of the questionnaire.
- Official poverty lines were estimated using the temporally comparable consumption aggregates rather than comprehensive consumption aggregates. As demonstrated in table 2.1, the comprehensive aggregate is higher due, in particular, to the inclusion of more types of durable goods and, most important, a better measure of the value of housing services. But using the new measure of housing services does not in itself lead to a higher poverty rate. We tested a modified comprehensive consumption aggregate that included a value of housing calculated using the original GSO-WB method and then calculated new poverty lines and poverty rates. The "old housing method" poverty rate was 21.3 percent, slightly higher than the "new housing method" poverty rate.
- Although food poverty lines are similar in the official and GSO-WB approaches, a decision was made to use a lower allocation for essential nonfood spending for the official poverty lines than indicated in the VHLSS data (see discussion in chapter 1).

TABLE 2.5 Poverty estimates for Vietnam, 2010: Comparing the GSO-WB methodology and the official methodology

Percent

Indicator	GSO-WB poverty estimates				Official poverty estimates		Share of total population
	Poverty		Extreme poverty				
	Rate	Contribution to total	Rate	Contribution to total	Rate	Contribution to total	
All Vietnam (national)	20.7	100	8	100	14.2	100	100
Urban	6	9	1.5	6	6.9	6	30
Rural	27	91	10.7	94	17.4	94	70
Red River Delta (Hanoi)	11.4	12	2.8	8	8.34	13	22
Northeastern mountains	37.3	21	17.9	26	24.2	20	11
Northwestern mountains	60.1	9	36.5	14	39.4	9	3
North-central coast	28.4	16	9.7	15	24	20	12
South-central coast	18.1	7	5.9	6	16.9	10	9
Central highlands	32.8	10	17	13	22.2	9	6
Southeast (Ho Chi Minh City)	8.6	7	3.1	7	2.3	4	18
Mekong Delta	18.7	17	4.8	11	12.6	17	19

Sources: 2010 VHLSS; GSO 2012 for official poverty estimates.

Other important differences between the two methodologies also might result in different poverty rates in the aggregate and across regions. For example,

- Official poverty rates for 2010 are calculated on the basis of per capita incomes in the full VHLSS,[9] with some adjustments at the provincial level following discussions with MOLISA. As described in box 2.2, income-based poverty estimates are typically different (and yield a different poverty profile) than consumption-based estimates.
- Income-based poverty rates are adjusted for spatial cost-of-living differences using a CPI-based regional deflator rather than the SCOLI. Consumption-based poverty rates are reestimated using CPI-based spatial cost-of-living adjustments instead of the SCOLI. The impact is small, raising the poverty rate (to 21.5 percent) rather than lowering it.

Neither set of lines is inherently better than the other. As noted in chapter 1, they are designed to serve different purposes. The strength of the GSO-WB approach lies in its consistency over time coupled with its independence from budgetary or political considerations. In contrast, Vietnam's official poverty lines are intended primarily to help the government to set targets and related resource allocations for poverty reduction programs and policies under Vietnam's 2011–15 SEDP. In this sense, they are administrative lines, constrained by resource availability. In response to a recent new directive on social protection (Resolution 15), MOLISA is revising its methodology to calculate average and minimum living standards taking into account many of the revisions described in this chapter. This new methodology will be used to identify potential beneficiaries of social assistance and social insurance policies and programs.

A poverty census was carried out in Vietnam at the end of 2010. Local surveys were used to identify poor and near-poor households (using short forms, proxy-means-test scorecards, and short income questionnaires), combined with village-level discussions to determine which households had incomes below the official poverty lines and were eligible to be on the list of poor households.[10] The lists are updated annually, again using a mix of survey methods and village-level discussions, often applied differently across the 10,000 or so communes in Vietnam. Analysis suggests that many of those included on the lists are poor, but not all poor households are included on the list (chapter 3). In short, errors of exclusion are a greater concern than errors of inclusion.

Comparing the new GSO-WB poverty lines with citizens' perceptions

An alternative methodology was used to estimate subjective poverty lines (Kapteyn 1994; Ravallion 2012; Ravallion and Lokshin 2002), drawing on additional questions added to the 2010 VHLSS that elicited households' own assessment of whether their consumption of important items, such as foods, foodstuffs, electricity, water, clothing, and housing, was sufficient to meet their needs (see annex 2C for technical details and Marra 2012). The following question was used to assess the adequacy of food (for example, rice, basic food grains, staples) and foodstuffs (for example, meats, vegetables, condiments):

11. Has consumption of food and foodstuff by your household [...] been sufficient to meet needs over the last 30 days?	
Insufficient 1	Food Foodstuff
Sufficient 2	☐ ☐
More than sufficient. 3	
No comment/not applicable 4	
Sufficient' means having met your household's minimum consumption needs.	

The intuition behind subjective poverty lines is straightforward: households whose observed incomes are above the subjective poverty line (that is, marked in green in figure 2.4, panel a) feel that they have enough or more than enough income to meet their needs, while households with observed incomes below the subjective line consider that their incomes are not adequate to meet their needs. The approach was implemented in a more disaggregated way for Vietnam, based on perceptions of the adequacy of specific items, for example, staple food, foodstuffs, and electricity. In the case of foodstuffs, panel b shows that, in 2010, poorer households

FIGURE 2.4 **Measuring subjective poverty in Vietnam**

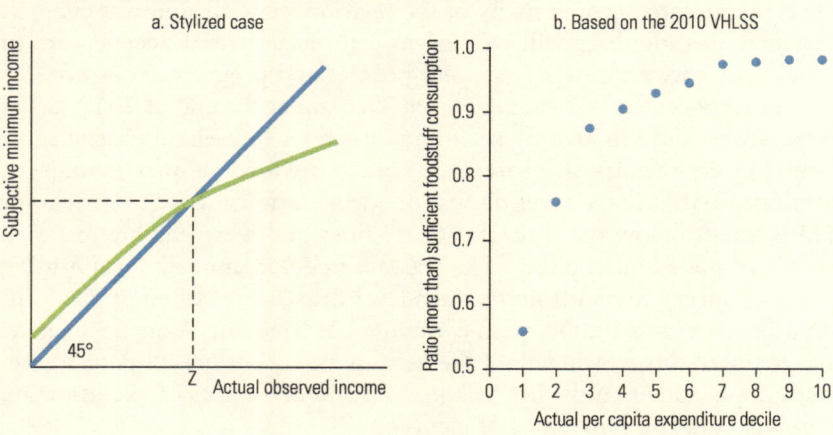

Source: 2010 VHLSS.

(deciles 1 and 2) were much less likely than better-off households to say that their consumption of foodstuffs is sufficient.

Based on responses in the 2010 VHLSS, less than 5 percent of Vietnam-ese households felt that they had consumed insufficient amounts of food in the 30 days preceding the survey. Acute hunger is no longer a major issue for Vietnam. However, 11.5 percent of households indicated insufficient consumption of foodstuffs, and the percentage was higher in rural than in urban areas—14 percent compared to 5 percent (figure 2.5). A surprisingly high percentage of households (25 percent in rural areas) reported that they were not able to consume sufficient electricity in the 30 days preceding the survey. This likely reflects supply-side problems with the quality and availability of electricity in 2010 rather than concerns about affordability; 2010 was a drought year in many parts of Vietnam, and load-shedding and brownouts were widespread.

Perceptions of sufficiency also differed across regions. Households in poorer regions (for example, the northern mountains and central high-lands) were more likely to report insufficient levels of consumption. Concerns about insufficient electricity were particularly high in regions in the north of Vietnam.

The responses to these questions were used to calculate a subjective poverty line, following an approach proposed in Pradhan and Ravallion (2000). The perceived sufficiency of consumption was regressed against characteristics of the household such as total consumption, size, gender composition, age, and education of members. Different regression models were used to test for the sensitivity of results. Based on regression results, subjective poverty lines were calculated as the minimum total expenditure

FIGURE 2.5 Perceived sufficiency of consumption in Vietnam, by urban and rural location, 2010

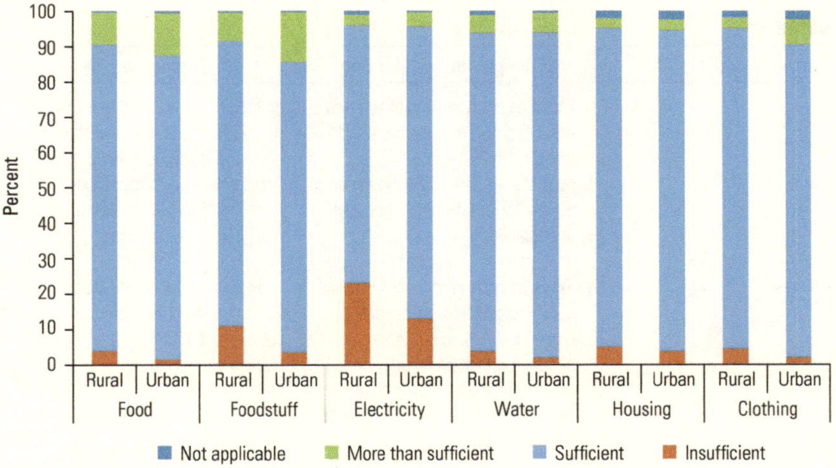

Source: 2010 VHLSS.

needed by a household to meet sufficient (foodstuff) consumption needs. Annex 2C provides a more detailed description of the derivation of subjective poverty lines.

Subjective poverty lines ranged from a high of D 888,000 per person per month to a low of D 616,000 per person per month depending on the exact specification of the regression model. All estimates of subjective poverty lines were higher than Vietnam's official poverty lines, and nearly all were higher than the new GSO-WB poverty line (D 653,000 per person per month). Most lines were clustered in the range of D 700,000 to D 800,000.

Estimates of subjective poverty lines suggest that the updated GSO-WB poverty lines and related poverty estimates do indeed reflect the aspirations and perceptions of the Vietnamese population.

Annex 2A Statistical tables

TABLE 2A.1 Differences between "temporally comparable" and comprehensive welfare aggregates

Item	Temporally comparable	Comprehensive
Food	Excludes consumption of tobacco and betel nut; assumes that food items listed in section 5A2 but not listed in 5A1 were consumed during Tet/holidays; Tet/holidays are considered 15.2 days long	Includes consumption of all 54 food items in VHLSS; assumes that the only food items consumed during Tet/holidays were those listed in section 5A1; Tet/holidays are considered 14 days long
Durables	Excludes consumption of certain durables: printers, photocopiers, mobile phones, microwaves, blenders, other transport; imputes using depreciation rates from the 1998 VLSS and a real interest rate of 5 percent	Includes all types of durables in 2010 VHLSS, but does not impute consumption for durables acquired more than 10 years prior; imputes using depreciation rates calculated from 2010 VHLSS data and real interest rate of 5%
Housing	Imputes housing consumption as 11.8% of other nonfood consumption for rural households and 21.4% for urban households	Imputes annual housing consumption as 2.88% of reported housing values. 2.88% is the median ratio of rental income to housing values for households in the 2010 VHLSS who are renters
Education	Equals total expenditures related to compulsory school subjects	Also includes supplemental expenditure on education, for tutors, typing classes, and so forth
Health	Equals spending on curative and preventive care, including out-of-pocket costs of inpatient and outpatient health services, expenditures for nonprescription medicine, and expenditures for medical tools	Also includes spending on health insurance
Utilities: Electricity, water, garbage	Simple sum of reported spending	Same
Other nonfood items (for example, clothing, fuel, kitchen items, and services)	Excludes spending on parties and celebrations and consumption of self-produced daily nonfood items from section 5B1	Same
Temporal deflator	GSO's rice, nonrice food, and nonfood monthly CPI	Same
Spatial deflator	GSO's regional CPI	2010 SCOLI

TABLE 2A.2 Reference food basket for Vietnam, by population group, 2010

	Average share of total calories					
	2.5–20th percentile					2.5–10th percentile
		Subpopulation				
Food item	All	Ethnic minorities	Ethnic majority	Urban	Rural	All
Plain rice (including fragrant and specialty rice)	66.4	64.2	68.2	63.1	66.7	69.1
Sticky rice	4.2	7.9	1.1	1.2	4.5	4.4
Maize (in seed equivalent)	1.6	2.7	0.6	1.1	1.6	2.6
Cassava (in fresh-type equivalent)	1.0	1.9	0.2	0.3	1.0	1.4
Potatoes of various kinds (in fresh-type equivalent)	0.3	0.3	0.3	0.3	0.3	0.2
Wheat grains, bread, wheat powder	0.3	0.2	0.4	0.5	0.3	0.2
Flour noodles, instant rice noodles/porridge	1.3	1.1	1.4	1.9	1.2	1.0
Fresh rice noodles, dried rice noodles	0.4	0.3	0.6	0.6	0.4	0.3
Vermicelli	0.1	0.0	0.1	0.1	0.1	0.1
Pork (in equivalent of the pork type with removed fat)	4.0	4.0	4.1	4.3	4.0	3.6
Beef	0.1	0.1	0.1	0.1	0.1	0.1
Buffalo meat	0.0	0.1	0.0	0.0	0.0	0.0
Chicken meat	0.9	1.0	0.8	0.9	0.9	0.8
Duck and other poultry meat	0.2	0.1	0.2	0.1	0.2	0.1
Other types of meat	0.0	0.0	0.0	0.1	0.0	0.0
Processed meat	0.1	0.1	0.1	0.1	0.1	0.1
Lard, cooking oil	4.2	4.0	4.3	4.4	4.1	3.9
Fresh shrimp, fish	1.4	0.8	1.9	1.8	1.4	1.2
Dried and processed shrimp, fish	0.3	0.4	0.3	0.3	0.3	0.3
Other aquatic products and seafood (crabs, snails, . . .)	0.1	0.1	0.1	0.1	0.1	0.1
Eggs of chickens, ducks, Muscovy ducks, geese	0.7	0.5	0.8	0.8	0.7	0.6
Tofu	0.6	0.6	0.7	0.6	0.6	0.6
Peanuts, sesame	0.5	0.5	0.6	0.5	0.5	0.4
Beans of various kinds	0.3	0.3	0.2	0.3	0.2	0.2
Fresh peas of various kinds	0.1	0.1	0.1	0.1	0.1	0.1
Morning glory vegetables	0.5	0.4	0.7	0.6	0.5	0.5

(Table continues next page)

TABLE 2A.2 (continued)

	Average share of total calories					
	2.5–20th percentile					2.5–10th percentile
	Subpopulation					
Food item	All	Ethnic minorities	Ethnic majority	Urban	Rural	All
Kohlrabi	0.1	0.0	0.1	0.1	0.1	0.1
Cabbage	0.1	0.1	0.1	0.2	0.1	0.1
Tomatoes	0.0	0.0	0.1	0.1	0.0	0.0
Other vegetables	0.7	0.7	0.6	0.8	0.6	0.6
Orange	0.0	0.0	0.0	0.1	0.0	0.0
Banana	0.6	0.6	0.5	0.5	0.6	0.6
Mango	0.0	0.0	0.0	0.0	0.0	0.0
Other fruits	0.4	0.3	0.5	0.6	0.4	0.3
Fish sauce	0.2	0.1	0.2	0.2	0.1	0.1
Salt	0.0	0.0	0.0	0.0	0.0	0.0
Sugar, molasses	1.3	0.8	1.7	1.6	1.3	1.0
Confectionery	0.6	0.6	0.7	0.8	0.6	0.6
Condensed milk, milk powder	0.2	0.1	0.2	0.2	0.2	0.1
Ice cream, yoghurt	0.0	0.0	0.0	0.1	0.0	0.0
Fresh milk	0.1	0.0	0.1	0.1	0.1	0.0
Alcohol of various kinds	1.3	1.7	0.9	1.0	1.3	1.3
Beer of various kinds	0.1	0.0	0.1	0.1	0.0	0.0
Bottled, canned, boxed beverages	0.1	0.0	0.1	0.2	0.1	0.1
Coffee powder	0.0	0.0	0.1	0.1	0.0	0.0
Other dried tea	0.4	0.3	0.4	0.3	0.4	0.3
Outdoor meals and drinks	3.3	2.1	4.3	7.6	2.9	2.1
Other food and drinks	1.0	0.8	1.1	1.3	0.9	0.8

Source: 2010 VHLSS.

Annex 2B Spatial cost-of-living estimates for 2010 VHLSS

A detailed price survey of 64 items was conducted in the main market in all communes in the October 2010 round of the VHLSS sample ($n = 1,049$) and in half the communes in the December 2010 round ($n = 539$). The 64 items included 45 specifically identified foods (including outdoor meals) and another 19 specifically identified nonfoods, including some durable goods and services.

To ensure consistency over space in the list of 64 items and to avoid problems with missing observations, surveyors were given detailed specifications (aided by photographs to ensure standardization) and were instructed to take two observations on the price of the detailed specification and to record whether that particular specification was the most common one in the market. A particular size—and brand name (for packaged goods)—was specified to avoid variation due to either bulk discounting or quality discounting. In almost 80 percent of the market-item combinations, the specification listed in the questionnaire was indeed the most common; it was available but not the most common in approximately 5 percent of markets. To deal with the problem of missing prices in the remaining market-item combinations, surveyors also collected the price of the most commonly available specification that was not the target specification. The price of the target specification was regressed against the prices of the alternate specifications (using brand-name fixed effects or, for unbranded items, creating quasi-brands by dividing products into intervals based on their unit prices) and a set of regional fixed effects. The regressions were used to impute the price of the target specification in about 10 percent of markets. District- or province-level average prices were used to impute the missing commune-level prices in the few cases remaining.

Various indexes are used to adjust for cost-of-living differences. The CPI is typically based on a Laspayres index. For purposes of the SCOLI, new prices were combined with regional budget shares from the 2010 VHLSS in order to calculate a Törnqvist price index. The Törnqvist index is the geometric average of the price relativities between region i and the base region, weighted by the arithmetic average of the budget shares for the two regions.

$$T = exp\left[\sum_{j=1}^{J}\left(\frac{S_{kj} + S_{ij}}{2}\right)\ln\left(\frac{P_{ij}}{P_{kj}}\right)\right], \tag{2B.1}$$

where P denotes prices in each region and S is the budget shares.

The Törnqvist index specifically accounts for the fact that consumers will substitute away from items that are expensive in their own region, relative to the base region, by using the budget shares of both the base region and their own region when weighting the price relativities. Technically, it closely approximates a true cost-of-living index for any arbitrary utility function, whereas the Laspeyres index (used for the CPI) is an exact measure of the cost-of-living index only when items are consumed in fixed proportions, without allowing for substitutions.

Because only 64 items had prices obtained in the SCOLI survey, compared to more than 100 consumption items listed in the VHLSS (including the consumption of housing services and the service flow from durables), prices were mapped to budget shares, and the price relativities for some closely related items were used as a proxy for the missing price relativities for other items. Two exceptions were for utilities, where the trimmed median unit value of electricity tariffs in each region and sector was used as the proxy to form a price relativity and flow of accommodation services from dwellings. For the imputed rents, detailed econometric analysis of the housing section of the VHLSS questionnaire was undertaken, to estimate a hedonic house value equation, which allowed for regional differences in the cost of constant-quality housing.

Annex 2C Subjective poverty in Vietnam

It is often argued that, as countries develop and become less poor, societies' standards also evolve. Even if the basic point of departure is to measure poverty with an "absolute" poverty line that is held fixed in real terms over time, societies will need to update this poverty line from time to time so that it remains relevant to a country's specific circumstances. As noted in chapter 2, as countries grow, their national poverty lines increase over time. Regardless of how carefully an absolute poverty line is developed, it is not possible to avoid some degree of arbitrariness. Challenges in setting a poverty line are grouped by Ravallion (2012) into (a) a referencing problem that includes the choice of reference group and basket and (b) an identification problem that involves translating households' utility function into measurable expenditures.

An alternative method for analyzing poverty that has received growing attention builds on subjective welfare questions included in household surveys. A *subjective* poverty line built up from such questions can offer an alternative entry point into the derivation of the poverty line and help with the interpretation of the conventionally derived CBN poverty line. This subjective poverty line exercise is particularly interesting in the context of Vietnam given the proposed update to the 2010 CBN poverty line.

Van Praag (1968) introduced subjective welfare assessment by constructing utility functions based on respondents' answers to the question asking how much income they regarded as "very bad," "bad," and so forth to "very good." A similar method, the minimum income question asks about the minimum income that respondents perceive to be necessary "to make ends meet" (Kapteyn 1994). However, applicability of the minimum income question methodology to the poorest countries has been debated (Deaton and Zaidi 2002; Pradhan and Ravallion 2000; Ravallion and Lokshin 2002; Krueger and Schkade 2008). Pradhan and Ravallion (2000) propose adapting Kapteyn's method by asking households if their consumption of food (and other things) has been adequate to "meet their needs." The 2010 VHLSS included a set of similar questions, allowing us to follow a similar estimation methodology. The exact framing of the question, asked of the household head, is the following:

---

11. Has consumption of food and foodstuff by your household [...] been sufficient to meet needs over the last 30 days?

		Food	Foodstuff
Insufficient.. 1		☐	☐
Sufficient 2			
More than sufficient................................... 3			
No comment/not applicable 4			

Sufficient' means having met your household's minimum consumption needs.

The same question was asked about "water," "electricity," "housing," and "clothing and footwear."

Out of total respondents to the 2010 VHLSS consumption section, 440 reported insufficient food consumption, 8,218 reported just sufficient food, and 686 indicated that their food consumption was more than sufficient (54 households did not respond). Satisfaction with the adequacy of food-stuff consumption (including higher-cost calories from meat, vegetables, oils, and condiments) was lower: 1,079 respondents reported inadequate consumption of foodstuffs, 7,580 indicated sufficient consumption, and 678 claimed that their consumption was more than sufficient.

To calculate a subjective poverty line, we follow Pradhan and Raval-lion (2000) in regressing perceived sufficiency of consumption on house-hold expenditure and household (head) characteristics, using sufficiency of foodstuff as the dependent variable. Responses of "not applicable" were excluded, and the other three categories were subjected to an ordered pro-bit regression including actual household consumption, household size, and characteristics of the household head. Regression coefficients, pre-sented in table 2C.1, were also used in calculating a range of subjective poverty lines, including those reported in the chapter.

TABLE 2C.1 **Subjective welfare regression and variables at country means**

	Regression results		Means of variables	
	Coefficient	S.E.	Mean	S.D.
Log total household expenditure	0.717***	0.029	10.978	0.731
Log household size	−0.475***	0.049	1.435	0.381
Household head is female	−0.092**	0.040	0.22	0.414
Household head has a wage job	−0.172***	0.031	0.407	0.491
Household has at least one widow(er)	−0.040	0.042	0.186	0.389
Highest grade household head	0.022***	0.005	7.313	3.683
Household head is registered within the commune	0.046	0.034	0.256	0.437
Household head is of ethnic majority (Kinh)	0.516***	0.044	0.854	0.353
Share of household < 18 years old	0.206***	0.078	0.256	0.206
Share of household > 59 years old	0.009	0.093	0.072	0.175
Log land area owned by household	0.029***	0.005	4.859	3.757
Urban	−0.148***	0.041	1.297	0.457
Cutoff 1	6.264***	0.277		
Cutoff 2	9.327***	0.289		
Number of observations	9,337			
Pseudo R²	0.139			

Note: The dependent variable is "perceived sufficiency of foodstuff consumption" with the following answer codes: 1 = insufficient, 2 = sufficient, and 3 = more than sufficient ("not applicable" is recoded as missing). The results are from an ordered probit regression. The natural logarithm is used for the log variables. The means of the variables and the regression are both weighted by population.
***$p < .01$, **$p < .05$.

Notes

1. The original GSO-WB poverty line was prepared as input to the 2000 poverty assessment, *Vietnam Development Report 2000: Attacking Poverty* (World Bank 1999).
2. A similar methodology was used in 2005 by a team of local and international experts, led by the Ministry of Labor, Invalids, and Social Affairs (MOLISA), to update Vietnam's official poverty lines for the 2006–10 Socio-Economic Development Plan (SEDP) and, led by MOLISA and, more recently, the GSO, to construct official poverty lines for the 2011–15 SEDP.
3. The decision to move to a fixed reference period was triggered by difficulties in measuring expenditures and prices during bouts of high inflation (for example, 2008) and an effort to capture seasonality in consumption patterns better.
4. These aggregates are in real terms; they are adjusted to January of the survey year and for regional cost-of-living differences.
5. The methodology is described in annex 2 of the *Vietnam Development Report 2000: Attacking Poverty* (World Bank 1999). Food consumption of the third quintile of households, ranked nationally based on per capita expenditures, was used to construct the reference food basket.
6. The group is restricted to the bottom 2.5–20 percent to avoid potential problems with outliers and measurement error.
7. Where α^* is defined as $\alpha^* \, \alpha + \beta_1 \log\left(\dfrac{1}{\alpha^*}\right)$.
8. Official estimates reflect the number of households, not the number of individuals, on the poverty list. To the extent that poor households are larger, on average, than nonpoor households, official estimates of the share of individuals below the poverty line would be higher than the share of households.
9. Each round of the VHLSS includes around 46,000 households. Detailed information on household income is collected for all households, but consumption information is collected for only 20 percent of households (three in each enumeration area) or 9,400 households in total. Only unit record data from the 20 percent sample (income plus consumption) are released to the public.
10. Prime Minister's Directive no. 1752/CT-TTg.

References

Banerjee, Abhijit. 2011. "Draw the Right Line." *Hindustan Times*, October 24. http://www.hinustantimes.com/StoryPage/Print/761099.aspx.

Deaton, Angus. 1988. "Quality, Quantity, and Spatial Variation in Price." *American Economic Review* 78 (3): 418–30.

———. 1997. *Analysis of Household Surveys: A Microeconometric Approach to Development Policy.* Washington, DC: Johns Hopkins University Press and World Bank.

Deaton, Angus, and Alessandro Tarozzi. 2005. "Prices and Poverty in India." In *The Great Indian Poverty Debate*, edited by Angus Deaton and Valerie Kozel, ch. 16, 381–411. New Delhi: Macmillan.

Deaton, Angus, and Salman Zaidi. 2002. "A Guide to Aggregating Consumption Expenditures." Living Standards Measurement Study Working Paper 135, World Bank, Washington, DC.

Gill, Nikhila. 2012. "Has Poverty Really Dropped in India?" *New York Times*, March 21. http://india.blogs.nytimes.com/2012/03/21/has-poverty-really-dropped-in-india/.

Haughton, Jonathan, Thi Thanh Loan Nguyen, and Bui Linh Nguyen. 2010. *Urban Poverty Assessment in Hanoi and HCMC*. Hanoi: UNDP and General Statistics Office.

India, Planning Commission. 2009. "Report of the Expert Group to Review the Methodology for Poverty Estimation." Government of India, Planning Commission, New Delhi.

Kapteyn, Arie. 1994. "The Measurement of Household Cost Functions: Revealed Preference versus Subjective Measures." *Journal of Population Economics* 7 (4): 333–50.

Kozel, Valerie, Ian Hinsdale, and Phong Nguyen. 2013. "Updated Methodologies for Poverty Monitoring in Vietnam." Background paper prepared for the 2012 Vietnam Poverty Assessment, World Bank, Washington, DC.

Krueger, Alan B., and David Schkade. 2008. "The Reliability of Subjective Well-Being Measures." *Journal of Public Economics* 92 (8–9): 1833–45.

Marra, Marleen. 2012. "Estimating Subjective Poverty Lines for Vietnam." Background paper prepared for the 2012 Vietnam Poverty Assessment, World Bank, Washington, DC.

MOH (Ministry of Health). 2006. "Proposed Nutrition Needs for the Vietnamese." Ministry of Health, Hanoi.

Pincus, Jonathan, and John Sender. 2008. "Quantifying Poverty in Vietnam: Who Counts?" *Journal of Vietnamese Studies* 2 (1, January): 108–50.

Pradhan, Menno, and Martin Ravallion. 2000. "Measuring Poverty Using Qualitative Perceptions of Consumption Adequacy." *Review of Economics and Statistics* 82 (3): 462–71.

Pradhan, Menno, Asep Suryahadi, Sudarno Sumarto, and Lant Pritchett. 2001. "Eating Like Which Joneses? An Iterative Solution to the Choice of a Poverty Line Reference Group." *Review of Income and Wealth* 47 (4): 473–87.

Ravallion, Martin. 1998. "Poverty Lines in Theory and Practice." Living Standards Measurement Study Working Paper 133, World Bank, Washington DC.

———. 2012. "Poor or Just Feeling Poor? On Using Subjective Data in Measuring Poverty." Policy Research Working Paper 5968, World Bank, Washington, DC.

Ravallion, Martin, and Benu Bidani. 1994. "How Robust Is a Poverty Profile?" *World Bank Economic Review* 8 (1, January): 75–102.

Ravallion, Martin, and Michael Lokshin. 2002. "Self-Rated Economic Welfare in Russia." *European Economic Review* 46 (8, September): 1453–73.

United Nations Statistics Division. 2005. *Handbook on Poverty Statistics: Concepts, Methods, and Policy Use; Special Project on Poverty Statistics*. New York: United Nations.

Van Praag, Bernard. 1968. *Individual Welfare Functions and Consumer Behavior: A Theory of Rational Irrationality*. Amsterdam: North Holland Publishing.

World Bank. 1999. *Vietnam Development Report 2000: Attacking Poverty*. Washington, DC: World Bank.

CHAPTER 3

Poverty Profile: Establishing the Facts about Poverty in Vietnam

The chapter characterizes the poor and the extreme poor and compares them with the rest of society along several key dimensions, including geographic location, ethnicity, sector of employment, source of income, educational attainment, ownership of durable goods, landholdings, household amenities, child poverty, and coverage under social protection and poverty reduction programs and policies. Statistical analysis is complemented by a rich body of qualitative research. It finds that the poor in Vietnam today are similar in important respects to the poor in the late 1990s. Among other factors, poverty is linked to rural and upland locations, agricultural livelihood, ethnic identity, low educational attainment, exposure to risk, and rising vulnerability.

Poverty reduction remains a challenge in Vietnam, albeit one that has changed dramatically in scope and nature over the last two decades. This chapter revisits the basic facts about poverty and the poor in Vietnam. It takes stock of what we know about poverty today and draws comparisons with the situation of the poor in the late 1990s, with the aim of highlighting both important areas of progress and remaining and new challenges. The chapter presents a new profile of the poor, using the 2010 General Statistics Office–World Bank (GSO-WB) poverty line and the updated (comprehensive) measures of household welfare proposed in chapter 2. The analysis is based primarily on the 2010 Vietnam Household Living Standards Survey (VHLSS), but also draws selectively on earlier rounds of the Vietnam Living Standards Survey (VLSS), particularly the 1998 VLSS, and other sources, such as recent participatory poverty assessments (PPAs), qualitative field studies, 2009 poverty maps, and other supplementary sources of information.

A poverty line only discriminates between poor and non-poor households. It ignores the fact that not all poor people are the same; some have incomes or consumption very close to the poverty line, while others live in much poorer conditions. Nor are the non-poor homogeneous; some live near the poverty line (referred to as the "near-poor" in Vietnam), while others are much more prosperous. The analysis presented in this chapter recognizes the broad economic diversity among poor and non-poor households in Vietnam. At the lower end of the welfare distribution, a distinction is drawn between the "extreme poor" (per capita expenditures below two-thirds of the poverty line) and the "poor" (per capita expenditures below the poverty line). The remainder of the population is analyzed on the basis of per capita expenditure *quintiles* and *deciles*. Specifically,

- Individuals are ranked by per capita expenditures from least well-off to most well-off and then divided into 5 equally sized population groups (quintiles) and 10 equally sized population groups (deciles). Quintile 1 constitutes the poorest 20 percent of the population, and quintile 5 constitutes the wealthiest 20 percent. Similarly, decile 1 constitutes the poorest 10 percent of the population, and decile 10 constitutes the wealthiest 10 percent.
- Individuals are also classified by *expanded* per capita expenditure quintiles. The poor are classified into two groups (the total poor and the extreme poor), and the non-poor are further classified by the standard per capita expenditure quintiles. Expanded quintiles thus constitute six groups: the extreme poor (individuals whose per capita expenditures are less than two-thirds of the poverty line, the poorest 8 percent of the population), the poor (individuals whose per capita expenditures are below the poverty line, the poorest 20.7 percent of the population), and quintiles 2 through 5 (as above).

In the context of the 2006–10 Socio-Economic Development Plan (SEDP), the Ministry of Labor, Invalids, and Social Affairs (MOLISA) introduced a "near-poor" classification, which includes households whose per capita income lies between the poverty line and 1.3 times the poverty line. If this definition is applied to the 2010 GSO-WB poverty line, roughly three-quarters of individuals in quintile 2 would fall into the near-poor group.

The World Bank recently launched a global initiative with the aim of eradicating extreme poverty by 2030 and promoting shared prosperity (defined as the growth rate for the poorest 40 percent). Research from around the world suggests that the poorest and most destitute are more difficult to reach than those living close to the poverty line; they face a range of structural barriers and specific constraints, and better policies and programs are needed to address these specific challenges. In many countries, including Vietnam, there is disquieting evidence that the extreme and destitute poor are falling further behind. This chapter develops profiles of the extreme poor as well as the poor, while recognizing that many of the near-poor (quintile 2) remain vulnerable to falling (back) into poverty.

In constructing the poverty profile, households and individuals are also categorized by socioeconomic group (ethnic minority, Kinh majority), sector (urban, rural), and economic region. The government of Vietnam has identified eight economic regions encompassing 63 provinces, more than 680 districts, and two major urban areas (Hanoi and Ho Chi Minh City). Annex 3A describes the eight economic regions, including the northeast region, northwest region, the Red River Delta (which houses Hanoi), the north-central coast, the south-central coast, the central highlands, the southeast (which houses Ho Chi Minh City), and the Mekong Delta. The northeast and northwest are mountainous regions where the majority of Vietnam's ethnic minorities reside. Ethnic minorities also live in upland areas of the central and southern regions, particularly the central highlands. The two deltas (Red River, Mekong) are major rice-growing regions, with the majority of Vietnam's rice exports coming from the Mekong Delta.

Stylized facts about poverty in Vietnam

The *Vietnam Development Report 2000: Attacking Poverty* (World Bank 1999) describes the key characteristics of poor households at the end of the 1990s, drawing on the 1993 and 1998 VLSS combined with a series of PPAs carried out in 1999. These early PPAs stressed core poverty concerns such as hunger; lack of productive assets; high exposure to adverse shocks such as drought, flooding, and illnesses; and social marginalization and isolation (particularly for ethnic minority groups). At that time, many poor households struggled to feed and educate large families, and child poverty was widespread. Landlessness was rising, and there were limited options for off-farm employment (box 3.1).

Many of these stylized facts are still true today. Although poverty has fallen dramatically, many of the factors that characterized the poor in the 1990s still characterize the poor today: low education and skills, dependency on subsistence agriculture, physical and social isolation, specific disadvantages linked to ethnic identity, and exposure to natural disasters and risks. Those who moved out of poverty acquired more schooling and job skills, diversified out of agriculture and into manufacturing and services, and reduced their exposure to seasonal hardships and shocks through income diversification and migration.

But some of the stylized facts have changed. For example, issues such as ethnic minority poverty that were only emerging as concerns in the late 1990s are much greater concerns today. Other issues, like poverty and vulnerability among migrants in urban areas, have become lesser concerns. Although income poverty remains very low in Vietnam's cities and towns, new forms of poverty are arising: urban households are particularly vulnerable to sharp bouts of inflation and a concomitant increase in the cost of living. Risks remain an important feature of the rural economy as well,

BOX 3.1 **Defining characteristics of poor households at the end of the 1990s**

By the end of the 1990s, poor households had the following defining characteristics:

- The poor lived in rural areas and were predominantly farmers with low levels of educational attainment, limited access to information, and low-function skills. In 1998, nearly four-fifths of the poor were agricultural households.
- Poor households had small landholdings, and landlessness was increasing, especially in the Mekong Delta. Households that were unable to make a living from the land found few opportunities to generate stable off-farm income. There was an urgent need for reforms to stimulate demand for off-farm employment.
- Households with many children or few laborers were disproportionately poor and were particularly vulnerable to rising and variable health and education costs. Newly formed households went through an initial phase of poverty, often aggravated by limited access to land. Poor households were also frequently caught in a debt trap.
- Poor households were vulnerable to seasonal hardship and household-specific and community-wide shocks, and some were socially and physically isolated.
- Poverty among ethnic minority groups had declined, but not as rapidly as among the majority population. Ethnic minorities faced many specific disadvantages that could best be addressed through an ethnic minority development program.
- Migrants to urban areas who were poor and had not secured permanent registration faced difficulties accessing public services, and some felt socially marginalized. Further work was needed to identify the best way to help these groups.
- Children were overrepresented in the poor population; they were less able to attend school and were trapped in a cycle of inherited poverty. Many felt insecure and uncertain about their future.

Source: World Bank 1999.

including weather-related risks and the emerging impacts of climate change for agriculture.

Spatial distribution of poverty

The poor still live in rural areas and are concentrated in upland regions. As shown in table 3.1, an estimated 20.7 percent of the population were poor in 2010, and 8 percent were extremely poor. Poverty remains a rural phenomenon; more than 90 percent of the poor and 94 percent of the extreme poor live in rural areas. The poor in urban areas live for the most part in smaller cities and towns. However, the qualitative studies carried

TABLE 3.1 Poverty headcount in Vietnam, by region and sector, 2010
Percent

	Poverty		Extreme poverty		Share of total population
	Rate	Contribution to total	Rate	Contribution to total	
National	20.7	100.0	8.0	100.0	100.0
Red River Delta	11.4	12.3	2.8	7.8	22.3
Northeastern mountains	37.7	20.8	17.9	25.8	11.5
Northwestern mountains	60.1	9.1	36.5	14.4	3.2
North-central coast	28.4	16.5	9.7	14.6	12.0
South-central coast	18.1	7.4	5.9	6.3	8.5
Central highlands	32.8	9.5	17.0	12.9	6.0
Southeast	8.6	7.2	3.1	6.9	17.5
Mekong Delta	18.7	17.1	4.8	11.4	19.0
Rural	27.0	91.4	10.7	94.4	70.3
Urban	6.0	8.6	1.5	5.6	29.7

Source: 2010 VHLSS.

for this book and recent research on urban poverty (Haughton, Nguyen, and Nguyen 2010) suggest that urban low-income households struggle with other (non-income) dimensions of poverty, such as poor sanitation, lack of adequate housing, limited coverage of social insurance, increasing exposure to risk, and continuing vulnerability to poverty.

The spatial distribution of poverty has changed over time. In the 1990s, poverty was widespread in Vietnam. Although poverty rates were higher in some regions than others (for example, in isolated and sparsely settled provinces in the northern mountains and central highlands), the majority of the poor lived in the more densely settled delta regions (figure 3.1, panel a). Poverty fell throughout Vietnam between 1998 and 2010, but it fell more rapidly in fast-growing regions around Hanoi and Ho Chi Minh City (that is, the Red River Delta and the southeast region). Uneven progress has resulted in substantial changes in the spatial distribution of poverty, with the remaining poor becoming more concentrated in the upland areas in the north of Vietnam and in the central highlands (figure 3.1, panel b). Chapter 4 examines the spatial distribution of poverty across provinces and districts using poverty-mapping methods.

Sector of employment

Many of the poor are farmers whose livelihoods are linked primarily to agriculture. In Vietnam, 32.9 percent of agricultural households[1] live below the poverty line, which is nearly three times higher than the national

FIGURE 3.1 Poverty in Vietnam, by region, 1998 and 2010

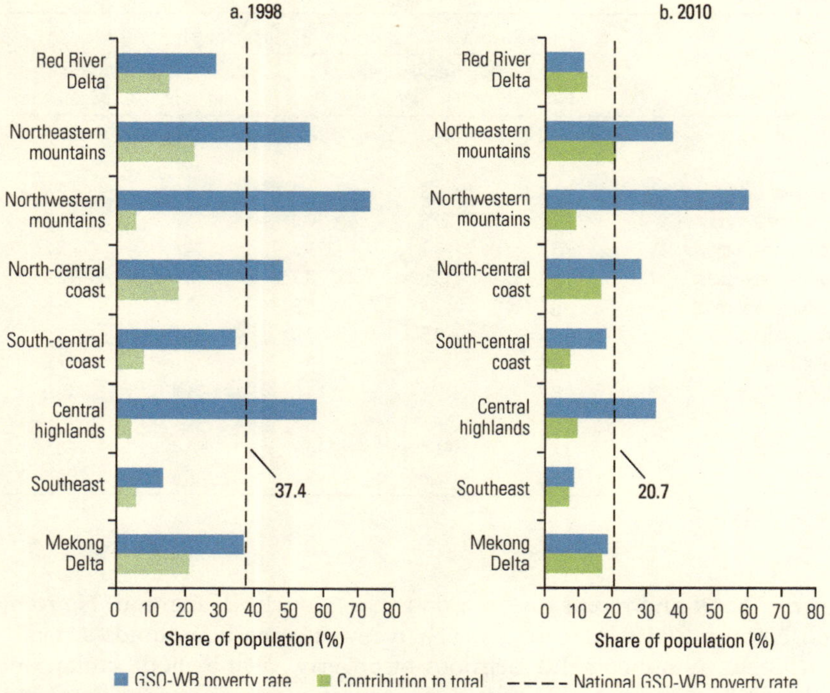

Source: 1998 VLSS; 2010 VHLSS.

poverty rate, and agricultural households make up 65 percent of the poor and 73 percent of the extreme poor compared with a population share of only 41 percent (table 3.2). Agricultural households also contribute disproportionately to the poverty gap and poverty severity.

The level and composition of household income across the expanded per capita expenditure quintiles are described in figure 3.2. The height of each bar reflects the average level of per capita income for each group. Figure 3.3 looks in greater detail at the composition of income for each group, broken down by income from agriculture (crop cultivation, livestock, forestry, aquaculture, and agriculture wages), nonfarm family enterprises, nonagricultural wages, social transfers, domestic and overseas remittances, and other sources. According to figure 3.3, poor households derive roughly half of their income from agricultural activities, including agricultural wages. However, what differentiates the incomes of the poor from those of wealthier households is not the amount of income from agricultural activities; crop incomes are surprisingly equal across wealth quintiles, reflecting Vietnam's broadly egalitarian distribution of agricultural land. What differenti-

TABLE 3.2 Poverty in Vietnam, by sector of employment of household head, 2010
Percent

	Poverty		Extreme poverty		Share of total population
	Rate	Contribution to total	Rate	Contribution to total	
National	20.7	100.0	8.0	100.0	100.0
Employment of household head:					
Not employed	13.2	9.1	5.3	9.6	14.4
Agriculture	32.9	64.8	14.1	72.5	40.9
Family business	5.9	4.4	1.2	2.3	15.4
Employed for wages in:					
Industry and manufacturing	13.2	4.0	2.7	2.1	6.3
Construction	19.3	7.7	5.1	5.3	8.3
Services	14.0	10.0	4.4	8.2	14.9

Source: 2010 VHLSS.

FIGURE 3.2 Level of household income in Vietnam, by expanded quintile, 2010

FIGURE 3.3 Composition of household income in Vietnam, by expanded quintile, 2010

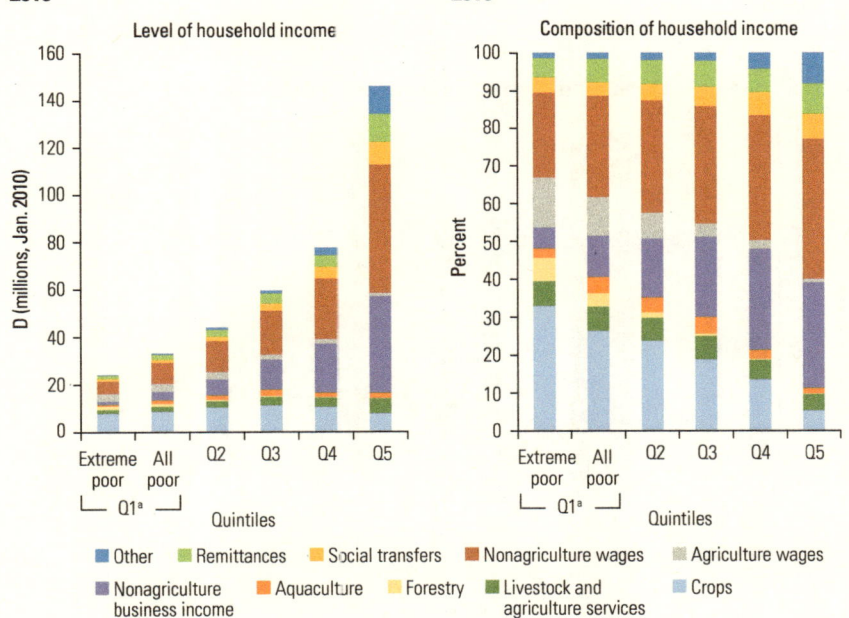

Source: 2010 VHLSS.

a. Quintile 1 is defined as "all poor," which comprised 20.7 percent of the population; of that 20.7 percent, 8 percent are considered "extreme poor."

ates the incomes of the poor from those of wealthier households is, instead, the extent to which households have successfully diversified into off-farm activities. Progress in the 1990s was driven by on-farm diversification—for instance, into cash crops, livestock, and (in some parts of the country) fish and shrimp farming (World Bank 1999). However, progress in recent years has been driven by diversification into business and trading and, even more important, by salaried employment in industry and manufacturing and jobs in the service sector. Even the extreme poor have income sources outside agriculture, although, as shown in the next section, this differs for poor minority households compared to poor Kinh households.

Poverty and ethnic identity

Ethnic identity matters even more for poverty. Although Vietnam's 53 ethnic minority groups make up only 15 percent of the population, they account for nearly half (47 percent) of the total poor and 68 percent of the extreme poor (figure 3.4). Although living conditions for many minorities have improved since the late 1990s, the concentration of minorities among the poor has nonetheless increased dramatically—by 25 percentage points for the extreme poor (from 43 percent in 1998 to 68 percent in 2010) and 19 percentage points for the poor (from 28 percent in 1998 to 47 percent in 2010).

FIGURE 3.4 Poor and better-off households in Vietnam, by ethnicity, 2010

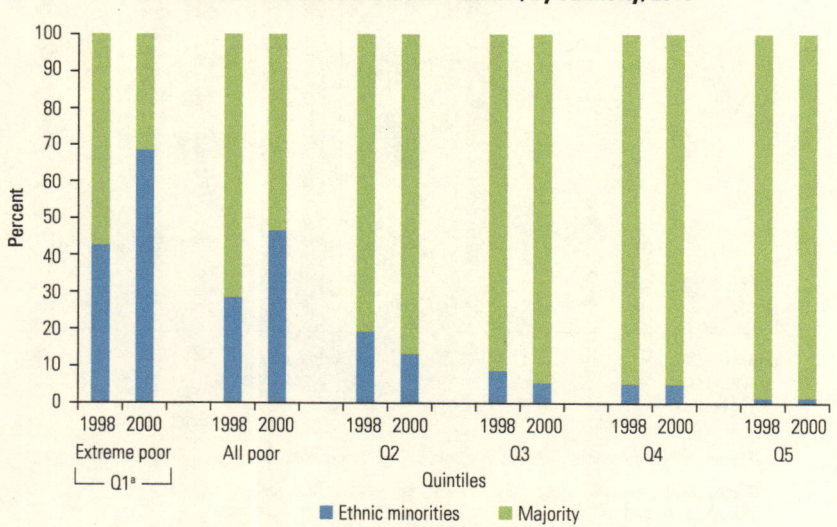

Sources: 1998 VLSS; 2010 VHLSS.
a. Quintile 1 is defined as "all poor," which comprised 20.7 percent of the population; of that 20.7 percent, 8 percent are considered "extreme poor."

TABLE 3.3 Poverty headcount among ethnic minorities in Vietnam, by region and sector, 2010

Percent

	Poverty		Extreme poverty		Share of total population
	Rate	Contribution to total	Rate	Contribution to total	
National	66.3	100.0	37.4	100.0	100.0
Red River Delta	13.1	0.2	0.0	0.0	1.0
Northeastern mountains	64.8	35.4	34.9	33.9	36.2
Northwestern mountains	72.8	18.9	45.5	20.9	17.2
North-central coast	71.2	14.0	34.8	12.1	13.0
South-central coast	78.4	5.3	50.7	6.1	4.5
Central highlands	76.6	15.2	50.4	17.7	13.1
Southeast	46.4	3.5	22.2	3.0	5.0
Mekong Delta	50.4	7.6	23.3	6.2	10.0
Rural	68.9	95.5	39.3	96.8	91.9
Urban	36.5	4.5	14.8	3.2	8.1

Source: 2010 VHLSS.

Despite progress, in 2010, 66.3 percent of minorities still lived below the poverty line, and 37.4 percent lived below the extreme poverty line (table 3.3). In comparison, only 12.9 percent of the Kinh majority population were still poor, and 2.9 percent lived below the extreme poverty line (table 3.4). Because the Kinh make up such a large share of the population in Vietnam, they still account for just over half (53 percent) of the total poor.

Minorities are more heavily concentrated among the extreme poor, as illustrated in table 3.5, and both the depth and severity of poverty are likewise substantially higher for minorities. These differences between Kinh poverty and ethnic minority poverty are illustrated graphically in figure 3.5: the distribution of welfare (per capita expenditures) for minorities who fall below the poverty line is skewed to the left, and the overall distribution has a much thinner tail than the distribution of welfare for the Kinh. Both the depth and severity of poverty are lower for Kinh living below the poverty line.

There are important differences in the spatial distribution of Kinh and ethnic minority populations in Vietnam. Minority populations remain heavily concentrated in the northern mountains, in the central highlands, and (to some extent) in the north-central coast. In contrast, the Kinh live primarily in large cities (including Hanoi and Ho Chi Minh City), in the Red River and Mekong deltas, and in lower elevations along the coast and inland areas. The spatial distribution of poverty tends to follow the spatial distribution of their respective populations: poor Kinh households are more likely to live in the deltas and in provinces along the north-

TABLE 3.4 Poverty headcount among the Kinh majority in Vietnam, by region and sector, 2010

Percent

	Poverty		Extreme poverty		Share of total population
	Rate	Contribution to total	Rate	Contribution to total	
National	12.9	100.0	2.9	100.0	100.0
Red River Delta	11.4	22.9	2.8	24.7	26.0
Northeastern mountains	14.4	8.0	3.3	8.2	7.2
Northwestern mountains	10.7	0.6	1.3	0.3	0.8
North-central coast	20.4	18.6	4.9	19.8	11.9
South-central coast	13.0	9.2	2.1	6.5	9.2
Central highlands	12.4	4.6	1.5	2.4	4.8
Southeast	6.9	10.5	2.3	15.3	19.7
Mekong Delta	16.1	25.5	3.3	22.7	20.5
Rural	17.0	87.7	3.9	89.1	66.6
Urban	4.8	12.3	1.0	10.9	33.4

Source: 2010 VHLSS.

TABLE 3.5 Poverty headcount, gap, and severity in Vietnam, by ethnicity, 2010

Percent

	Poverty		Extreme poverty		Poverty severity	
	Rate	Contribution to total	Rate	Contribution to total	Rate	Contribution to total
Poor						
Kinh-Hoa	12.9	53.3	2.7	39.7	0.9	31.1
Ethnic minorities	66.3	46.7	24.3	60.3	11.3	68.9
Extreme poor						
Kinh-Hoa	2.9	31.5	0.5	21.5	0.1	15.1
Ethnic minorities	37.4	68.5	9.7	78.5	3.7	84.9

Source: 2010 VHLSS.

central coast. In contrast, most poor minority households live in upland areas, with the northern mountains and central highlands accounting for a somewhat higher share of poor ethnic minorities than their share in the population. Notably, across all locations (with the exception of Red River Delta, where very few ethnic minorities reside), poverty rates among ethnic minorities average between four and seven times higher than poverty rates among the Kinh (figure 3.6). Majority populations living in areas with high minority populations have, on average, substantially better living conditions than minorities living in these same areas.

FIGURE 3.5 **Distribution of welfare in Vietnam, by ethnicity, 2010**

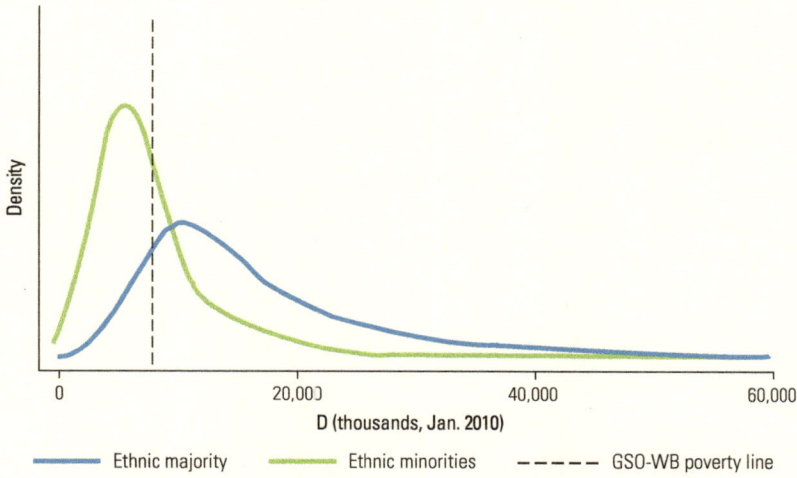

Source: 2010 VHLSS.

FIGURE 3.6 **Level of poverty in Vietnam, by ethnicity and region, 2010**

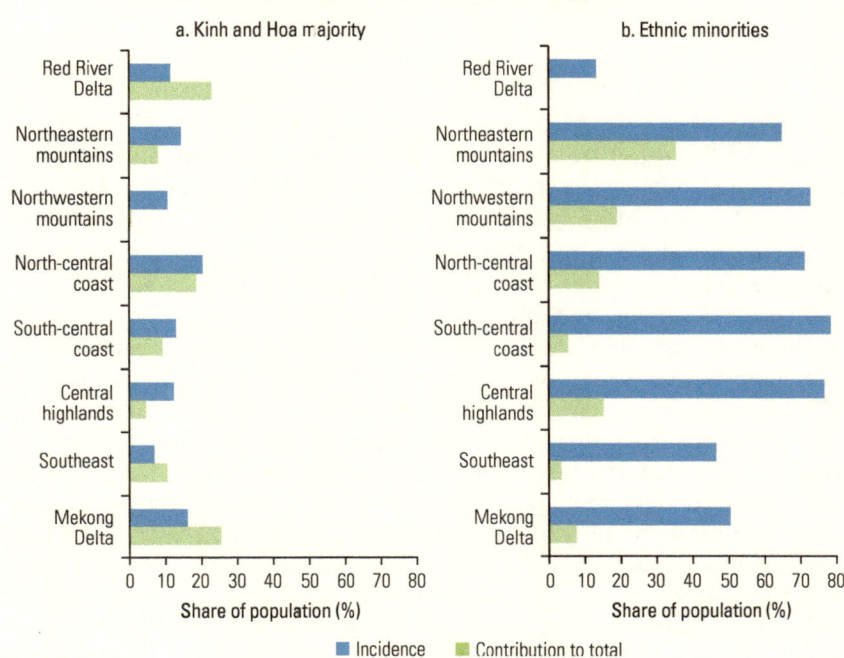

Source: 2010 VHLSS.

MAP 3.1 Spatial distribution of the poor in Vietnam, by ethnicity, 2010

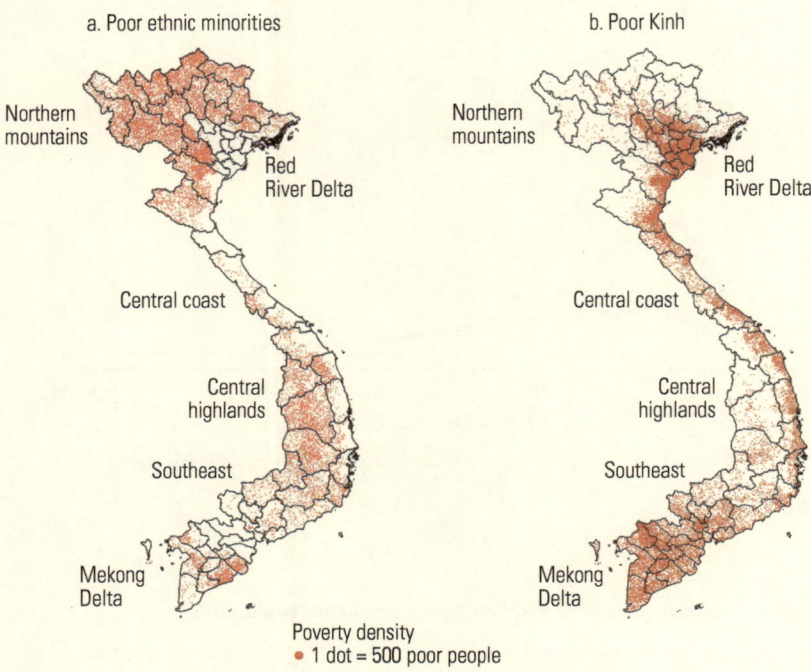

a. Poor ethnic minorities

Northern
mountains

Red
River Delta

Central coast

Central
highlands

Southeast

Mekong
Delta

b. Poor Kinh

Northern
mountains

Red
River Delta

Central coast

Central
highlands

Southeast

Mekong
Delta

Poverty density
● 1 dot = 500 poor people

Source: Estimates based on the 2009 Housing and Population Census and the 2010 VHLSS.

Map 3.1 illustrates the strong spatial segregation between poor minority and poor majority households in Vietnam. Poor minorities are heavily concentrated in the northeastern and northwestern mountains, upland areas in the north-central coast, and the central highlands. In contrast, poor people from the majority population are concentrated in the Red River Delta, along coastal regions, and in the Mekong Delta.

There are important differences in livelihood strategies and employment patterns between poor majority and minority households (figure 3.7). Poor minorities earn three-quarters of their total income from agriculture and allied activities, including wage employment in agriculture. In contrast, poor majority households earn only 42 percent from agriculture and allied activities and a much higher share from off-farm activities, both salaried nonfarm employment and family enterprises. Forestry is important for minorities, but much less so for poor majorities, in large part reflecting differences in location. However, the composition of income is similar between ethnic minorities and the majority in the wealthiest quintile.

FIGURE 3.7 Composition of income for extreme poor, poor, and top quintile in Vietnam, by ethnicity, 2010

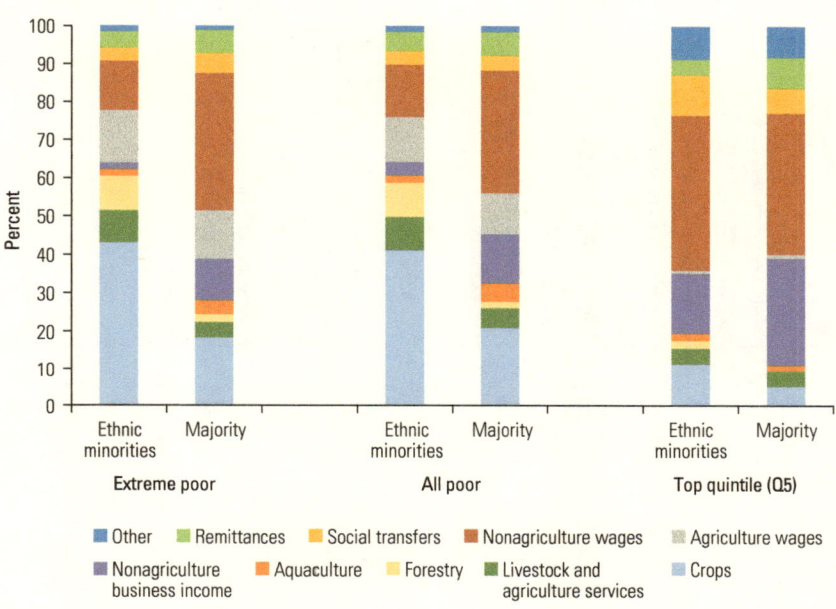

Source: 2010 VHLSS.

Poverty and educational attainment

Poverty is still linked to low educational attainment (figure 3.8). Vietnamese today are far better educated than they were a decade ago. Primary completion rates were already high by the end of the 1990s, as evidenced in the first panel of figure 3.8. Since then, enrollments at lower- and upper-secondary levels have risen rapidly, leading to an increase in the number of students who attend colleges and universities. However, lack of education continues to be an important determinant of poverty, and this was highlighted by respondents in both urban and rural areas as a cause of rising inequality (chapter 6).

According to table 3.6, individuals living in households whose head did not complete primary school had the highest poverty rate in 2010 (nearly 40 percent or twice the national average) as well as the highest extreme poverty rate (nearly 19 percent or 2.5 times the national average). The inverse relationship between education and poverty has become stronger over time: in 1998, households whose heads had completed primary or

FIGURE 3.8 Schooling achievement in Vietnam, by age cohort, 1998 and 2010

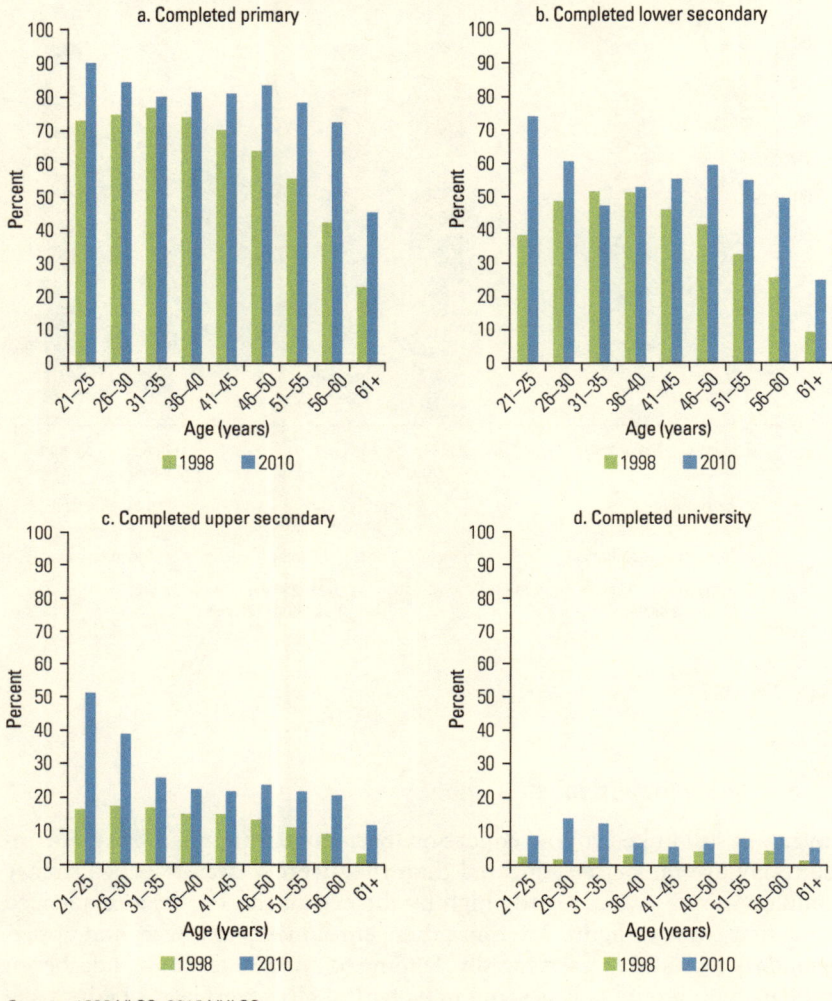

Sources: 1998 VLSS; 2010 VHLSS.

less schooling accounted for 55 percent of the total poor. By 2010, they accounted for 75 percent of the poor. Rising levels of education, coupled with rapid income diversification, has been a powerful force for poverty reduction in Vietnam.

Table 3.7 describes the distribution of education for persons 21 years and older across expanded per capita expenditure quintiles, illustrating in yet another way the strong relationship between rising levels of education and increasing wealth in Vietnam. By 2010, 40 percent of persons 21 years

TABLE 3.6 Poverty headcount in Vietnam, by education of household head, 2010
Percent

	Poverty		Extreme poverty		Share of total population
	Index	Contribution to total	Index	Contribution to total	
National	20.7	100.0	8.0	100.0	100.0
Household head's highest educational qualification:					
None	39.8	46.1	19.3	58.1	24.0
Primary	23.5	28.5	7.9	25.0	25.1
Lower secondary	15.3	18.4	4.2	13.2	24.9
Upper secondary	8.7	4.2	2.1	2.6	9.9
Vocational	5.8	2.6	0.8	0.9	9.4
Higher education	0.7	0.2	0.1	0.1	6.6

Source: 2010 VHLSS.

and older in the richest quintile had completed a university degree; in contrast, less than 2 percent in the poorest quintile were university graduates. In fact, more than a quarter of those in the poorest quintile had not even completed primary school by 2010.

Table 3.7 also highlights the gap in education between ethnic minorities and the Kinh majority. Even among the poor, minorities are substantially less educated than their Kinh economic peers: for example, 39 percent of poor minorities had not completed primary school compared to only 16 percent of poor Kinh. Achievement gaps are, in part, due to a historical legacy of lower educational achievement among many minority populations, but they also reflect lower (albeit increasing) current enrollment rates. Figure 3.9 illustrates the relationship between education and total per capita expenditures for Kinh and minorities that is documented in table 3.7.

High levels of current enrollments indicate that future generations of workers will be better prepared to participate in Vietnam's modernizing economy than previous generations. However, gaps in enrollments between children from poor and better-off households have persisted (table 3.8), including gaps between enrollments for Kinh and for ethnic minority children (table 3.9). Most primary-school-age children—rich and poor, minority and majority—are enrolled in school. But enrollments among (poor) minorities drop off at the lower-secondary level, and children from lower-income households are much less likely to be enrolled in upper-secondary schools than children from better-off households. Chapter 6 analyzes the links between education and rising inequality, including the role of inequality in opportunities (especially education) in perpetuating poverty across generations.

TABLE 3.7 **Distribution of completed education in Vietnam, by ethnicity and expanded quintiles (persons 21 years of age and older), 2010**

	None	Primary	Lower secondary	Upper secondary	Vocational	Higher education
National						
All poor	26.7	29.7	28.7	12.3	1.3	1.4
Extreme poor	37.1	28.3	23.4	9.3	1.2	0.7
Quintile 2	12.4	26.6	34.7	20.7	3.4	2.3
Quintile 3	6.6	21.6	31.8	27.0	6.1	6.9
Quintile 4	4.7	14.2	23.1	30.3	9.8	17.8
Quintile 5	2.0	7.7	15.6	25.6	9.2	40.0
Rural	13.1	23.1	30.6	21.9	4.7	6.7
Urban	4.7	12.5	17.6	25.9	9.0	30.3
National	10.6	20.0	26.7	23.1	5.9	13.7
Majority						
All poor	16.4	31.2	34.5	14.2	1.8	2.0
Extreme poor	21.7	25.1	33.6	16.1	2.5	1.0
Quintile 2	10.7	26.2	36.0	21.2	3.3	2.6
Quintile 3	6.3	21.6	32.2	27.0	6.0	6.9
Quintile 4	4.5	14.6	23.4	30.3	9.8	17.4
Quintile 5	2.0	7.8	15.7	25.6	9.0	39.9
Ethnic minorities						
All poor	38.6	28.0	21.9	10.1	0.9	0.6
Extreme poor	44.2	29.8	18.7	6.1	0.6	0.6
Quintile 2	23.3	28.5	25.8	17.5	3.9	0.9
Quintile 3	12.2	21.5	25.3	26.1	8.2	6.8
Quintile 4	9.3	7.2	18.3	29.0	10.0	26.3
Quintile 5	4.2	1.7	9.2	23.0	17.1	45.0

Source: 2010 VHLSS.
Note: "All poor" represents 20.7 percent of the population (or Quintile 1); of that 20.7 percent, 8 percent are considered extreme poor.

Gender gaps in minority school enrollments have received a lot of attention in Vietnam. These gaps have closed at the primary level but persist at the secondary level and above. However, reverse gender gaps—substantially higher enrollments for girls than for boys at the secondary level—have started to emerge at the secondary level, particularly among children from less-well-off Kinh households and in the central highlands, the southeast, and the Mekong Delta. Concerns have been raised that boys from poor households are leaving school earlier than girls to take up jobs in the service sector and manufacturing, "pushed" by poverty and economic imperatives and "pulled" by expanding employment opportunities in nearby cities and towns. While leaving school after six or eight years of education may make

FIGURE 3.9 Educational achievement in Vietnam, by ethnicity and expanded quintiles (persons 21 years and older), 2010

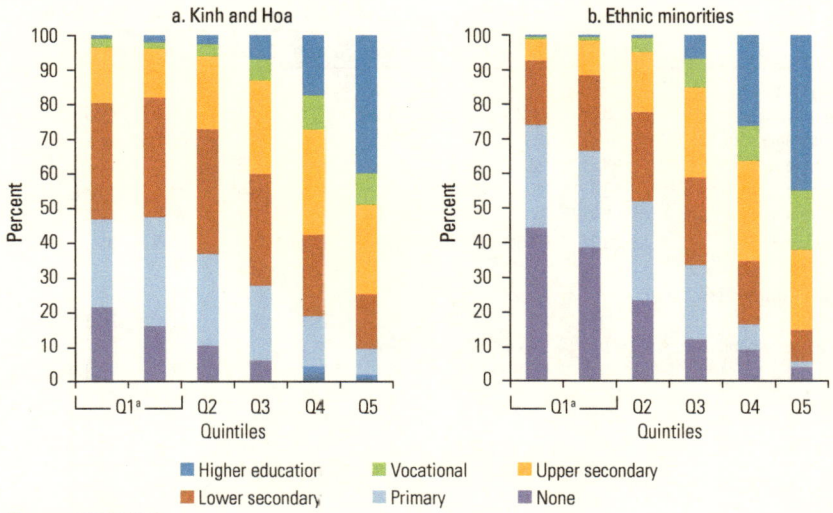

Source: 2010 VHLSS.

a. Quintile 1 is defined as "all poor," which comprised 20.7 percent of the population; of that 20.7 percent, 8 percent are considered "extreme poor."

TABLE 3.8 Net school enrollment rates for boys and girls in Vietnam, by expanded quintile and region, 2010

	Primary			Lower secondary			Upper secondary		
	Male	Female	Total	Male	Female	Total	Male	Female	Total
All poor	90.2	90.2	90.2	68.6	75.6	72.2	28.1	36.1	32.4
Extreme poor	91.6	83.8	90.2	62.2	70.8	66.6	16.4	28.1	22.9
Quintile 2	93.7	92.6	93.2	77.5	82.6	79.9	50.0	56.5	53.0
Quintile 3	94.1	92.9	93.5	84.9	85.5	85.2	58.1	62.5	60.3
Quintile 4	92.5	93.7	93.1	90.5	90.4	90.5	66.0	73.6	69.5
Quintile 5	93.3	97.6	95.3	86.1	90.3	88.0	76.2	85.6	80.9
Red River Delta	95.0	93.5	94.3	89.6	91.9	90.6	69.2	67.2	68.2
Northeastern mountains	93.0	90.9	91.9	85.2	83.0	84.1	56.0	60.7	58.3
Northwestern mountains	93.3	93.9	93.6	80.9	65.5	74.2	47.4	38.8	42.7
North-central coast	90.9	91.1	91.0	83.8	87.6	85.8	54.7	58.9	56.8
South-central coast	92.1	90.7	91.4	89.5	86.4	88.1	58.4	69.6	64.0
Central highlands	95.4	87.7	91.9	67.3	78.2	73.1	45.6	52.5	49.3
Southeast	90.3	97.9	94.1	76.1	81.8	78.4	52.8	63.1	58.0
Mekong Delta	91.4	92.7	92.0	66.1	76.5	71.2	39.2	50.5	44.1
Rural	92.4	91.9	92.2	78.9	82.8	80.7	49.3	54.5	51.8
Urban	92.9	95.2	94.1	83.5	85.0	84.2	68.8	76.2	72.5
National	92.5	92.8	92.6	80.0	83.3	81.5	53.9	60.1	57.0

Source: 2010 VHLSS.

TABLE 3.9 **Net school enrollment rates for boys and girls in Vietnam, by expanded quintile and ethnicity, 2010**

	Primary			Lower secondary			Upper secondary		
	Male	Female	Total	Male	Female	Total	Male	Female	Total
Majority									
All poor	88.3	94.2	91.0	71.9	85.8	79.5	34.2	46.4	40.8
Extreme poor	92.4	96.4	94.5	69.7	94.1	81.8	27.6	48.5	39.9
Quintile 2	93.2	92.1	92.7	75.7	84.2	79.6	50.7	57.7	54.0
Quintile 3	93.8	93.0	93.4	85.2	85.7	85.4	58.1	63.3	60.7
Quintile 4	92.4	94.6	93.5	91.0	90.5	90.7	66.7	75.4	70.7
Quintile 5	93.2	97.5	95.3	86.0	90.2	87.9	76.8	85.3	81.0
Ethnic minorities									
All poor	92.5	86.5	89.3	65.5	63.1	64.4	22.4	26.3	24.5
Extreme poor	91.4	86.1	88.7	59.4	62.5	61.0	12.4	19.2	16.1
Quintile 2	97.4	96.1	96.8	90.1	72.2	81.6	46.1	48.3	47.1
Quintile 3	100.0	90.5	95.4	78.0	82.1	80.3	57.9	43.4	53.1
Quintile 4	94.5	74.9	85.5	80.1	88.9	84.4	58.4	41.2	52.3
Quintile 5	100.0	100.0	100.0	100.0	100.0	100.0	25.7	100.0	75.1

Source: 2010 VHLSS.

sense given short-run incentives, education choices made today will follow these children for the rest of their lives. These young workers may not have the education and skills to get good jobs in the future as the economy continues to grow and modernize, and Vietnam's economic development will be constrained by the lack of an educated and skilled labor force. Skills gaps are already a growing concern among Vietnamese employers, particularly in export sectors (World Bank 2013).

There are many reasons why children from poor and ethnic minority households do not stay in school. As discussed in chapter 1, high out-of-pocket costs are one factor. Location is another. In upland regions, particularly in the northern mountains, upper-secondary schools are often located at some remove from rural communities, and students are forced to board rather than commute to school each day from their homes. Background qualitative studies carried out for this report also highlight widespread concerns about the poor quality of schools in rural areas.

Land distribution

Vietnamese farmers have small landholdings, and landlessness is rising. An early and strong commitment by the government to distribute land use rights equitably among farmers in Vietnam has resulted in a pattern of land distribution that remains remarkably equitable by international standards. Rural growth and on-farm diversification were the driving forces for poverty reduction in the 1990s. Most rural households continue to have small landholdings, and in recent years, few households were able to improve substantially their living conditions through expanded cultivation of annual crops. A high percentage of Vietnamese farmers continue to grow rice, in part driven by state restrictions on the use of land. Land use restrictions are in place primarily for rice production and affect land in the Mekong and Red River deltas (Markussen, Tarp, and van den Broeck 2009). Except in the Mekong Delta, rice is grown primarily for own consumption rather than as a source of cash income. In Vietnam, 72 percent of poor households grew rice according to the 2008 VHLSS; 90 percent of this rice was consumed at home, and only 18 percent of poor households were net sellers of rice. Instead, rising wealth among rural households is linked to on-farm diversification into cash crops and, even more important, diversification into off-farm activities. The last decade is notable for rapidly expanding opportunities to generate stable off-farm income, including in industrial centers and nearby towns.

Less-well-off rural households cultivated, on average, more land than better-off rural households in 2010 (table 3.10). However, these statistics should be interpreted with care; much of the land cultivated by ethnic minorities is in upland regions and often of lower quality due to sloping and rocky terrain and lack of dependable irrigation. Better-off households cultivate more perennial cropland, which is used for commercial activities (including coffee, an important cash crop).

The proportion of landless rural households has risen in all regions since the late 1990s (table 3.11). However, with the exception of the Mekong Delta, landlessness is not associated with higher poverty. In fact, initial analysis suggests a positive relationship between rural landlessness and wealth in most regions in the north of Vietnam (table 3.12). But 54 percent of the rural poor living in the southeast region and 48 percent of the rural poor living in the Mekong Delta are landless (the landless rates among the extreme poor are similar). Concerns have been raised over the years about the links between landlessness and poverty. In particular, some observers were concerned that legislation enacted in the late 1990s that led to the

TABLE 3.10 **Average landholdings for rural households in Vietnam, by consumption quintile, 2010**

Square meters

	Quintile				
	1	2	3	4	5
All land	8,235	6,049	5,901	5,723	5,608
Annual crop land	3,765	3,322	2,927	2,826	2,302
Perennial land	698	1,031	1,145	1,640	2,463

Source: 2010 VHLSS.

TABLE 3.11 **Share of rural households in Vietnam without allocated or swidden land, by region, 1993–2010**

	1993	1998	2010
Northern mountains	2.0	3.7	8.1
Red River Delta	3.2	4.5	13.4
North-central coast	3.8	7.7	15.5
South-central coast	10.7	5.1	19.7
Central highlands	3.9	2.6	17.3
Southeast	21.3	28.7	58.9
Mekong Delta	16.9	21.3	33.6
National	8.2	10.1	22.5

Sources: For 1993 and 1998, from World Bank 1999, table 2.4; for 2010, estimates from 2010 VHLSS.
Notes: Swidden land is land cleared for cultivation by cutting and burning the vegetation. "Land" includes annual cropland, perennial cropland, forestry land, water surface, and shifting-cultivation farmland. It excludes gardens, ponds, and land classified as "other."

TABLE 3.12 **Share of rural households in Vietnam without allocated or swidden land, by region and quintile, 2010**

	Extreme poor	Quintile				
		1	2	3	4	5
Red River Delta	2.2	4.6	4.8	7.9	14.6	30.5
Northeastern mountains	0.7	2.2	4.8	9.6	20.9	31.4
Northwestern mountains	0.5	0.6	5.3	5.5	38.7	56.9
North-central coast	7.9	7.9	9.9	14.9	22.6	52.0
South-central coast	2.5	10.6	14.6	16.7	21.7	25.3
Central highlands	13.2	9.6	17.0	27.6	21.1	23.9
Southeast	43.4	53.9	43.4	53.6	56.5	68.5
Mekong Delta	50.3	47.5	29.0	29.7	30.6	34.9

Source: 2010 VHLSS.

opening up of land markets would encourage poor farmers to sell land for quick profits, leaving them without adequate means of livelihood; others argued that land markets would promote greater efficiency (Ravallion and van de Walle 2008a, 2008b). The picture is mixed. Respondents living in Tra Vinh Province in the Mekong Delta interviewed for one of the background studies for this book noted expanding opportunities for land-poor households in the Mekong and southeast to diversify into higher-paid off-farm activities. However, off-farm diversification requires relevant education and skills. Although young workers can acquire these skills, the situation is more complicated for households with older workers. More work is needed to understand the complex links between landlessness and poverty in Vietnam's southern provinces.

Housing and local infrastructure

Housing and local infrastructure have improved substantially since the late 1990s. Housing conditions are an important measure of quality of life, both as ends in themselves and as means toward achieving better living standards. For example, access to sanitation interacts with health care, good nutrition, and water supply to influence the health of individuals. Homes built with more durable building materials provide safer shelter and reduce labor costs for repairs and new construction.

Vietnam has achieved widespread improvements in the quality of housing and access to neighborhood amenities and local infrastructure in recent years. These are evident in recent rounds of the VHLSS and were also reported in related field studies. For example, respondents in a study of the long-run drivers of poverty reduction (Nguyen and Hoang 2012) describe substantial improvements in rural infrastructure since the early 1990s and increased access to associated social and economic services, markets, and information. These include better road and bridge access for rural communes and remote villages, new irrigation facilities, and rapid expansion of media services and technologies into rural areas. Associated with this, many households have invested in new types of assets that improve mobility and access to information, including motorbikes, televisions, mobile phones, and even computers in urban areas. These widespread improvements in economic and social infrastructure are the result of the combined efforts of many government infrastructure investment programs across the different infrastructure sectors. They provide a good foundation for growth of the rural economy and continued reductions in rural poverty in the coming years.

Although the poor still own fewer durable goods than better-off households, the comparative statistics in table 3.13 indicate substantial increases

TABLE 3.13 Household ownership of durable goods in Vietnam, 1998 and 2010
% of households

	National		Poor		Extreme poor	
	1998	2010	1998	2010	1998	2010
Car	0.2	1.3	0.0	0.0	0.0	0.0
Motorbike	20.3	75.9	2.4	50.9	0.4	39.6
Mobile phone	—	69.8	—	37.1	—	24.2
TV	55.7	89.3	30.2	73.6	11.9	61.3
Computer	0.7	16.8	0.0	0.3	0.0	0.4
Refrigerator or freezer	9.0	42.6	0.0	5.3	0.0	2.2
Air conditioner	0.7	8.2	0.0	0.1	0.0	0.2
Electric fan	68.4	85.2	45.9	65.2	26.3	49.4
Rice cooker or electric stove	19.3	77.6	1.1	45.6	0.0	28.3

Source: 2010 VHLSS.
Note: — = not available.

in the ownership of durable goods since 1998. For example, in 2010, 51 percent of the poor owned a motorbike compared to 2 percent in 1998; 74 percent owned a television compared to 30 percent in 1998; 46 percent owned a rice cooker or electric stove compared to 1 percent in 1998; and 37 percent owned a mobile phone. The extreme poor owned very little in 1998; however, by 2010, 40 percent owned a motorbike, 61 percent owned a television, 28 percent owned a rice cooker or stove, and 24 percent owned a mobile phone. Wider access to transport, televisions, and mobile phones has improved the spread of information and helped the poor to become less socially isolated and more integrated into the wider economy.

Despite improvements, many of the poor still do not have access to clean water (36 percent of households in the bottom quintile, 14 percent in the second quintile) or adequate sanitation (21 percent of households in the bottom quintile, and 8 percent in the second quintile do not have flush or semiflush toilets). Although Vietnam has done a remarkable job of making electricity widely available (more than 95 percent of households are connected to the grid) and improving the reliability of supply, 11 percent of households in the bottom quintile are still not connected to the electricity grid (table 3.14). Many of the households that still lack access to clean water, adequate sanitation, and electricity are ethnic minorities living in less accessible upland regions of Vietnam. These households are deprived not only in terms of income, but also in terms of access to public goods and services (chapter 1).

Urban poverty

Urban poverty is low and concentrated in smaller cities and towns. The 2010 poverty rate was only 6 percent in urban areas compared to 27 percent in rural areas. Because only 30 percent of the population live in urban areas, the urban poor constitute less than 9 percent of the poor in Vietnam.

TABLE 3.14 Share of households with access to housing and neighborhood amenities in Vietnam, by quintile, 2010

% of households

	Quintile					
	1	2	3	4	5	Total
Tap water	7.5	13.3	21.7	32.8	59.2	26.9
Clean (nontap) water	56.4	72.8	71.2	62.3	39.7	60.5
Flush toilet	12.8	31.2	48.4	67.6	88.7	49.7
Semiflush toilet	66	61.3	46.8	30.7	10.9	43.1
Solid house	12	19.7	26.9	34.5	62.5	31.1
Semisolid house	64.9	66.2	64.7	60.7	36.3	58.6
Household with electricity	89	97.9	99.4	99.3	99.6	97

Source: 2010 VHLSS.

Although poverty in Vietnam has been primarily a rural phenomenon, understanding and addressing urban poverty are becoming increasingly important. Vietnam is urbanizing rapidly; the urban population grew 3.4 percent per year between 1999 and 2009 compared to annual population growth of only 0.4 percent in rural areas. The urban population is forecast[2] to reach 45 percent of the total population by 2020—a major increase over the 30 percent registered in the 2009 Housing and Population Census. In light of this rapid change, it is vital to understand better the factors that influence the living conditions of low-income urban households, including how poverty is distributed across urban areas.

City size is one important correlate of poverty. The sample size of the 2010 VHLSS is too small to estimate poverty rates for different types of cities. Instead, poverty-mapping methods (chapter 4) were used to estimate poverty rates by city size, ranging from very large "special cities" (for example, Hanoi and Ho Chi Minh City) to small (class 5) cities, which include district towns with 4,000 or fewer inhabitants. Table 3.15 presents poverty statistics by city size ranging from extra large cities (that is, Hanoi and Ho Chi Minh City) to extra small towns (classes 4 and 5).

Not surprising, poverty levels decrease with city size. Measured by the 2010 GSO-WB poverty line,[3] only 1.9 percent of the population in the country's six largest cities are poor, compared to 11.2 percent of the population living in small cities and towns. The depth and severity of poverty also decrease with city size. Thus the urban poor are overwhelmingly concentrated in small cities and towns, which account for only 43 percent of the urban population but more than 70 percent of the urban poor. Conversely, 32 percent of Vietnam's urban population live in Hanoi and Ho Chi Minh City, but only 11 percent of the urban poor live there.

Smaller towns are similar in many ways to rural villages, in terms of both infrastructure and services as well as characteristics of the population. Table 3.16 provides an overview of housing, local services, and education levels for urban areas, categorized by city size, and for rural areas.

TABLE 3.15 Poverty in Vietnam, by city size, 2009

City class	Extra large Special city	Large Class 1	Medium Class 2	Small Class 3	Extra small Class 4, 5	Rural
Number of cities in category	2	7	14	45	634	
Average population (thousands)	4,075	467	225	86	11	
Share of total population (%)	9.5	3.8	3.7	4.5	8.1	70.4
Share of urban population (%)	32.1	12.9	12.4	15.3	27.3	
Poverty rate (%)	1.9	3.8	4.2	5.8	11.2	25.6
Poverty gap (%)	0.4	0.6	0.7	1.1	2.4	6.8
Share of urban poor (%)	11	8.8	9.2	5.9	55	

Source: Estimates based on the 2009 Housing and Population Census and the 2010 VHLSS.

TABLE 3.16 **Share of households with specific characteristics in Vietnam, by city size, 2009**
% of households

	Extra large	Large	Medium	Small	Extra small	Rural
Primary education	20.2	21.8	20.7	23.7	26.2	30
Secondary education	19	21	20.5	20.1	22.6	27
Tertiary education	49.7	41.7	46.5	40.1	30.6	14.9
Dwelling walls of solid material	98.2	90.6	92.4	86.7	79.9	69.5
Dwelling walls of semisolid material	1.2	4.5	5	8.4	11.9	16
Dwelling walls of temporary material	0.6	4.9	2.6	4.9	8.2	14.5
Dwelling roof of solid material	35.1	21.5	25.2	19.5	17.9	13.4
Dwelling roof of semisolid material	6	11.5	18.1	20.7	26.6	39.6
Dwelling roof of temporary material	58.8	67	56.8	59.8	55.5	47.1
Flush toilet	99.3	89.6	92.7	82.9	69.6	38.8
Other kind of toilet	0.5	9.9	5	14.6	24.9	50.4
No toilet	0.2	0.5	2.3	2.5	5.5	10.9
Drinking water from pipe	74.2	74.3	75.5	57.2	33.6	8
Drinking water from well	25.3	15.9	21.3	35.6	52.2	58.3
Drinking water other source	0.6	9.9	3.2	7.2	14.2	33.8
Electricity for lighting	99.7	99.7	99.8	99.6	99	94.1
Electricity for cooking	2.1	1.4	1.1	1.9	1.8	1.5
Gas for cooking	89.3	70.7	75.5	66.9	55.6	22.9
Firewood for cooking	0.7	12	7.2	15.7	32.2	64.6

Source: Estimates based on 2009 Population Census.
Note: Education level is highest level attained by the household head.

Although access to electricity is universal across all types of cities, smaller cities lag larger ones in most other basic services. For example, firewood is used much more extensively for cooking than gas, access to piped water is generally limited, and very few households report having flush toilets. People living in small towns have, on average, lower levels of education and skills than people living in larger cities.

Demographic Factors

Poverty is less correlated with demographic factors, but aging is an emerging issue and child poverty remains a concern. Compared to the 1990s, demographic factors such as high dependency ratios and having a female head of household have become less linked to poverty. Comparisons between 1999 and 2009 population "pyramids" for Vietnam highlight the sharp reduction in the proportion of children in the population and an increase in the proportion of older adults (GSO 2010; figure 3.10). Recent qualitative studies carried out for this book (Nguyen and Hoang 2012) identify important links between changing household structures and the dynamics of income and well-being. The nationwide family planning campaign, active since the late 1980s, was widely acknowledged at all

FIGURE 3.10 **Population pyramid for Vietnam, by gender, 1999 and 2009**

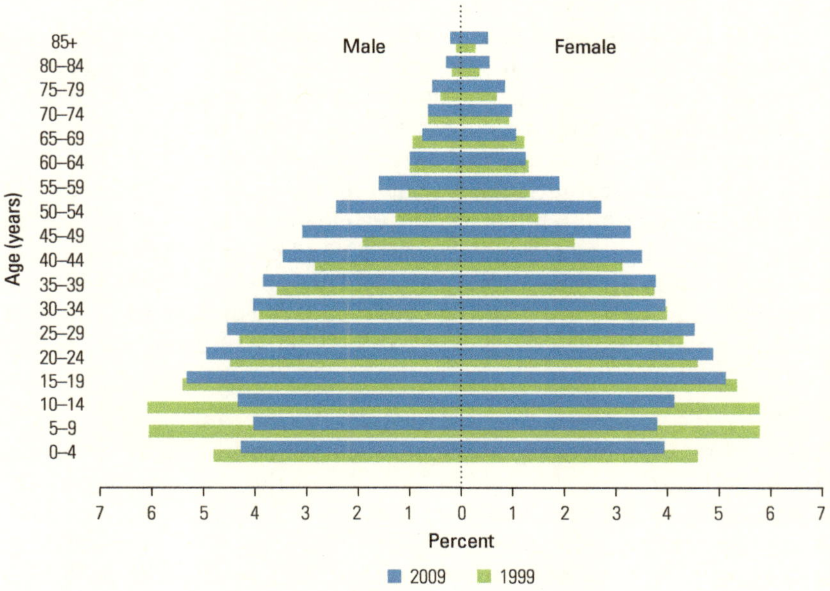

Source: GSO 2010.

field sites as having made an important contribution to poverty reduction. Most couples (nearly 80 percent according to the 2010 VHLSS) now have only two children, which helps to reduce household spending on basic services like education and health and allows for more "quality" spending on children.

The qualitative research on long-run drivers of poverty reduction, with its two-decade reference period, also identifies some positive impacts for large families. The Vietnamese economy has been expanding and creating new jobs. Although poor rural households struggled to raise and educate children born in the 1980s and early 1990s, these children are now grown, and many are working in off-farm activities or have migrated to work in urban areas. Rather than being a burden, they contribute to supporting their parents and younger siblings who stay home.

Female-headed households with children were identified in several sites as more vulnerable to poverty, in large part because they depend only on the earnings of the female household head. Many respondents felt that two working parents are required to support a family in Vietnam. Moreover, men in rural areas are better paid than most women because they take on different (heavier and more dangerous) tasks. Single mothers struggle with the lack of adequate daycare facilities, particularly in rural areas, and often do not receive support from the extended family.

Aging is another important source of vulnerability. Vietnam has a high proportion of widows; according to the 2010 VHLSS, 19 percent of households include a widow, and 12.5 percent are currently headed by a widow. The proportion of widows in an age cohort rises sharply with age: 47.6 percent of women 66–70 years of age are widowed compared to only 9.7 percent of men in the same age cohort; 67.6 percent of women 76–80 years of age are widowed compared to 24.5 percent of men in the cohort. PPAs and recent qualitative studies carried out, for instance, by Oxfam, highlight the vulnerability of households headed by elderly persons—in particular, widows—which is linked, in part, to the limited coverage of social insurance and pensions for Vietnam's aging population (UNFPA 2011). Vulnerability linked to aging is a growing challenge in Vietnam, and additional research on the links between poverty, vulnerability, and aging is needed.

Aging and economies of scale in consumption

Additional research on aging and household economies of scale and composition was carried out for this book to address the concern that conventional poverty profiles based on per capita consumption tend to underreport poverty among small households (particularly those with only elderly members) and to overreport poverty among large households (including those with many children). The work examines different methods to adjust for economies of scale (size) in household welfare. While some types of consumption such as food are more directly a function of household size (although young children eat less than adults), other types of consumption such as spending on electricity and housing are fixed costs and less directly linked to household size. To adjust for economies of scale, individual welfare is redefined as

$$y^* = \frac{Y}{(N)^\theta}, \tag{3.1}$$

where Y is total household expenditures, N is the number of household members, and θ is a scale parameter, which ranges from 1 to 0. When $\theta = 1$, individual welfare is equal to per capita expenditures (no economies of scale). Engel's curve analysis undertaken as part of the study suggests that moderate scale economies hold for Vietnam (that is, $\theta = 0.68$).

Table 3.17 presents poverty rates for different demographic groups and different household demographic compositions using conventional measures of per capita expenditure ($\theta = 1$) and moderate ($\theta = 0.8$) and more substantial ($\theta = 0.6$) adjustments for economies of scale. Conventional measures show conventional results—higher poverty—than the national average for minority households and for large households with more dependents (two or more children). Even after adjusting for economies of scale, households with three or more children (around 10 percent of households in 2010) are more likely to be poor. Child poverty remains a

TABLE 3.17 **Demographic characteristics and scale economies for the poor in Vietnam, 2010**

	Population (%)	Household size	Share of poor (%)		
			$\theta = 1$	$\theta = 0.8$	$\theta = 0.6$
All households	100.0	4.5	20.7	21.2	21.9
No widow	81.0	4.4	20.3	20.5	21.2
With widow	19.0	4.8	23.6	24.1	25.2
Female-headed	24.8	4.0	14.9	16.5	18.2
Male-headed	75.2	4.6	22.6	22.5	23.0
Widow-headed	12.5	4.1	21.5	23.2	26.0
Ethnicity = Kinh	82.2	4.4	13.2	13.4	14.3
Ethnicity = not Kinh	17.8	5.1	62.2	63.0	62.9
Household composition					
Single adult	0.7	1.0	4.0	11.3	19.9
Single elderly/widow/ widower	0.7	1.0	14.9	29.6	51.1
2 adults	3.8	2.0	6.8	10.9	16.9
Single parent	0.6	2.0	21.4	26.7	34.5
2 elderly	1.2	2.0	22.3	31.9	46.0
Other 2-member household	1.2	2.0	17.0	23.6	34.3
Nuclear, 1 child	6.5	3.0	14.0	16.8	19.3
Nuclear, 2 children	14.0	4.0	25.1	26.8	28.3
Nuclear, 3+ children	5.3	5.3	47.3	45.1	42.9
Extended family, no children	20.4	3.9	8.7	9.7	11.1
Extended family, 1 child	19.9	4.8	15.0	14.8	15.1
Extended family, 2 children	12.0	5.6	26.2	24.0	22.2
Extended family, 3+ children	4.7	7.5	56.3	52.4	46.7
Joint family, no elderly	6.0	5.7	29.9	26.4	24.0
Joint family, with elderly	3.0	6.0	20.9	18.4	17.0

Source: 2010 VHLSS.

concern. In addition, small households with elderly members emerge as a new group of vulnerable poor when we include progressive adjustments for economies of scale. The number of these households is likely to increase as the population ages and Vietnam becomes more urbanized. Ongoing efforts to develop a modern social protection system for Vietnam should consider (single) elderly and widow or widower households as target populations deserving special attention.

Childhood poverty and long-term development

Children face multiple deprivations that could affect their long-term development.[4] They are at higher risk of poverty than adults, and poverty affects them differently. They have different dietary requirements, for example, and the role of education is vital at this stage of life. A child-specific approach to measuring poverty can highlight those needs that are especially crucial for children and their development and enable the design of more effective poverty reduction objectives, strategies, and policies.

According to the 1998 VLSS, 47.2 percent—nearly half—of all children were living in poverty. By 2010, this figure had fallen to 29.2 percent. Extreme child poverty fell more slowly—from 16.8 percent in 1998 to 12.5 percent in 2010. Furthermore, in households with three or more children, child poverty remains high, as noted in the previous section. But the monetary approach to measuring child poverty reflects only one dimension of well-being and does not capture the intra-household distribution of resources. The conventional methodology has thus been extended to assess child poverty along additional dimensions.

In 2008, MOLISA and the United Nations Children's Fund (UNICEF) developed a Vietnam-specific approach to measuring multidimensional child poverty, based on the Convention on the Rights of the Child. The approach incorporates eight domains, including deprivations in education, nutrition, health, shelter, water and sanitation, child labor, leisure, and social inclusion and protection. The prevalence of poverty (deprivation) can be calculated for any one of these domains, and a multidimensional child poverty (MDCP) rate can be constructed to measure the percentage of children who are poor (deprived) in at least two domains. MDCPs were calculated for 2004, 2006, and 2008 using the respective VHLSS.

UNICEF's monetary child poverty (MCP) rate measures the proportion of children living in households whose welfare levels fall below the GSO-WB poverty line. In contrast, the MDCP rate identifies the proportion of children suffering from deprivation in at least two of the eight selected domains. It is systematically higher than the MCP, indicating that around one-third of children living in Vietnam—or an estimated 7 million—are considered multidimensionally poor, in contrast to around one in five who are poor according to conventional income or expenditure criteria (figure 3.11).

The MCP and the MDCP approaches identify different, albeit overlapping, groups of poor children. While some children are identified as poor according to both methods, there is also a group that is only identified as poor by the multidimensional approach and likewise for the monetary approach. Using the 2006 VHLSS data, the GSO and MOLISA estimate that 18 percent of children are captured exclusively by the MDCP and would not have been considered poor by the MCP. This result underlines the stark difference between child and overall poverty and the importance of using a multidimensional measure to complement the standard monetary measurement of poverty.

Figure 3.12 highlights the disparities that exist among subgroups of the national population. The MDCP declined for both ethnic categories from 2006 to 2010, but children from ethnic minority households were still almost three times more likely to be multidimensionally poor in 2010 than their Kinh and Hoa peers. The figures also provide evidence of a sig-

FIGURE 3.11 Monetary and multidimensional child poverty in Vietnam, 2006–10

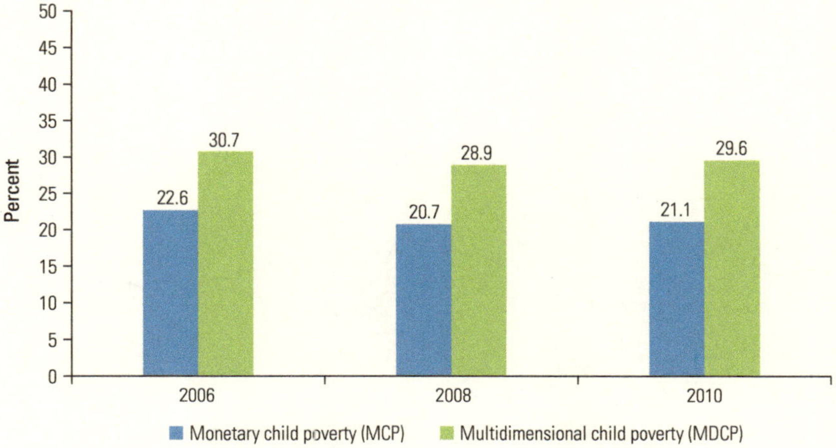

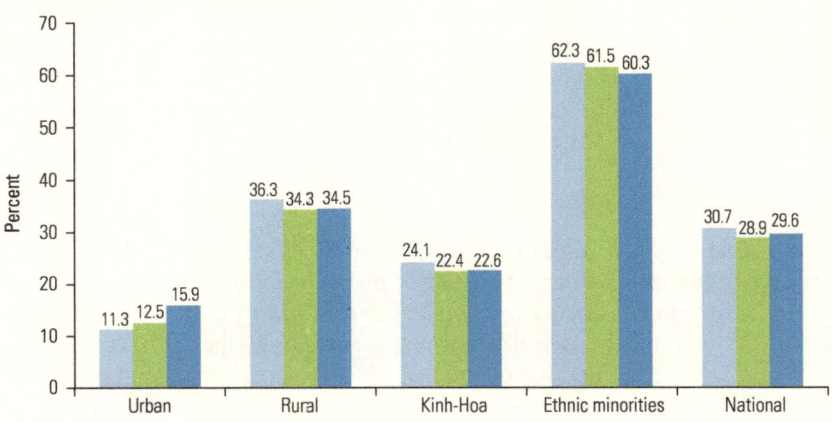

Sources: 2006, 2008, 2010 VHLSS.

FIGURE 3.12 Multidimensional child poverty in Vietnam, by selected social and demographic measures, 2006–10

Sources: 2006, 2008, 2010 VHLS

nificant urban-rural divide; children in rural areas are twice as likely to be multidimensionally poor as children in urban areas. While child poverty in rural areas has declined some in recent years, the MDCP indicates that child poverty in urban areas is rising.

Figure 3.13 provides a breakdown by domain of the 2010 MDCP. Health, water and sanitation, and leisure are clearly the domains of most

FIGURE 3.13 Child poverty rate in Vietnam, by domain, 2010

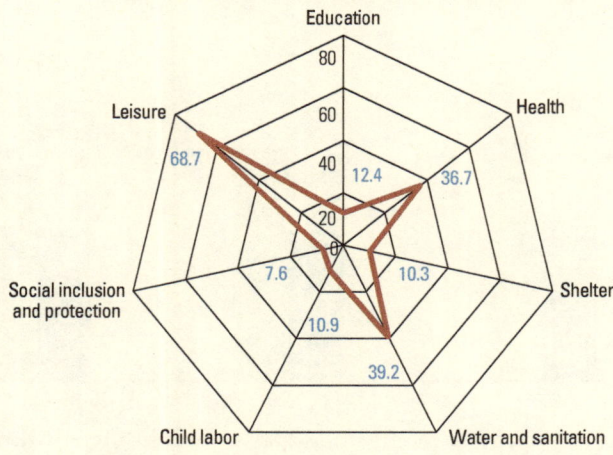

Sources: 2006, 2008, 2010 VHLSS.

concern. These figures indicate that more than one in three children 2 to 4 years of age (36.7 percent) was not fully immunized and had not visited a health facility in the prior 12 months (health); almost two out of five children 0 to 15 years of age (39.2 percent) lived in dwellings without hygienic sanitation or safe drinking water (water and sanitation); and more than two out of three children 0 to 4 years of age (68.7 percent) did not have any toys or books (leisure).

Vulnerability to weather shocks

Poor households are vulnerable to weather shocks. Located in one of the earth's five typhoon centers, Vietnam is prone to natural disasters, including frequent tropical storms and flooding. The 2008 VHLSS collected information on whether households had experienced weather shocks between 2003 and 2008 and the types of shocks. Results are presented in table 3.18. Households in rural areas are much more likely to experience weather shocks than their urban counterparts, and the poor are more exposed to shocks than the nonpoor. Households in the central highlands are more likely than those in any other region to experience droughts, while those in the central coastal regions are most likely to experience storms or flooding (Le, Nguyen, and Phung 2012).

Coverage of poverty reduction and social protection programs

Poverty reduction and social protection programs provide limited coverage. Vietnam's social protection system includes three main components:

TABLE 3.18 **Share of households experiencing natural disasters in Vietnam, by region, 2003–08**

% of households

	Drought	Flood, storm	Landslide	Other forms of extreme weather
National	6.7	12.9	0.7	15.2
Rural	8.6	15.5	0.9	19.4
Urban	´.8	6.3	0.1	4.3
Red River Delta	2.6	10.3	0.4	28.6
Northeastern mountains	9.4	7.0	1.7	23.0
Northwestern mountains	8.1	14.3	1.3	22.6
North-central coast	15.8	29.3	1.1	30.3
South-central coast	7.3	25.9	0.4	7.4
Central highlands	13.2	10.9	0.4	4.9
Southeast	2.9	5.1	0.3	1.3
Mekong Delta	3.5	10.2	0.5	1.4
Poor	14.2	17.9	1.2	22.9
Nonpoor	5.6	12.2	0.6	14.1

Source: 2010 VHLSS.

labor market policies and programs, social insurance (for example, pensions, retirement benefits, and survivorship), and social assistance, broadly focused on addressing the needs of poor and vulnerable households. Access to poverty reduction programs and policies can be an important aspect of well-being for low-income households. But concerns have been raised about both the targeting and coverage of Vietnam's existing poverty reduction programs. These issues are examined briefly using information collected in the 2010 VHLSS: each round of the survey includes information on whether households have been formally classified as poor—that is, whether they are on the official MOLISA poverty list—and thus are eligible for benefits under existing government programs, most notably the National Targeted Program for Sustainable Poverty Reduction (NTP-SPR). Each round of the VHLSS also collects information on whether the household received program benefits. This information can be used to assess coverage and targeting of Vietnam's social protection programs.

Analysis suggests that, although coverage is problematic (a substantial number of households that should be on the MOLISA poverty list are not), targeting is less of a concern (most households on the list are from the poorest groups). However, the 2010 VHLSS was administered before the results of the government's new poverty census were used to update the official poverty list. Thus, while the official poverty rate for 2010 was 14.2 percent, only 10.6 percent of households surveyed in the 2010 VHLSS reported being on the (old) MOLISA poverty list.

TABLE 3.19 Share of households officially classified as poor in Vietnam, by expanded quintile, 2010

% of households

	2010
All poor	36.0
Extreme poor	52.0
Quintile 2	12.2
Quintile 3	6.3
Quintile 4	2.6
Quintile 5	0.4

Source: 2010 VHLSS.

Table 3.19 shows the percentage of households (by expanded expenditure quintile) that report being on the official MOLISA poverty list. Just over half of the extreme poor (52 percent) were on the official poverty list and only 36 percent of poor. Although coverage is low, leakage of benefits to the nonpoor is very modest; only 12.2 percent of households in the second quintile and 6.3 percent of households in the third quintile reported being on the official poverty list.

Figure 3.14 presents the distribution of households on the poverty list by welfare decile. The great majority—nearly 70 percent—of households that are classified as poor live below the GSO-WB poverty line. Only 11.5

FIGURE 3.14 Distribution of households on the official poverty list in Vietnam, by expanded quintile, 2010

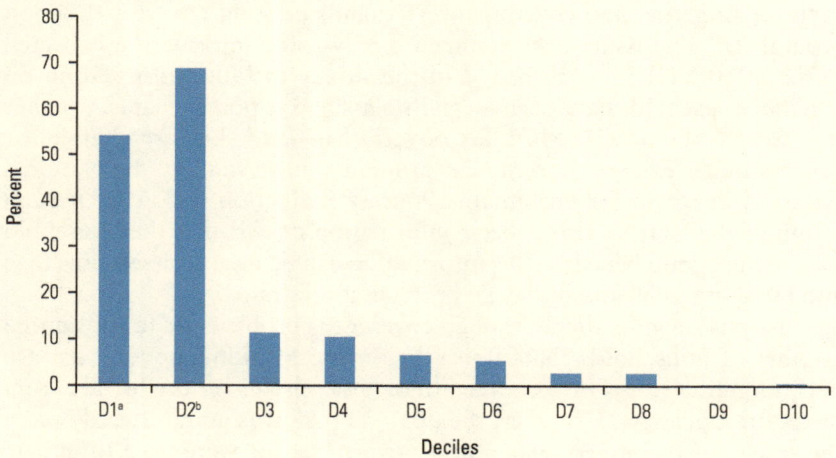

Source: 2010 VHLSS.
a. D1 = extreme poor (8 percent of the population).
b. D2 = all poor (20.7 percent of the population; the 20.7 includes D1).

percent of those officially classified as poor are in the upper half of the welfare distribution. While there is room for improvement, these targeting results are better than in many other countries, where program benefits are frequently captured by better-off households and rural elites. This being said, there are clearly problems with program coverage, including coverage of the poorest households. Deeper analysis of coverage and targeting at the regional level indicates that coverage is lower in high-poverty provinces, such as in the northwest and northeast, and higher in some better-off provinces and urban areas. MOLISA may face pressure to spread program benefits more equitably across provinces. Given the increasing concentration of the poor in high-poverty regions, doing so would lead to even more reductions in program coverage.

Table 3.20 looks in detail at the coverage of Vietnam's various social protection and poverty reduction policies by expanded expenditure quintile (Nguyen and Vu 2012). Coverage rates are low in general, and social insurance programs are not well targeted to the poor. For example, few households reported receiving vocational training in 2010. Analysis of the coverage of social assistance measures presents a more nuanced picture.

TABLE 3.20 Coverage of social protection and poverty reduction policies in Vietnam, by expanded quintile, 2010

% of people in households receiving a particular type of assistance

People in households receiving:	Total	Extreme poor	All poor	Quintiles 2	3	4	5
All transfers and programs	72.6	88.8	77.2	68.1	67.8	70.6	74.5
All social insurance	32.1	11.2	14.3	20.4	28.0	41.1	58.1
Employment subsidy	1.5	1.2	0.8	1.3	1.6	1.8	1.7
Pension	9.2	2.9	2.2	5.4	7.0	11.6	19.5
Having social insurance	26.7	7.5	11.9	15.6	23.4	34.1	50.0
Vocational training	0.1	0.2	0.3	0.2	0	0	0
All social assistance	56.6	87.4	72.0	60.6	54.7	47.9	41.0
Allowances for veterans, merit households	4.0	2.9	2.8	5.2	4.8	4.6	2.6
Allowances for policy households	4.9	11.8	8.8	5.0	4.1	3.3	1.6
Health subsidy allowances	32.7	29.6	31.3	34.3	34.9	29.8	33.7
Education subsidy allowances	8.3	36.0	15.0	7.6	4.0	4.2	2.3
Allowance for recovery from disaster, fire	4.9	7.4	6.7	7.4	5.7	3.8	1.0
Loan from Vietnam Bank for Social Policies	13.1	33.7	25.6	14.2	10.3	8.6	3.2
Health program	12.0	54.7	29.3	11.9	5.2	2.3	0.7
Education fee reduction and exemption	5.5	25.8	14.9	5.4	1.9	0.7	0.1
Housing program	1.1	4.4	2.9	1.3	0.4	0.2	0
Cultivation land for ethnic minorities	0.1	0.1	0.5	0.3	0	0	0
Agricultural extension	7.8	25.5	14.4	7.3	6.1	4.7	1.9
Clean water	1.9	9.1	4.5	2.1	0.6	0.5	0.2
Food supports	5.2	24.9	10.4	5.6	2.0	1.9	0.2
Production support	9.0	27.9	14.5	9.0	8.0	5.6	2.1

Source: Nguyen and Vu 2012.

Many of the policies included under the NTP-SPR are well targeted toward the poor (for example, reduced and subsidized education fees, production support, food support), but consistent with the analysis above, coverage rates are generally low: less than a third of the extreme poor were covered by these poverty reduction policies in 2010. The coverage of (subsidized) health insurance is better, but benefits accrue to households across the welfare distribution.

Table 3.21 presents similar estimates stratifying for urban versus rural households and for Kinh majority versus ethnic minorities. Minorities report substantially lower coverage of social insurance programs, but greater access to NTP-SPR support and greater access to social assistance programs more generally. Higher coverage is not surprising given the very high poverty rates among ethnic minorities.

TABLE 3.21 Coverage of social protection and poverty reduction policies in Vietnam, by urban or rural location and ethnicity, 2010

% of people in households receiving a particular type of assistance

People in households receiving:	Total	Urban	Rural	Kinh-Hoa	Ethnic minorities
All transfers and programs	72.6	75.3	71.5	70.3	86.1
All social insurance	32.1	56.2	22.0	35.2	14.0
Employment subsidy	1.5	2.0	1.3	1.6	0.8
Pension	9.2	17.9	5.5	10.1	4.0
Having social insurance	26.7	48.9	17.3	29.3	11.0
Vocational training	0.1	0	0.1	0	0.6
All social assistance	56.6	44.0	61.9	52.2	82.0
Allowances for veterans, merit households	4.0	2.6	4.6	4.2	2.4
Allowances for policy households	4.9	2.3	5.9	4.1	9.4
Health subsidy allowances	32.7	31.9	33.0	33.0	30.7
Education subsidy allowances	8.3	3.5	10.3	4.1	32.7
Allowance for recovery from disaster, fire	4.9	1.3	6.4	4.8	5.6
Loan from Vietnam Bank for Social Policies	13.1	6.8	15.8	9.7	33.2
Health program	12.0	3.4	15.6	6.4	44.1
Education fee reduction and exemption	5.5	1.8	7.1	3.2	18.8
Housing program	1.1	0.2	1.5	0.4	4.8
Cultivation land for ethnic minorities	0.1	0	0.2	0	0.8
Agricultural extension	7.8	1.1	10.6	4.7	25.9
Clean water	1.9	0.2	2.7	0.6	9.7
Food supports	5.2	1.4	6.8	2.8	19.1
Production support	9.0	1.4	12.1	6.0	26.2

Sources: VHLSS 2010; Nguyen and Vu 2012.

Notes: Program coverage is the portion of population in each group that receives the transfer. Specifically, coverage is the number of individuals in the group who live in a household where at least one member receives the transfer divided by the number of individuals in the group. Program coverage is calculated as the household expansion factor multiplied by the household size.

Annex 3A Overview of Vietnam's eight economic regions

Vietnam's eight regions include the east and west northern mountains, the Red River Delta, the north-central coast, the south-central coast, the central highlands, the southeast, and the Mekong Delta.

The east northern mountains lie to the north of the Red River Delta. It includes nine provinces, with a population of 8.2 million. The Viet (Kinh) people make up the majority, with the exception of areas where a number of minority groups reside. Economic development in the region is based mainly on mining, especially coal and various minerals, forestry, perennial crops, vegetables, and tourism at sites like Ba Be Lake, Tam Dao, and Ha Long Bay.

The west northern mountains are in the mountainous northwestern part of the country, bordering China and the Lao People's Democratic Republic. The region covers six provinces, with a population of 4.2 million. The Thai people make up the majority, but more than 20 other ethnic groups live in northwest region. High mountains make communications difficult. The economy is based on agriculture and industrial crops such as tea and maize. The soil contains various minerals that have not yet been exploited.

The Red River Delta's population is 18.8 million inhabitants, a majority of which (96.2 percent) are Viet people who live in 10 provinces. The region is the economic, political, and cultural center of the country, with the capital Hanoi and the port of Haiphong. The economic engines are industrial production and services. It is also the second-largest rice producer in the country.

The north-central coast has about 10.1 million inhabitants consisting of 25 ethnic groups, with the majority group made up of Viet people. The region is located between the Lao PDR border and a long coastal line. It offers good conditions for overseas trading and tourism.

The south-central coast encompasses eight provinces with a combined population of 8.9 million. Most of the population are Viet people, but other minorities include Bana, Cham, and RaGlai. Economic development is based mainly on industrial production, especially in Da Nang and Khanh Hoa provinces, and in new industrial centers, namely the Chu Lai economic zone and the Dung Quat economic zone (with the Dung Quat refinery). The long coastline offers good potential for development of the region's marine economy.

The central highlands region has a population of 5.3 million that is ethnically dominated by the Bana, Coh, Ede, and Giarai. It shares a border with Cambodia and Lao PDR and covers the poorest areas of the country, with sluggish economic development and weak infrastructure. Its fertile soil is good for cash crops such as coffee, pepper, and rubber.

The southeast consists of seven provinces and 14.9 million people: Viet people are the majority, and Cham and Kh'mer are the main ethnic minorities. This region is the most economically developed and also the most urbanized region in Vietnam, with the economic hub of Ho Chi Minh City. Other provinces of the region such as Binh Duong, Dong Nai, and Ba Ria-Vung Tau are industrialized and contribute significantly to the region's economic development.

The Mekong Delta includes 13 provinces and 17.3 million people, of which Viet is the main group and Hoa and Khmer are the minorities. It is the largest rice-growing area and produces half of Vietnam's total rice production. In addition, it is home to a large aquacultural industry of catfish and shrimp and a variety of fruits.

Notes

1. Defined as households where the head's main job is in agriculture.
2. Ministry of Construction Plan, as part of Decree 10/1998/QD-TTg (GSO 1998).
3. Several of Vietnam's largest cities have developed their own poverty lines; for instance, Hanoi recently announced a new poverty line of D 750,000 per person per month for the 2011–15 SEDP, and Ho Chi Minh City uses a poverty line of D 1 million per person per month.
4. Information in this section was provided by UNICEF/Hanoi and is reported in GSO (2011).

References

GSO (General Statistics Office of Vietnam). 1998. "Decision to Approve the Orientations of the Master Plan for the Development of Vietnam's Urban Centers till 2020." Decree 10/1998/QD-TTg, Hanoi, January 23.

———. 2010. "Migration and Urbanization in Vietnam: Patterns, Trends, and Differentials." Report prepared with support from the United Nations Population Fund based on 2009 Housing and Population Census, 15 Percent Sample, GSO, Hanoi.

———. 2011. "Report on Multidimensional Child Poverty in Vietnam." Report prepared by UNICEF and the GSO, Hanoi, September.

Haughton, Jonathan, Thi Thanh Loan Nguyen, and Bui Linh Nguyen. 2010. "Urban Poverty Assessment in Hanoi and HCMC." Report prepared by the United Nations Development Programme and the GSO, Hanoi.

Le, Dang Trung, Cuong Viet Nguyen, and Tung Phung Duc. 2012. "Natural Shocks, Vulnerability to Poverty in Vietnam." Background paper prepard for the 2012 Vietnam Poverty Assessment, Hanoi.

Markussen, Thomas, Finn Tarp, and Katleen van den Broeck. 2009. *The Forgotten Property Rights: Restrictions on Land Use in Vietnam.* Discussion Paper 09-21. Copenhagen: University of Copenhagen, Department of Economics.

Nguyen, Cuong Viet, and Linh Vu. 2012. "Poverty Targeting and Social Protection Strategies in Vietnam." Background paper prepared for the 2012 Vietnam Poverty Assessment, Hanoi.

Nguyen, Tam Giang, and Xuan Thanh Hoang. 2012. "Long-Run Drivers of Poverty Reduction in Vietnam between 1992 and 2011." Background paper prepared for the 2012 Vietnam Poverty Assessment, Hanoi.

Ravallion, Martin, and Dominiqe van de Walle. 2008a. "Land and Poverty in Reforming East Asia." *Finance and Development* 45 (3): 38–41.

———. 2008b. *Land in Transition: Reform and Poverty in Vietnam.* New York: Palgrave Macmillan; Washington, DC: World Bank.

UNFPA (United Nations Population Fund). 2011. "The Aging Population in Vietnam: Current Status, Prognosis, and Possible Policy Responses." United Nations Population Fund, Hanoi.

World Bank. 1999. *Vietnam Development Report 2000: Attacking Poverty.* Washington, DC: World Bank.

———. 2013. *Vietnam Development Report 2013: Skilling up Vietnam: Preparing the Workforce for a Modern Market Economy.* Washington, DC: World Bank.

CHAPTER 4

Spatial Dimensions of Poverty: 1999 and 2009 Poverty Maps

New poverty and inequality maps were created using Vietnam's 2009 Population and Housing Census in combination with the 2010 Vietnam Household Living Standards Survey. Poverty rates are highest in rural, inland, and upland areas and especially among ethnic minorities. Regions with high poverty are also characterized by high inequality. Poverty is becoming more spatially concentrated over time.

Household surveys are an important source of information on poverty and living conditions in countries throughout the world. But there is also widespread demand for information on poverty at a more disaggregated level, such as districts, communes, and villages, than is available through national household surveys. Knowing where poor people live is important information for designing effective poverty reduction policies and programs, including targeted poverty reduction programs and policies to promote infrastructure investment and improve access to public goods and services in poor areas.

Spatial targeting requires reliable information on poverty outcomes at the local level. To determine eligibility for support under the National Target Program for Sustainable Poverty Reduction (NTP-SPR) and other social programs, the Ministry of Labor, Invalids, and Social Affairs (MOLISA) uses a bottom-up process of local surveys combined with village-level discussions to produce poverty estimates at the commune level. But analysis suggests that coverage is uneven, and better information is needed on poverty outcomes at the local level (Nguyen, Lanjouw, and Marra 2012). Estimation of poverty for small geographic units (for example, districts and communes) is data intensive. While household surveys like the Vietnam Household Living Standard Survey (VHLSS) collect detailed information on household incomes and expenditures, the sample sizes are too small to yield reliable estimates of poverty at the district or commune level. In contrast, Vietnam's decennial population and housing censuses do not suffer from small-sample problems; they cover the whole population. Censuses also collect valuable information on individual and household characteristics that provide insights into living standards. But the census does not collect the detailed information on income or expenditures needed to measure poverty directly.

Small-area estimation techniques (often referred to as poverty-mapping methods) have been developed to estimate poverty at the small-area level. One popular approach, introduced by Elbers, Lanjouw, and Lanjouw (2002, 2003), combines household survey data and census data at the unit record level. The approach exploits a census's coverage of the entire population and a household survey's detailed information on income and expenditure. First, an expenditure (or income) model is estimated using the household survey data. The dependent variable is expenditure (or income), and the explanatory variables are a set of household and community characteristics that are comparable and available in both the household survey and the census. Subsequently, the parameter estimates from the expenditure model are applied to the census data in order to predict expenditure for all households in the population. From there it is a straightforward procedure to estimate poverty measures in small areas such as communes and districts. Annex 4A describes the methodology and data.

The small-area estimation method has been applied in a large number of countries to produce maps not only of poverty measures but also of other welfare indicators (see Bedi, Coudouel, and Simler 2007 for a review of applications). In Vietnam, many poverty maps have been developed in the past using the small-area estimation method of Elbers, Lanjouw, and Lanjouw (2002, 2003). For example, Minot, Baulch, and Epprecht (2003) combined the 1993 Vietnam Living Standard Survey (VLSS) and the 1994 Agricultural Census to estimate poverty at the local level in rural areas of Vietnam. They also constructed a poverty map using the 1998 VLSS and a 33 percent sample of the 1999 Population and Housing Census. Nguyen (2009) applied the 2002 VHLSS to the 33 percent sample of the 1999 Population and Housing Census to produce a poverty map for 2002. Nguyen, Tran, and van der Weide (2010) further updated the rural poverty map for 2006 using the 2006 VHLSS and the 2006 Rural Agriculture and Fishery Census.

The General Statistics Office completed a new census of the population in 2009 and a new round of the Vietnam Household Living Standards Survey in 2010. We use these data sets to construct new poverty and inequality maps for Vietnam. This chapter documents these new estimates of poverty at the province and district level[1] of Vietnam, using the new General Statistics Office–World Bank (GSO-WB) poverty lines and comprehensive consumption aggregates described in chapter 2. The estimates are based on the 15 percent sample of the 2009 Population and Housing Census in combination with the 2010 VHLSS. In addition, poverty is estimated at the province and district level for different groups, including rural, urban, Kinh-Hoa, and ethnic minority subpopulations. Estimates of province- and district-level inequality are also presented, as is a complementary set of "wealth maps"—that is, maps showing which provinces and districts account for the wealthiest 15 percent of the Vietnamese population.

The chapter then turns to an assessment of spatial changes in poverty based on the 1999 and 2009 poverty maps. Although poverty at the national level has fallen substantially over this period, the rate of progress has not been uniform across all localities. Against a background of substantial aggregate growth and poverty reduction, poverty has become more concentrated in certain regions of the country and within certain socioeconomic groups. Building on these findings, the mapping methodology is used to assess whether the 62 "poorest districts" identified under Program 30A are indeed among the poorest in Vietnam. Initial findings from policy simulations to assess the gains from spatial targeting in 2010 compared to 1999 are also described. The policy message emerging from both exercises is that spatially targeted poverty reduction policies, including, for example, area-based schemes, will continue to play an important role in Vietnam.

2009 poverty maps

Small-area estimation methods are used to construct per capita expenditure-based poverty rates for regions, provinces, and districts in Vietnam. Table 4.1 provides regional estimates of the poverty rate and per capita expenditure that are computed using per capita expenditure data from the 2010 VHLSS and regional estimates from the poverty-mapping method. The 2012 VHLSS is representative at the regional level, and the regional poverty rate that is directly estimated from expenditure data can be regarded as the benchmark against which to compare the poverty map estimates. As shown in table 4.1, estimates of the poverty rate are quite similar across the two approaches.

Table 4.2 presents estimates using poverty-mapping methods of the mean of per capita expenditure and the estimated poverty rate, the absolute number of poor people, and the contribution to national poverty for all 63 provinces in Vietnam. Lai Chau, Ha Giang, and Dien Bien are the three poorest provinces, with a poverty rate of more than 70 percent. As expected, Hanoi and Ho Chi Minh City are the least-poor cities, followed by Da Nang, Hai Phong, Quang Ninh, Binh Duong, and Ba Ria-Vung Tau. Similar estimates for Vietnam's 668 districts are presented, along with provincial estimates, in the figures and maps that follow (Nguyen, Lanjouw, and Marra 2012).

Map 4.1 shows the spatial distribution of poverty by provinces and districts in 2009. Poverty rates are highest in the mountainous northern areas and lowest in the Mekong and Red River deltas. Disaggregating

TABLE 4.1 Per capita expenditures and poverty indexes in Vietnam, by region, 2009 or 2010

	Estimates from the 2010 VHLSS				Estimates from small-area estimation method			
	Per capita expenditure (dong, thousands)	P0	P1	P2	Per capita expenditure (dong, thousands)	P0	P1	P2
Northern mountains	10,927.1	44.87	0.156	0.070	10,826.4	43.85	0.148	0.068
	(250.2)	(1.54)	(0.007)	(0.004)	(340.9)	(1.76)	(0.008)	(0.005)
Red River Delta	21,546.0	11.95	0.027	0.009	20,515.2	10.65	0.020	0.006
	(605.6)	(0.85)	(0.003)	(0.001)	(592.2)	(1.02)	(0.003)	(0.001)
Central coast	14,222.6	23.73	0.064	0.025	14,002.1	22.48	0.052	0.018
	(267.3)	(1.33)	(0.005)	(0.003)	(268.7)	(1.05)	(0.003)	(0.001)
Central highlands	13,069.0	32.74	0.115	0.054	12,931.0	33.29	0.115	0.054
	(490.9)	(2.75)	(0.013)	(0.008)	(351.8)	(1.25)	(0.006)	(0.003)
Southeast	24,297.4	7.02	0.017	0.006	23,350.9	7.07	0.014	0.004
	(935.9)	(0.96)	(0.004)	(0.002)	(844.9)	(0.84)	(0.002)	(0.001)
Mekong Delta	14,858.2	18.71	0.043	0.014	14,497.9	17.45	0.036	0.011
	(265.8)	(1.10)	(0.003)	(0.002)	(280.7)	(1.08)	(0.003)	(0.001)

Sources: Estimates based on the 2009 Vietnam Population and Housing Census and the 2010 VHLSS.
Note: Standard errors are in parentheses. P0 = poverty headcount, P1 = depth of poverty, P2 = severity of poverty.

TABLE 4.2 Per capita expenditure and poverty rates of provinces in Vietnam, 2009

Province	Number of People	Share of total population	Per capita expenditure (dong, thousands) Mean	Per capita expenditure (dong, thousands) Standard error	Poverty rate (%) Mean	Poverty rate (%) Standard error	Number of poor people	Share of total poverty
Northern mountains								
Ha Giang	724,352	0.84	7422.70	448.1	71.46	2.99	517,586	3.07
Cao Bang	510,884	0.60	9,325.70	515.1	53.11	3.26	271,348	1.61
Bac Kan	294,660	0.34	10,136.10	792.0	45.97	5.32	135,448	0.80
Tuyen Quang	725,467	0.85	11,238.30	917.9	39.95	5.41	289,798	1.72
Lao Cai	613,074	0.71	9,711.50	817.8	56.77	3.90	340,010	2.06
Dien Bien	491,046	0.57	7,625.90	611.7	71.06	3.65	348,953	2.07
Lai Chau	370,134	0.43	6,809.20	465.3	76.41	2.99	282,805	1.68
Son La	1,080,641	1.26	8,326.00	590.3	63.60	4.02	687,305	4.08
Yen Bai	740,904	0.86	10,621.90	794.5	45.33	4.72	335,860	1.99
Hoa Binh	786,963	0.92	10,439.00	675.5	47.31	4.23	372,330	2.21
Thai Nguyen	1,124,785	1.31	14,170.50	1,117.1	21.99	3.42	247,386	1.47
Lang Son	731,886	0.85	10,292.10	715.1	45.69	4.29	334,364	1.98
Bac Giang	1,555,720	1.81	12,823.40	889.4	23.83	4.33	370,722	2.20
Phu Tho	1,313,926	1.53	13,535.90	806.9	23.62	3.20	310,380	1.84
Red River Delta								
Ha Noi	6,448,837	7.52	29,344.60	1,375.70	4.94	0.89	318,488	1.89
Quang Ninh	1,144,381	1.33	18,538.00	1,243.90	12.12	1.81	138,656	0.82
Vinh Phuc	1,000,838	1.17	15,743.10	869.0	11.99	2.83	119,989	0.71
Bac Ninh	1,024,151	1.19	17,590.40	1,145.40	10.19	2.37	104,327	0.62
Hai Duong	1,703,492	1.99	15,261.30	827.50	14.84	2.73	252,716	1.50
Hai Phong	1,837,302	2.14	20,316.90	1,140.20	7.93	1.62	145,625	0.86
Hung Yên	1,128,702	1.32	16,063.40	812.60	12.78	2.36	144,273	0.86

(Table continues next page)

TABLE 4.2 Continued

Province	Number of People	Share of total population	Per capita expenditure (dong, thousands)		Poverty rate (%)		Number of poor people	Share of total poverty
			Mean	Standard error	Mean	Standard error		
Thai Binh	1,780,953	2.08	13,578.20	873.7	18.95	3.86	337,435	2.00
Ha Nam	785,057	0.92	14,269.80	1,011.8	16.56	4.07	130,009	0.77
Nam Dinh	1,825,770	2.13	14,866.40	814.6	14.04	2.70	256,321	1.52
Ninh Binh	898,458	1.05	14,955.30	878.3	15.28	3.33	137,314	0.81
Central coast								
Thanh Hoa	3,400,238	3.96	13,118.20	474.9	26.48	2.09	900,393	5.34
Nghe An	2,913,054	3.40	13,356.40	576.6	26.74	2.57	778,900	4.62
Ha Tinh	1,227,554	1.43	13,222.90	578.5	21.55	2.97	264,499	1.57
Quang Binh	846,924	0.99	13,847.20	798.8	23.20	4.14	196,475	1.17
Quang Tri	597,984	0.70	12,567.10	621.0	29.55	3.15	176,710	1.05
Thua Thiên Hue	1,087,578	1.27	14,453.70	955.1	19.43	3.03	211,283	1.25
Da Nang	887,068	1.03	23,087.90	1,311.7	2.39	1.05	21,218	0.13
Quang Nam	1,419,502	1.65	12,703.20	528.7	23.47	2.73	333,146	1.98
Quang Ngãi	1,217,159	1.42	12,955.10	573.2	23.65	2.80	287,827	1.71
Binh Dinh	1,485,943	1.73	14,498.90	834.9	16.68	3.16	247,882	1.47
Phú Yên	861,993	1.00	13,377.20	793.1	22.08	3.47	190,348	1.13
Khanh Hoa	1,156,902	1.35	16,778.10	1,244.5	15.51	2.87	179,462	1.06
Ninh Thuan	564,128	0.66	11,626.10	799.1	34.52	4.36	194,759	1.16
Binh Thuan	1,169,450	1.36	13,428.50	693.8	21.44	3.04	250,692	1.49

Central Highlands

Province								
Kon Tum	430,036	0.50	11,112.5	796.7	47.58	3.37	204,624	1.21
Gia Lai	1,272,791	1.48	11,222.1	439.8	43.34	2.07	551,562	3.27
Dak Lak	1,728,380	2.01	13,445.5	639.8	30.32	2.03	524,104	3.11
Dak Nong	489,441	0.57	11,719.4	500.0	32.50	2.83	159,063	0.94
Lâm Dong	1,186,786	1.38	15,173.1	687.8	21.96	1.97	260,629	1.55
South East								
Binh Phuoc	874,961	1.02	14,370.4	849.9	17.20	3.58	150,477	0.89
Tay Ninh	1,066,402	1.24	15,459.4	737.6	11.78	2.51	125,615	0.75
Binh Duong	1,482,635	1.73	18,378.5	1,168.5	7.82	2.10	115,901	0.69
Dong Nai	2,483,210	2.89	17,293.1	1,129.8	11.73	2.21	291,223	1.73
Ba Ria-Vung Tau	994,836	1.16	18,704.2	1,336.3	9.97	2.22	99,206	0.59
Ho Chi Minh	7,123,340	8.30	29,431.0	1,342.5	2.94	0.51	209,427	1.24
Mekong Delta								
Long An	1,436,913	1.67	16,334.8	703.5	10.97	1.64	157,596	0.93
Tien Giang	1,670,215	1.95	16,578.6	875.9	9.53	2.14	159,215	0.94
Ben Tre	1,254,588	1.46	16,022.7	745.8	10.00	2.00	125,506	0.74
Tra Vinh	1,000,932	1.17	13,507.1	688.8	22.28	3.09	222,988	1.32
Vinh Long	1,028,365	1.20	16,038.5	887.7	11.76	2.26	120,947	0.72
Dong Thap	1,665,420	1.94	13,820.8	605.6	15.58	2.42	259,532	1.54
An Giang	2,144,772	2.50	13,739.4	595.5	18.22	2.50	390,808	2.32
Kiên Giang	1,683,149	1.96	13,057.1	580.7	24.02	2.62	404,319	2.40
Can Tho	1,187,088	1.38	17,911.6	1,029.2	11.70	1.97	138,868	0.82
Hau Giang	756,625	0.88	13,369.3	690.7	19.68	3.41	148,915	0.88
Soc Trang	1,289,441	1.50	12,561.6	604.5	27.28	3.10	351,709	2.09
Bac Liêu	856,249	1.00	12,533.0	670.7	23.30	3.74	199,528	1.18
Ca Mau	1,205,107	1.40	12,456.9	682.5	26.36	3.48	317,609	1.88

Sources: Estimates based on the 2009 Population and Housing Census and the 2010 VHLSS.

MAP 4.1 **Predicted poverty rates in provinces and districts of Vietnam, 2009**

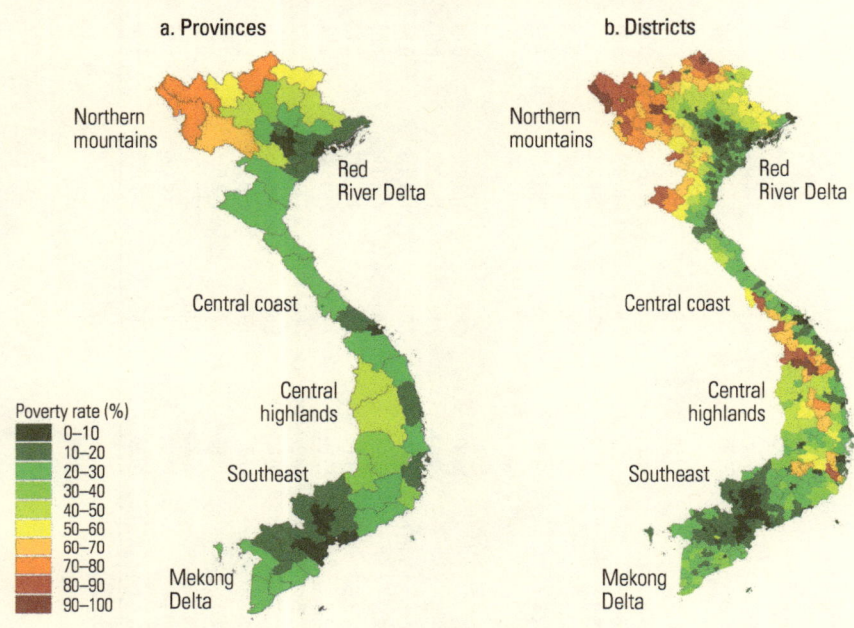

Sources: Estimates based on the 2009 Population and Housing Census and the 2010 VHLSS.

down to the district level reveals a greater degree of heterogeneity in terms of both pockets of extreme poverty and pockets of particularly low levels of poverty. As discussed later, such heterogeneity across subnational locali- ties translates into better spatial targeting of public resources for poverty reduction.

Map 4.2 graphs the density of the poor across the country. Because of their large populations, the Mekong and Red River delta regions still account for a significant number of poor people in Vietnam. In the late 1990s, the incidence of poverty was highest in more sparsely populated localities, which thus accounted for only a modest fraction of the poor. Today, although poverty rates remain spatially concentrated, the distri- bution of poor people is spread more evenly across the country. Conse- quently, Vietnam's poorest communities now account for a larger share of the poor population.

Inequality

Inequality is higher in poorer regions. In Vietnam, the relationship between poverty and inequality (measured by the Gini index) is positive. A more equal distribution in well-being is associated with a lower poverty rate at the province and district level (figure 4.1), while regions with high pov-

MAP 4.2 Spatial density of poverty in Vietnam, 2009

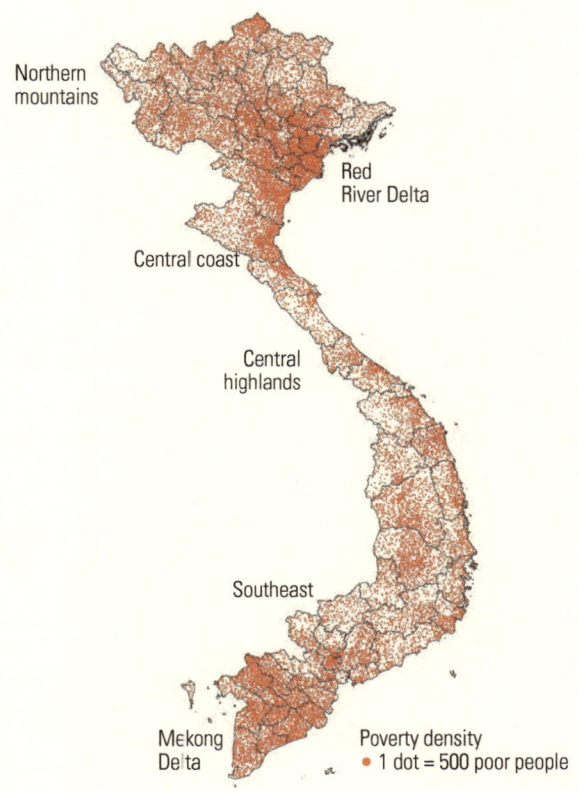

Sources: Estimates based on the 2009 Population and Housing Census and the 2010 VHLSS.

erty rates tend to be more unequal. This result is driven, in large part, by persistent gaps in welfare between ethnic minorities and the Kinh majority (see chapter 5). However, there remains a great deal of heterogeneity in inequality outcomes, particularly when results are disaggregated to the district level.

Relationship between poverty and other characteristics

Although Vietnam is still heavily rural, the pace of urbanization is accelerating. According to the most recent census, an estimated 30 percent of people now reside in urban areas. Overall, urban areas tend to have lower poverty levels (Ravallion, Chen, and Sangraula 2007). According to figure 4.2, poverty rates are negatively correlated with the share of urban population at the province and district level, but, again, with considerable variability across space.

FIGURE 4.1 Relationship between the poverty rate and Gini index in provinces and districts of Vietnam, 2009

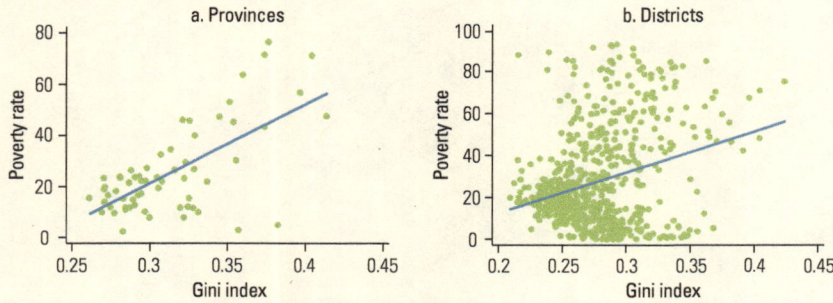

Sources: Estimates based on the 2009 Population and Housing Census and the 2010 VHLSS.

FIGURE 4.2 Poverty rate and proportion of urban population in Vietnam, 2009

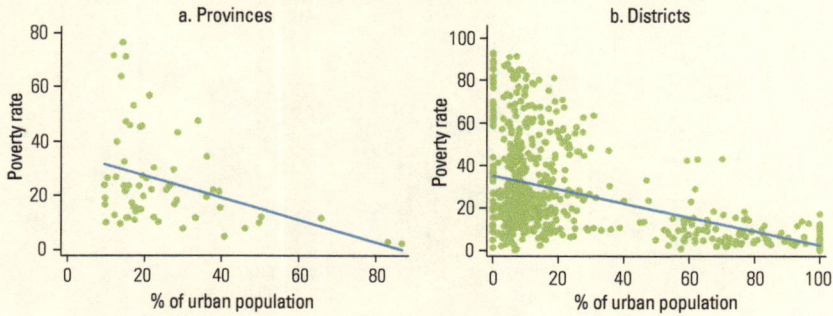

Sources: Estimates based on the 2009 Population and Housing Census and the 2010 VHLSS.

FIGURE 4.3 Poverty rate and proportion of ethnic minorities in provinces and districts of Vietnam, 2009

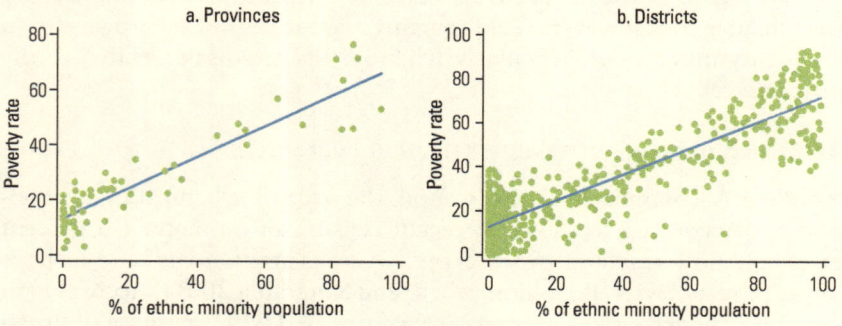

Sources: Estimates based on the 2009 Population and Housing Census and the 2010 VHLSS.

MAP 4.3 **Urban and rural poverty rates in provinces and districts of Vietnam, 2009**

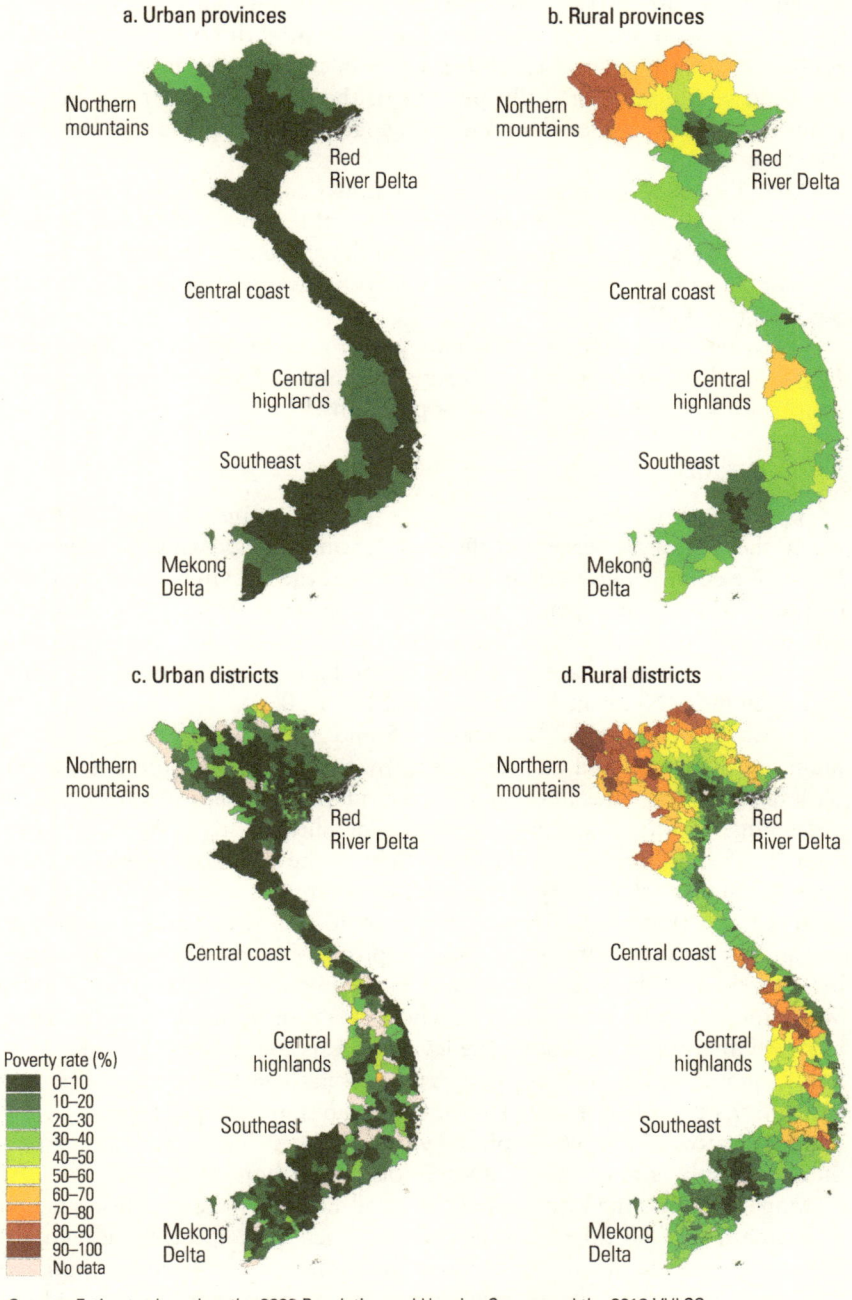

Sources: Estimates based on the 2009 Population and Housing Census and the 2010 VHLSS.

Map 4.3 compares poverty rates in urban and rural areas at both the province and the district levels. Urban poverty is found to be uniformly lower than rural poverty, and there are substantial differences in poverty rates between urban and rural areas within a given province or district. As discussed in chapter 3, 70 percent of the urban poor live in smaller cities and towns, rather than Vietnam's large (special, class 1, and class 2) cities.

Analysis based on mapping methods also confirms that poverty has become increasingly concentrated among ethnic minority populations, and there is a strong correlation between the share of ethnic minorities in the population and the poverty rate, at both the province and the district levels (figure 4.3).[2]

Consistent with chapter 3, Vietnam's poor are increasingly concentrated in the northern mountains and central highlands, where there are high proportions of minorities in local populations.

Inequality and wealth maps

Mapping methods are used to estimate the percentage of people belonging to the richest 20 percent of the population at the province and district levels. We employ two measures of inequality, the Gini index and the ratio of the 90th to 10th expenditure percentile (a better measure of absolute inequality). Provincial results are presented in table 4.2. Province- and district-level estimates are presented in the figures and maps that follow and elsewhere (Nguyen, Lanjouw, and Marra 2012).

Consistent with table 4.2, maps 4.5 and 4.6 show that inequality is higher in provinces and districts with low average expenditures. Districts with high poverty rates in the northern mountains (which also have a high percentage of minorities) have higher expenditure inequality than other regions. This finding is noteworthy in light of the common (often implicit) view in Vietnam that everyone in poor communities is similarly poor and with the view that inequality is a more common feature in urban areas. But the finding also resonates with other empirical studies of inequality at the local level (see Elbers, Lanjouw, and Lanjouw 2002; Elbers et al. 2004). While there may be poor localities where everyone is similarly poor, more in-depth analysis at the commune level suggests that there is still substantial inequality at low levels of geographic disaggregation (see the targeting simulations described in annex 4A). Communes in Vietnam typically consist of four to six villages; empirical work suggests that villages tend to be more ethnically and economically homogeneous than communes.

Map 4.7 shows the locations of the wealthiest 20 percent of households in Vietnam—the so-called middle class and rich. As expected, individuals in the top quintile of the per capita expenditure distribution are spatially concentrated in the delta regions, especially in Hanoi and Ho Chi Minh City and in the immediate surrounding areas.

MAP 4.4 Poverty rates in provinces and districts of Vietnam, by ethnicity, 2009

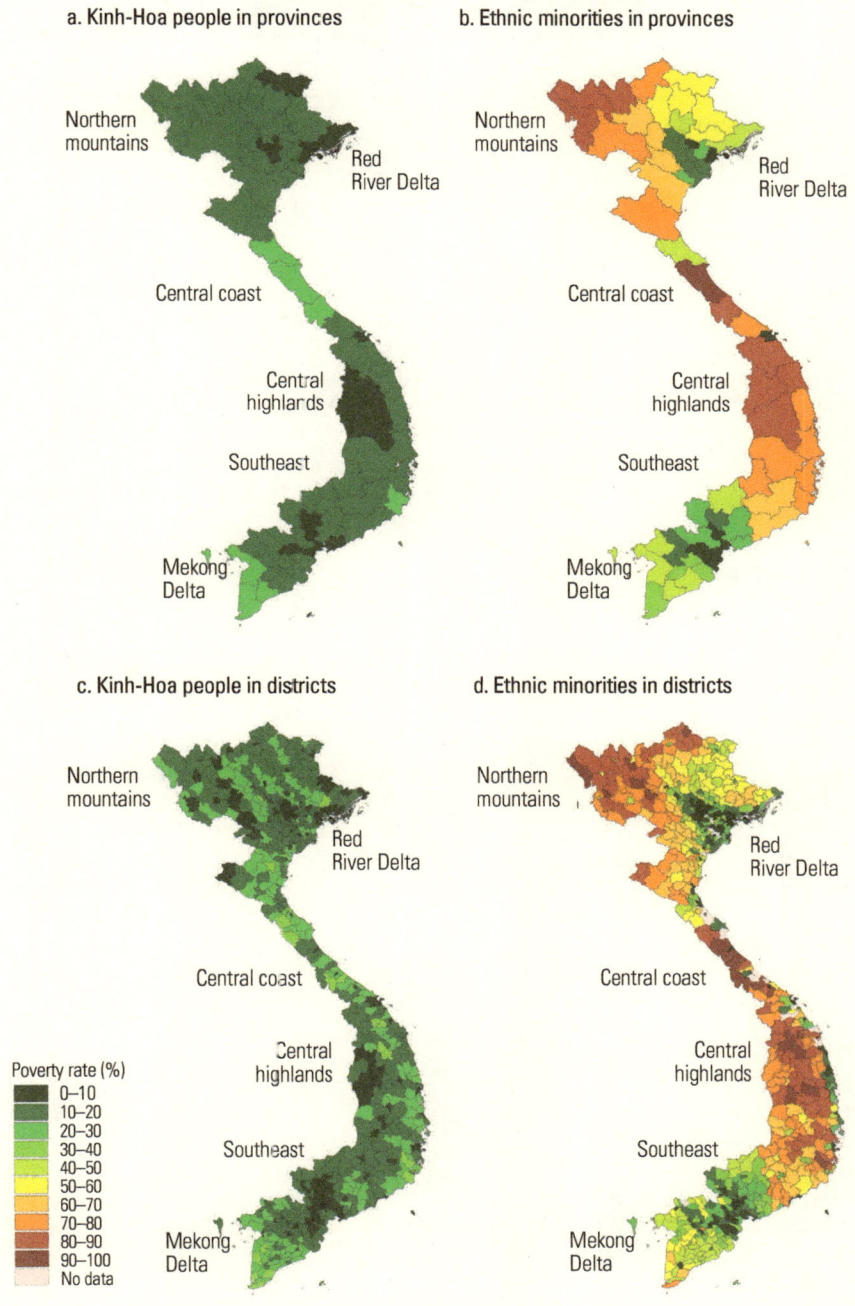

a. Kinh-Hoa people in provinces

b. Ethnic minorities in provinces

c. Kinh-Hoa people in districts

d. Ethnic minorities in districts

Poverty rate (%)
0–10
10–20
20–30
30–40
40–50
50–60
60–70
70–80
80–90
90–100
No data

Sources: Estimates based on the 2009 Population and Housing Census and the 2010 VHLSS.

TABLE 4.3 **Inequality and wealth measures for provinces in Vietnam, 2009**

Provinces	Gini index		Ratio of 90th to 10th expenditure percentile		Percentage of people in the richest quintile	
	Mean	Std. error	Mean	Std. error	Mean	Std. error
Northern mountains						
Ha Giang	0.374	0.018	4.93	0.35	3.55	0.89
Cao Bang	0.351	0.016	5.10	0.40	4.73	1.14
Bac Kan	0.321	0.018	4.21	0.32	5.31	1.62
Tuyen Quang	0.329	0.021	4.38	0.37	7.54	2.13
Lao Cai	0.397	0.019	6.12	0.53	7.38	1.99
Dien Bien	0.404	0.023	5.82	0.56	4.51	1.29
Lai Chau	0.376	0.017	4.82	0.29	2.99	0.80
Son La	0.36	0.013	4.82	0.27	4.20	1.02
Yen Bai	0.354	0.019	5.20	0.46	7.24	1.91
Hoa Binh	0.345	0.018	4.70	0.35	6.83	1.57
Thai Nguyen	0.308	0.021	4.11	0.42	13.33	3.44
Lang Son	0.325	0.018	4.31	0.32	5.77	1.69
Bac Giang	0.281	0.012	3.60	0.22	8.55	2.29
Phu Tho	0.305	0.013	4.01	0.26	11.30	2.21
Red River Delta						
Ha Noi	0.382	0.013	6.02	0.40	49.03	2.16
Quang Ninh	0.324	0.015	4.50	0.34	25.76	3.65
Vinh Phuc	0.275	0.012	3.47	0.19	15.81	2.73
Bac Ninh	0.297	0.014	3.85	0.26	22.08	3.55
Hai Duong	0.289	0.013	3.63	0.18	14.49	2.33
Hai Phong	0.322	0.014	4.32	0.28	30.29	3.26
Hung Yên	0.29	0.012	3.68	0.21	16.96	2.49
Thai Bình	0.271	0.014	3.36	0.19	9.40	2.33
Ha Nam	0.273	0.015	3.41	0.23	11.33	2.95
Nam Dinh	0.271	0.014	3.40	0.19	12.97	2.50
Ninh Bình	0.283	0.016	3.57	0.24	13.63	2.55
Central coast						
Thanh Hoa	0.316	0.011	3.95	0.15	10.11	1.15
Nghe An	0.328	0.016	4.15	0.21	10.88	1.33
Ha Tinh	0.287	0.009	3.45	0.14	9.40	1.39
Quang Binh	0.322	0.017	3.99	0.26	11.75	1.81
Quang Tri	0.323	0.012	4.42	0.25	9.45	1.51
Thua Thiên Hue	0.305	0.016	3.90	0.29	13.22	2.80
Da Nang	0.283	0.011	3.63	0.21	40.11	4.16
Quang Nam	0.281	0.009	3.55	0.17	8.04	1.42
Quang Ngãi	0.29	0.012	3.76	0.20	8.72	1.58
Binh Dinh	0.293	0.015	3.57	0.23	12.42	2.28
Phú Yên	0.297	0.015	3.60	0.22	9.69	2.02

(Table continued next page)

TABLE 4.3 **Continued**

Provinces	Gini index		Ratio of 90th to 10th expenditure percentile		Percentage of people in the richest quintile	
	Mean	Std. error	Mean	Std. error	Mean	Std. error
Khanh Hoa	0.325	0.017	4.44	0.35	20.18	3.50
Ninh Thuan	0.313	0.015	4.19	0.30	7.28	1.92
Binh Thuan	0.287	0.012	3.64	0.19	10.02	1.91
Central highlands						
Kon Tum	0.414	0.011	7.60	0.47	9.97	2.04
Gia Lai	0.374	0.008	6.18	0.24	8.87	1.16
Dak Lak	0.356	0.011	5.34	0.25	12.50	1.70
Dak Nong	0.307	0.007	4.44	0.15	7.03	1.19
Lâm Dong	0.337	0.010	4.98	0.23	16.80	2.00
South East						
Binh Phuoc	0.294	0.009	3.53	0.16	11.53	1.91
Tay Ninh	0.287	0.008	3.35	0.14	13.49	1.79
Binh Duong	0.300	0.008	3.62	0.15	22.47	3.65
Dong Nai	0.319	0.014	3.93	0.27	19.47	3.27
Ba Ria - Vung Tau	0.331	0.015	4.14	0.28	23.46	3.70
Ho Chí Minh	0.357	0.009	4.73	0.18	51.17	2.87
Mekong Delta						
Long An	0.285	0.009	3.57	0.13	17.55	2.15
Tien Giang	0.277	0.010	3.46	0.14	18.18	2.72
Ben Tre	0.269	0.009	3.36	0.13	16.29	2.33
Tra Vinh	0.294	0.009	3.76	0.15	10.49	1.80
Vinh Long	0.284	0.011	3.58	0.17	16.81	2.66
Dong Thap	0.261	0.007	3.18	0.10	9.59	1.60
An Giang	0.278	0.009	3.39	0.13	9.98	1.49
Kiên Giang	0.293	0.010	3.72	0.14	9.43	1.48
Can Tho	0.328	0.017	4.29	0.33	22.59	2.76
Hau Giang	0.271	0.008	3.39	0.12	9.22	1.70
Soc Trang	0.298	0.011	3.79	0.16	8.44	1.46
Bac Liêu	0.271	0.010	3.32	0.13	7.25	1.56
Ca Mau	0.288	0.012	3.58	0.17	7.76	1.63

Sources: Estimates based on the 2009 Population and Housing Census and the 2010 VHLSS.

Evolution of spatial poverty between 1999 and 2009

Chapter 1 documents Vietnam's rapid reduction in poverty since the early 1990s based on a range of poverty lines applied to successive rounds of the VHLSS. However, the VHLSS is only representative at higher levels of spatial aggregation—that is, by region and urban and rural sector. The 2009 poverty maps can be compared with 1999 poverty maps to measure progress at the province and district levels and to look at changes in the spatial distribution of poverty over time. This section describes spatial

MAP 4.5 **Expenditure Gini indexes for provinces and districts in Vietnam, 2009**

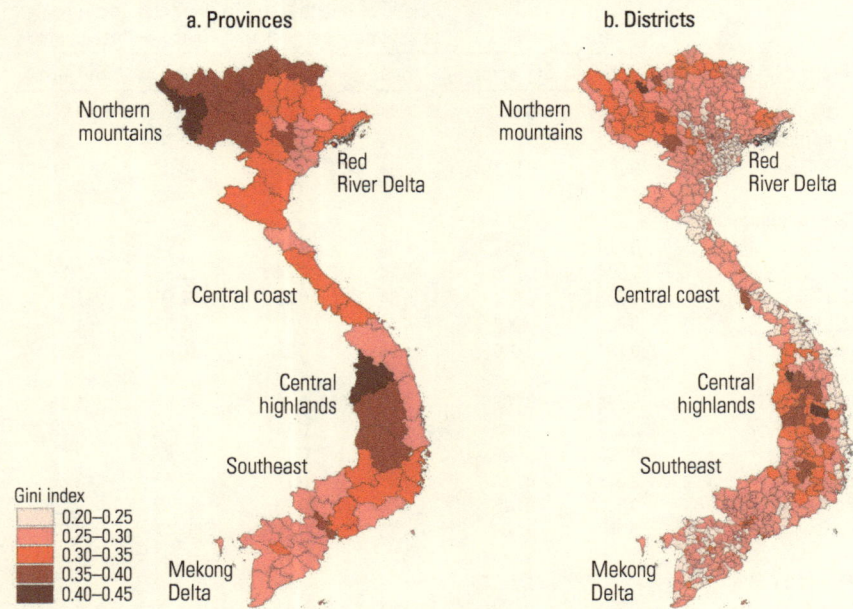

Sources: Estimates based on the 2009 Population and Housing Census and the 2010 VHLSS.

MAP 4.6 **Absolute inequality in provinces and districts in Vietnam: Ratio of the 90th to the 10th expenditure percentile, 2009**

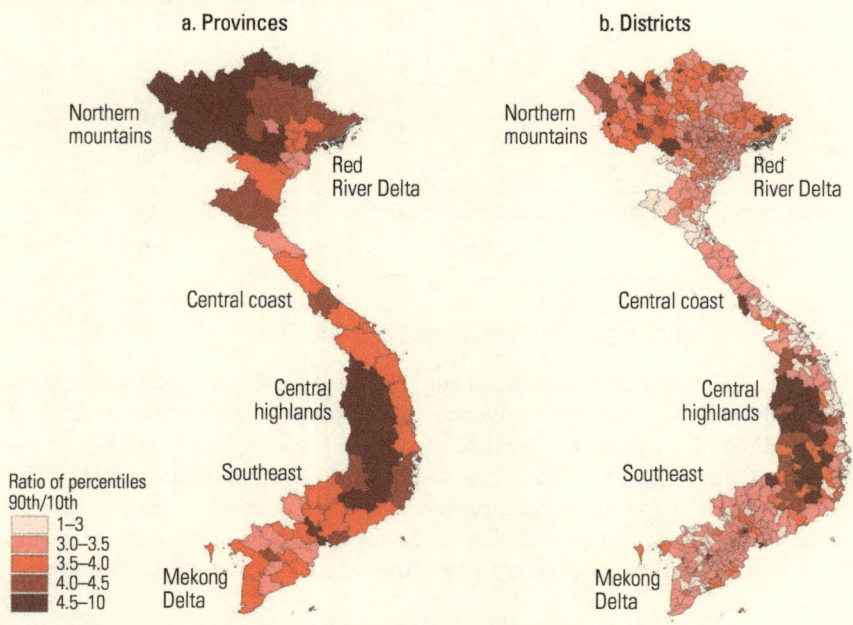

Sources: Estimates based on the 2009 Population and Housing Census and the 2010 VHLSS.

MAP 4.7 Spatial distribution of individuals in the wealthiest expenditure quintile in provinces and districts of Vietnam: A wealth map, 2009

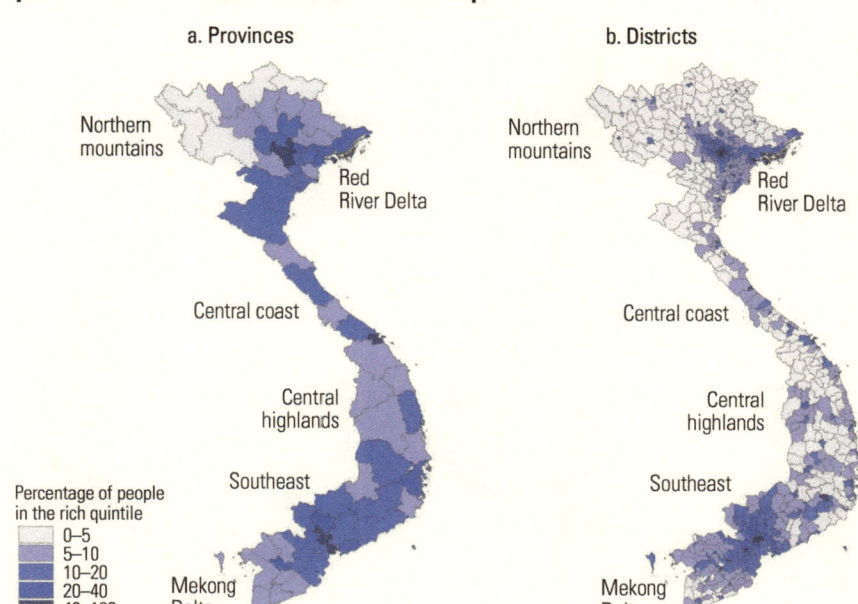

a. Provinces

b. Districts

Northern mountains

Red River Delta

Central coast

Central highlands

Southeast

Mekong Delta

Percentage of people in the rich quintile
- 0–5
- 5–10
- 10–20
- 20–40
- 40–100

Sources: Estimates based on the 2009 Population and Housing Census and the 2010 VHLSS.

patterns of poverty, leaving for future work in-depth analysis of the causal mechanisms that underpin these patterns.

Comparisons of maps 4.8 and 4.9 show that poverty fell most rapidly between 1999 and 2009 in the provinces and districts in the two deltas. Provinces and districts in the northern mountains and central highlands experienced substantially lower rates of poverty reduction. District-level maps highlight the variation within provinces, such as in the central highlands.

The areas with a high incidence of poverty are not necessarily the areas with the highest number of poor people. For example, provinces in the northern mountains have a high incidence of poverty but low population densities and thus account for only a small share of the total poor in Vietnam. Map 4.10 shows the density of the poor across the country in 1999 and 2009. In 1999, the poor were heavily concentrated in the Red River Delta and Mekong Delta; these areas had moderate poverty rates but high population densities. By 2009, however, poverty had become less spatially concentrated. Poverty fell rapidly in the two delta regions, but much less in the northern mountains and central highlands.

Nearly all provinces and districts experienced a decline in poverty between 1999 and 2009 (figure 4.4). But the rate of progress was slower in areas that had very high or very low rates of poverty in 1999 and much

MAP 4.8 Provincial poverty rates in Vietnam, 1999 and 2009

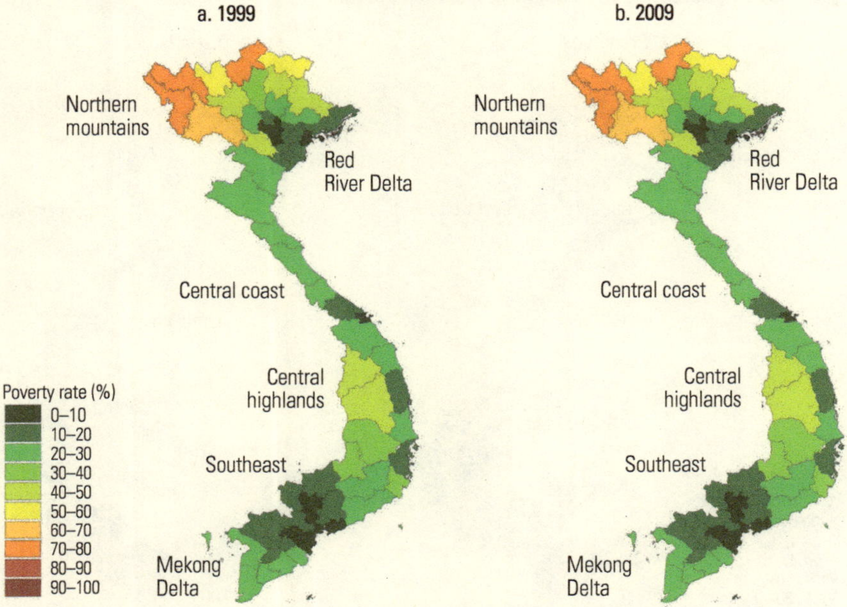

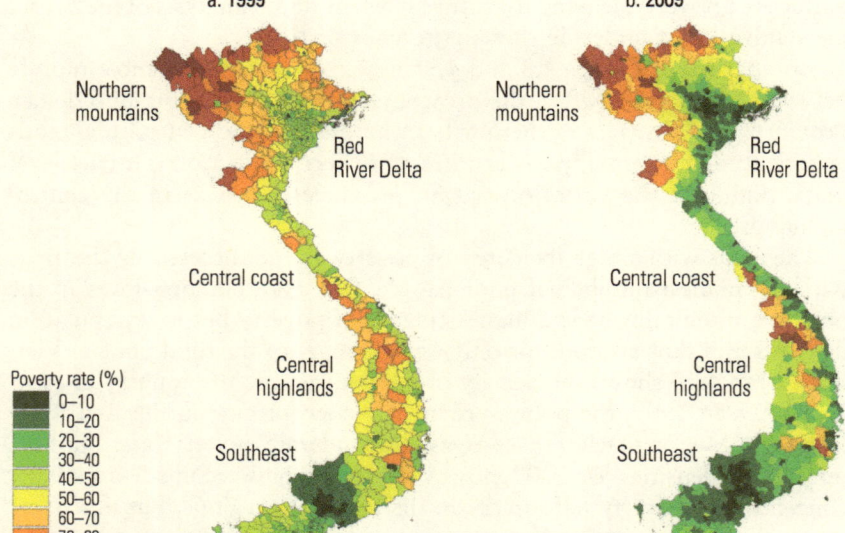

a. 1999   b. 2009

Poverty rate (%)
0–10
10–20
20–30
30–40
40–50
50–60
60–70
70–80
80–90
90–100

Sources: Estimates based on the 2009 Population and Housing Census and the 2010 VHLSS. The 1999 poverty rates are from Minot, Baulch, and Epprecht 2003.

MAP 4.9 District poverty rates in Vietnam, 1999 and 2009

a. 1999   b. 2009

Poverty rate (%)
0–10
10–20
20–30
30–40
40–50
50–60
60–70
70–80
80–90
90–100

Sources: Estimates based on the 2009 Population and Housing Census and the 2010 VHLSS. The 1999 poverty rates are from Minot, Baulch, and Epprecht 2003.

MAP 4.10 Density of poverty in Vietnam, 1999 and 2009

a. 1999
b. 2009
Northern mountains
Red River Delta
Central coast
Central highlands
Southeast
Mekong Delta
Northern mountains
Red River Delta
Central coast
Central highlands
Southeast
Mekong Delta
Poverty density
1 dot = 500 poor people

Sources: Estimates based on the 2009 Population and Housing Census and the 2010 VHLSS. The 1999 poverty rates are from Minot, Baulch, and Epprecht 2003.

FIGURE 4.4 Poverty rates in provinces and districts of Vietnam, 1999 and 2009

a. Provinces
b. Districts
2009 poverty rate
1999 poverty rate
0
20
40
60
80
100

Sources: Estimates based on the 2009 Population and Housing Census and the 2010 VHLSS. The 1999 poverty rates are from Minot, Baulch, and Epprecht 2003.

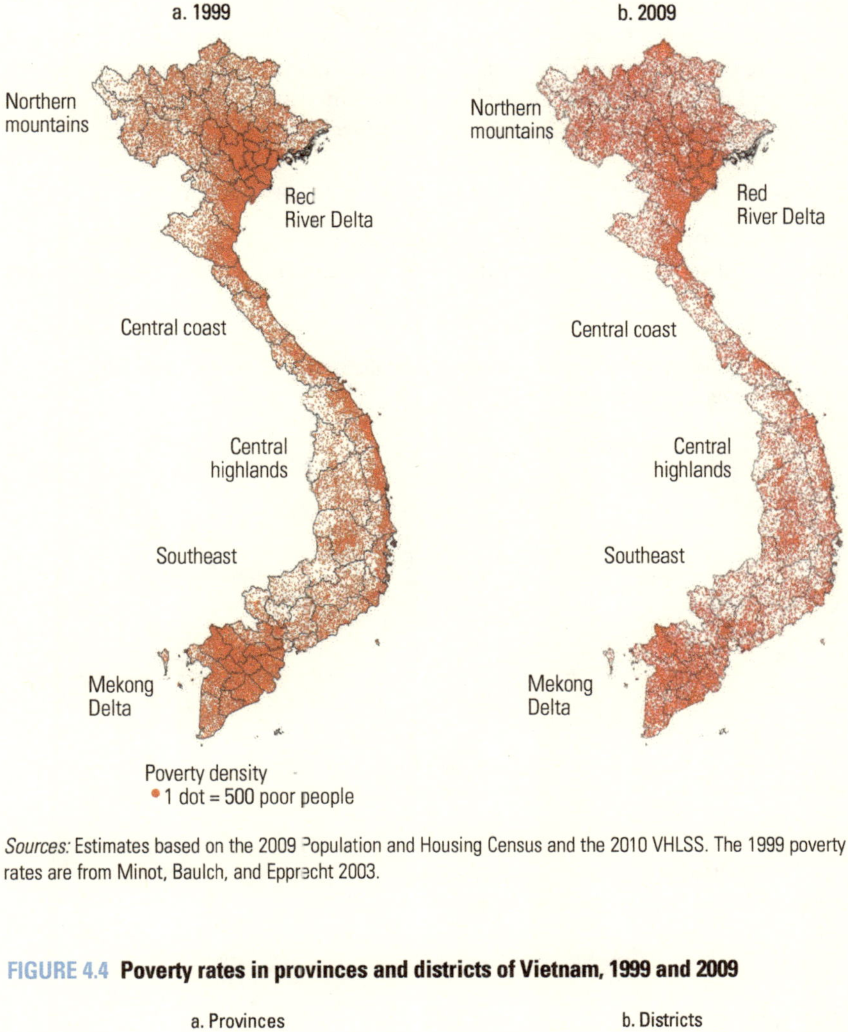

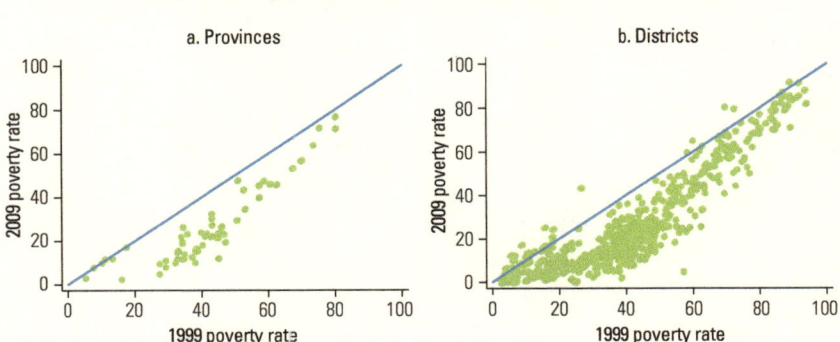

faster in areas that started the period in the middle ranges—that is, with a poverty headcount of 25 to 55 percent (figure 4.5).

Provinces with lower levels of inequality in 1999 generally achieved a bigger reduction in poverty. This largely reflects the growing gap between Kinh and ethnic minority households; high-inequality areas typically have a high proportion of ethnic minorities (figure 4.6).

Contribution of the rural nonfarm sector to poverty reduction

Various factors are responsible for differential rates of progress across provinces and districts in Vietnam. Income and employment diversification has

FIGURE 4.5 Changes in poverty in provinces and districts of Vietnam, 1999–2009, by initial poverty rate in 1999

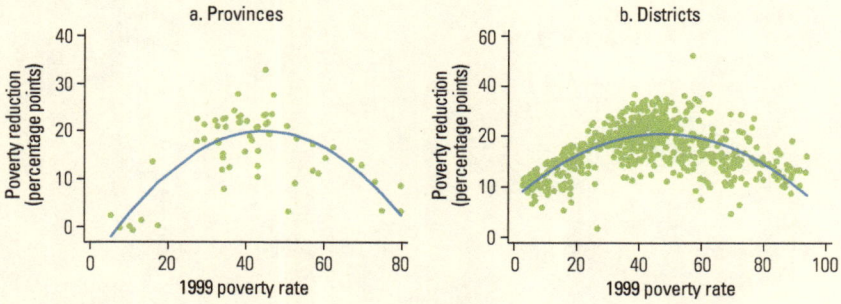

Sources: Estimates based on the 2009 Population and Housing Census and the 2010 VHLSS.
Note: The 1999 poverty rates are from Minot, Baulch, and Epprecht 2003.

FIGURE 4.6 Change in poverty in provinces and districts of Vietnam, 1999–2009, compared to the initial Gini index, 1999

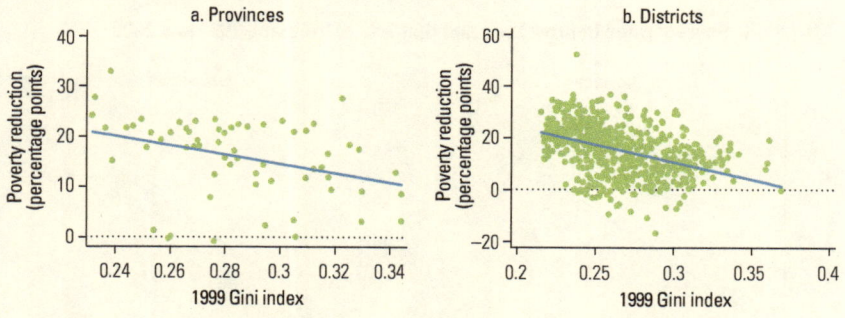

Sources: Estimates based on the 2009 Population and Housing Census and the 2010 VHLSS.
Note: The 1999 poverty rates are from Minot, Baulch, and Epprecht 2003.

been a strong force for growth and poverty reduction. Much attention has been paid to diversification linked to rural-to-urban migration and the role of remittances. In some other countries, the expansion of the rural non-farm sector has played a beneficial role in promoting rural development and improving the lives of the poor. The rural nonfarm sector can help to absorb excess agricultural labor, provide insurance against agricultural shocks, reduce rural-to-urban migration, and, more generally, promote a more equitable distribution of income (see, for example, Ferreira and Lanjouw 2001; Lanjouw and Lanjouw 2000; Oseni and Winters 2009).

Between 1999 and 2009, a major shift occurred in rural occupations in Vietnam. While in 1999, more than 81 percent of the working population worked in agriculture, by 2009, this had fallen to 71 percent. The growth of the rural nonfarm sector has been primarily due to expansion in the number of low-skilled blue-collar occupations in the construction, manufacturing, trade, and food preparation sectors. More than half of the increase in fast-growing blue-collar nonfarm industries in rural Vietnam is the result of an expanding construction sector (table 4.4).

Results from the district-level poverty maps, augmented with data from the 1999 and 2009 Population and Housing Census, are used to explore the determinants of rural nonfarm diversification and its contribution to poverty reduction. Proximity to an urban center is found to stimulate rural nonfarm employment—in particular, proximity to large cities (Lanjouw and Marra 2013). In terms of economic significance, the nonfarm sector of rural districts that are, on average, 10 kilometers farther from the nearest city grew 1.63 percentage points more slowly than in similar districts that are 10 kilometers closer between 1999 and 2009. Although the absolute magnitude may seem small, providing jobs for around 2 percent of the working population for every 10 kilometers of urban proximity is substantial. In addition, analysis suggests that growth of the rural nonfarm sector did indeed contribute to poverty reduction between 1999

TABLE 4.4 Rural employment in Vietnam, 1999 and 2009

% of the working population

	Description	1999	2009
Farm	All agriculture and forestry and fishing	81.4	71.2
Nonfarm	Self-employed nonfarm, nonfarm wage labor, rural-urban commuters	18.6	28.8
White-collar nonfarm	Finance, consulting, science, government, television, health care, education, employed by the Communist party	5.9	5.8
Blue-collar nonfarm	Mining, processing, construction, reparation, trading, food preparation, transportation, cleaning	12.6	23
Construction	All construction, site preparation, building activities	1.6	7.5
Other blue-collar nonfarm	All other blue-collar nonfarm jobs	11	15.5

Sources: 1999 and 2009 Vietnam Population and Housing Census.

and 2009; the poverty headcount was reduced by 0.0186 (1.86 percent) for a 10 percentage point increase in the growth in the nonfarm sector. A similar picture emerges when we consider reductions in the severity of poverty (P1); even the poorest of the poor, captured in reductions in the squared poverty gap (P2), are found to benefit from an expanding nonfarm sector. These findings stand in contrast to those of Hoang et al. (2012), which suggest that the very poor do not benefit from expansion in the rural nonfarm sector because they lack the education and skills to access nonfarm jobs. It is clearly important to look beyond the household level to understand the potential indirect labor market effects of an expanding nonfarm sector.

Policy design and evaluation

This chapter has documented changing patterns in the spatial distribution of poverty between 1999 and 2009. But what do these imply for the design of policy? A series of simulations were carried out to assess how much the spatial disaggregation provided by poverty maps can help to improve area-based targeting schemes in Vietnam (details provided in annex 4A). The simulations are based on a hypothetical transfer scheme that aims to minimize poverty at the national level (focusing on the squared poverty gap or severity of poverty) by using spatial targeting at different levels of geographic disaggregation—that is, the province, district, and commune. The initial results clearly show that in both 1999 and 2009 there were potentially large gains in targeting performance by disaggregating to the local level. An important corollary of these findings is that the benefits from spatial targeting increase as more spatially disaggregated data on poverty become available. The simulations show that a given impact on poverty can be achieved at considerably less expense using detailed spatial targeting than using a uniform transfer.

A second key finding is that the benefits from spatial targeting, at any level of geographic disaggregation, clearly were greater in 2009 than in 1999. This finding follows directly from the evidence presented in the previous section on the changing spatial distribution of poverty in Vietnam over time. As Vietnam has prospered, moderately poor households living in relatively well-off areas in 1999 (for example, Red River Delta) have been able to cross the poverty line, so that by 2009 these areas contributed much less to national poverty levels. Instead, poverty has become more concentrated in poor districts. This is an important finding for policy makers because it suggests a stronger rationale for using spatial targeting to reach the poor today than was the case in earlier years.

However, these simulations should be viewed as only illustrative. They do not take account of important practical and political considerations such as how the hypothetical transfers would be financed, the costs of

BOX 4.1 **Overview of Program 30A**

Program 30A, named after Prime Minister Decision 30A in 2008, is a comprehensive poverty reduction program targeted at 61 (now 62) of the country's poorest districts through 2020. These districts lie in 20 provinces throughout the country, but most of the districts are located in the northeastern mountainous region. The program focuses on four primary areas: (a) increasing income through production, job creation, and labor exports; (b) improving education standards; (c) improving the quality of local administrators; and (d) investing in infrastructure.

Funding commitments for the different components are made in three-year tranches. According to MOLISA, state budget funding for 2009–11 was D 8.5 trillion. For 2012–15, funding is D 7.2 trillion. A substantial portion of the funding goes toward boosting incomes by paying citizens to protect specified areas of forest. However, as with Program 135-II, the vast majority of funds are invested in infrastructure. Thus far, no attempt has been made to evaluate the impact of this program.

The 62 districts selected under Program 30A do not receive direct support only through Program 30A. Their designation as particularly needy districts also makes them eligible for other targeted programs. For example, in order to improve cadre quality, Program 30A is linked to the 600 Deputy Chairman Program, which is run by the Ho Chi Minh Youth League and the Ministry of Home Affairs. This program, initiated in 2011, targets 600 communes in the 62 districts and brings in trained manpower to support the work of the People's Committees in 600 very poor communes.

administering such a scheme, possible behavioral responses of households, and the possibility of local capture linked to power and influence. The anticipated, albeit hypothetical, gains from targeting must be juxtaposed against the potential costs and political-economy considerations and should be scrutinized against other possible policy objectives. In practice, a combination of geographic targeting of villages and means-tested targeting of poor households within villages is likely to be the best way forward for Vietnam.

We close this chapter with a brief assessment of the targeting performance of Program 30A, one of MOLISA's newer area-based targeted poverty reduction programs. A welfare ranking of districts was drawn up, based on criteria developed by MOLISA (incorporating information on income, as opposed to expenditures, and other indicators of well-being), and the poorest 62 districts on the list were singled out for specific policy interventions (box 4.1). Mapping methods were used to see whether the 62 poorest districts identified by MOLISA's criteria are also the poorest as measured by the per capita expenditure criteria underpinning the Vietnam poverty map for 2009. Figure 4.7 illustrates the close correlation

between the two approaches; the districts targeted by MOLISA are also
among the poorest identified by the independent mapping methodology.
Spatial targeting in Vietnam is not only warranted on empirical and conceptual grounds, but appears administratively and logistically feasible, as
evidenced by one well-established program.

**FIGURE 4.7 Poverty by district in Vietnam; 2010 MOLISA compared to poverty map
estimates**

Sources: MOLISA 2014; GSO 2009 (mapping estimates based on the 2009 Population and Housing Census and
the 2010 VHLSS).

Annex 4A Spatial distribution of poverty and the gains from spatial targeting

This chapter documents changing patterns in the spatial distribution of poverty between 1999 and 2009. But what do these patterns imply for the design of policy? Simulations were carried out to assess how much the spatial disaggregation provided by poverty maps can help to improve area-based targeting schemes in Vietnam.[3] We consider here the distribution of a hypothetical budget to the population of Vietnam. We assume that we have no information about the poverty status of this population other than the geographic location of residence and the level of poverty in each location. As a benchmark case, we make the extreme assumption of no knowledge whatsoever about the spatial distribution of poverty, in which case our given budget is distributed uniformly to the entire population. We set up a series of comparisons to this benchmark, where we assume knowledge about poverty levels in progressively smaller subpopulations. For a given level of disaggregation, we ask how knowledge about poverty outcomes across localities can be incorporated into the design of a transfer scheme so as to improve the overall targeting performance relative to the benchmark case. In light of the observations made above, concerning the evolving spatial distribution of poverty in Vietnam, we ask whether and how our conclusions differ between 1999 and 2009.

We consider a transfer scheme that makes use of our knowledge of the spatial distribution of poverty to minimize poverty at the national level. We consider the gains from spatial targeting at alternative levels of disaggregation. We focus on the squared poverty gap, a measure of poverty that is particularly sensitive to the distance between a poor person's income level and the poverty line.[4] We specify a poverty line that accords with a poverty rate of around 20 percent nationally, in each respective year, and we consider a modest hypothetical budget that would be insufficient, in and of itself, to eliminate all poverty, even if it were perfectly targeted at the household level.

The results from this exercise show clearly that, in both 1999 and 2009, disaggregating to the local level produces potentially large gains in the performance of targeting. These benefits are clearly seen when we examine the squared poverty gap as our poverty measure of choice. The impact on the poverty headcount rate is more muted, given that we do not "optimize" our transfer scheme with respect to this poverty measure. An important corollary of these findings is that the benefits from spatial targeting become increasingly evident as more and more disaggregated data on poverty are used. We show that a given impact on poverty can be achieved at considerably less expense by using detailed spatial targeting rather than a uniform transfer.

The results from this exercise also show that the benefits from spatial targeting, at any level of disaggregation, are more clearly evident for 2009 than for 1999. This finding follows directly from the evidence presented on the changing spatial distribution of poverty in Vietnam over time. As Vietnam has prospered, moderately poor households living in relatively well-off areas in 1999 were able to traverse the poverty line, so that by 2009, such relatively well-off areas no longer contributed as much to overall poverty levels. Poverty has become more spatially concentrated. For policy makers, this is an important finding because it indicates that there may be an even stronger rationale for spatial targeting of resources today than was the case a decade ago.

Transfer scheme

We postulate that the government has a budget, S, available for distribution and wishes to transfer this budget in such a way as to reduce poverty. We specify a baseline case in which the government is assumed to have no knowledge of who the poor are or where they are located. It is therefore unable to distribute its budget in any manner other than as a lump-sum transfer to the entire population of size N. We thus calculate the impact of transferring S/N to the entire population.

Kanbur (1987) shows that, to minimize poverty summarized by the Foster-Greer-Thorbecke (FGT) class of poverty measures with parameter value $\alpha > 1$, the group with the highest $FGT(\alpha - 1)$ should be targeted on the margin.[5] Hence to minimize the squared poverty gap (equal to a poverty measure from the FGT class with $\alpha = 2$), target populations should be ranked by the poverty gap (FGT with $\alpha = 1$), and lump-sum transfers should be made until the poverty gap of the poorest locality becomes equal to that of the next poorest one, and so on until the budget is exhausted.

Budget and poverty lines

We assume that the budget available for distribution has been exogenously set. As is intuitively clear, the potential benefits from targeting will vary with the overall size of budget. In the limit, as the budget goes to infinity, there is no need for targeting, as even a uniform transfer will eliminate poverty. As a benchmark, we identify the per capita consumption value of the 25th percentile of the consumption distribution.[6] We scale this consumption value by the total population. Our benchmark budget is set to equal 5 percent of this total value.

Gains from targeting also vary with the choice of poverty line. The higher the poverty line, the less need for targeting, as leakage to the nonpoor diminishes to zero. In this study, we select as the benchmark a poverty line that yields a poverty rate of exactly 20 percent in both 1999 and 2009.

Simulating the impact of uniform transfers

Our policy simulation in the case of uniform transfers is calculated in a very straightforward manner. Budget S is divided by total population N. The resulting transfer a is added to each predicted expenditure in our database to yield $y(r)ch + a$. For each replication r we estimate post-transfer national poverty. The average across the r replications of the estimated post-transfer poverty rates yields the expected poverty rate associated with the benchmark, untargeted lump-sum transfer scheme. This new estimated poverty rate can be compared to the original national poverty estimate from the poverty map to gauge the impact of the transfer.

Simulating the impact of "optimal" geographic targeting

Simulating the impact of the "optimal" targeting scheme is slightly more complicated. Following Kanbur (1987), we want to equalize the following expression across the poorest locations of a country:

$$G_c(a_c) = \int_0^z (z - y - a_c)^+ \, dF_c(y), \qquad (4A.1)$$

which is z times the poverty gap in location c, after every person in the location has received a transfer a_c. $F_c(y)$ is the average of the R simulated expenditure distribution of c. The function $(x)+$ gives the "positive part" of its argument, that is, $(x)+ = x$, if x is positive, otherwise 0. Transfers ac (which must be nonnegative) add up to a given budget S:

$$\sum_c N_c a_c = S, \qquad (4A.2)$$

where Nc is the population size of location c. After transfers, there is a group of locations all sharing the same (maximum) poverty gap rate in the country. These are the only locations receiving transfers. We describe below how this problem is solved given that we are working with a database of incomes for every household in the 15 percent sample of the population census.

Solving the problem: "Optimal" geographic targeting

As described in Elbers et al. (2004), given our interest in minimizing the FGT2, optimal geographic targeting implies that after transfers there is a group of locations all sharing the same (maximum) poverty gap in the country. We determine the level of transfers going to each location by first solving a different problem. Following the notation introduced above, consider the minimum budget $S(G)$ needed to bring down the poverty gap of all locations to at most level G/z. This amounts to transferring an amount $a_c(G)$ to locations with before-transfer poverty gaps above G/z, such that $G_c[a_c(G)] = G$. Once we know how to compute $S(G)$, we simply adjust G until $S(G)$ equals the originally given budget for transfers S. To implement this scheme, we must solve the following equation for ac:

$$G = \int_0^z (z - y - a_c)^+ \, dF_c(y).$$ (4A.3)

In what follows we drop the location index c for ease of notation. Using integration by parts, it can be shown that

$$G(a) = \int_0^z (z - y - a_c)^+ \, dF(y) = \int_0^{z-a} F(y) \, dy.$$ (4A.4)

In other words, we need to compute the surface under the expenditure distribution between expenditure levels $y = 0$ and $y = z - t$, for values of t up to z. Instead of computing $G(t)$ exactly, we use a simple approximation. For this to work, we split the interval $[0,z]$ in n equal segments and assume that the "poverty-mapping" software has generated expected headcounts for poverty lines $z \, k/n$, where $k = 0, \ldots, n$. In other words we have a table of $F(z \, k/n)$. Using the table, we approximate $F(y)$ by linear interpolation for y between table values. With the approximated expenditure distribution, it is easy to solve for transfers as a function of G. In practice, we find that $n = 20$ gives sufficiently precise results.[7]

The computational setup is as follows (note that the numbering we adopt means going from z in the direction of 0 rather than the other way around). Define $b0 = 0$, and for $k = 1, \ldots, n$, bk as the surface under the (approximated) expenditure distribution between $z - kz/n$ and $z - (k - 1)$ z/n, divided by z:

$$b_k = \frac{1}{2n} \left\{ F(z - kz/n) + F[(z - (k-1)z/n] \right\}$$ (4A.5)

Let $g0$ be the original poverty gap, or in terms of the discussion above, $g0 = G(0)/z$. For $k = 1, \ldots n$, put

$$g_k = g_{k-1} - b_k.$$ (4A.6)

The gk are the poverty gaps of the approximated expenditure distribution for successively lower poverty lines $z - kz/n$. Let ak be the per capita transfer needed to bring down the poverty line to $z - kz/n$:

$$a_k = kz/n.$$ (4A.7)

We can now solve for per capita transfers as a function of the intended poverty gap $g < g0$: find k such that $g_{k+1} \leq g < g_k$. The per capita transfers resulting in poverty gap g are

$$a(g) = a_k + \frac{g_k - g}{g_k - g_{k+1}} \cdot \frac{z}{n}.$$ (4A.8)

This scheme can be implemented using standard spreadsheet software.

Results

Table 4A.1 presents the basic results from our simulations. Using disaggregated data on poverty to allocate transfers gives better results than making a uniform lump-sum transfer across the entire population. Targeting transfers to poor localities, in accordance with the optimization scheme outlined above, yields lower values of the national FGT2 than when the budget is transferred as a uniform lump-sum transfer to the entire population. Second, the more disaggregated the poverty map, the greater the improvement over a uniform lump-sum transfer. Our simulations suggest that using estimates of poverty at the province, district, and commune levels results in non-negligible improvements in the FGT2 with a given budget. However, while the general patterns we observe are similar across our two poverty maps for 1999 and 2009, they are not identical. Notably, while commune-level targeting in 1999 would reduce the FGT2 from a level of 0.0110 following a uniform transfer to 0.0058 (a 43 percentage point reduction), commune-level targeting in 2009 would achieve a 66 percentage point reduction—the FGT2 would decline from 0.0166 to 0.0057 (table A4.1). With district-level targeting rather than commune-level targeting, the gains are slightly less marked but are still evident.[8]

Table 4A.2 repeats the simulations presented in table A4.1, focusing on the headcount, or FGT0, measure of poverty. As mentioned above, the optimization procedure outlined in Kanbur (1987) applies to the squared poverty gap or FGT2 measure. There is no analogous optimization algorithm for the FGT0 measure. We report in table 4A.2, however, the result-

TABLE 4A.1 Impact on FGT2 of targeting at different levels of geographic disaggregation: Optimal targeting scheme, 1999 and 2009

	1999	2009
Original FGT2	0.0159	0.0234
FGT2 after:		
i) Uniform transfer	0.011	0.0166
ii) Province-level targeting[a] (61/63 Provinces)	0.008	0.0096
iii) District-level targeting[b] (614/685 Districts	0.0066	0.007
iv) Commune-level targeting[c] (10474/10896 communes)	0.0058	0.0057
Original FGT2	1.00	1.00
FGT2 after:		
i) Uniform transfer	0.69 (1.00)	0.71 (1.00)
ii) Province-level targeting[a] (61/63 Provinces	0.50 (0.72)	0.41 (0.58)
iii) District-level targeting[b] (614/685 Districts)	0.42 (0.61)	0.30 (0.42)
iv) Commune-level targeting[c] (10474/10896 communes)	0.36 (0.57)	0.24 (0.34)

Note: Budget = 5 percent of (total population × 25th percentile per capita expenditure); poverty line = per capita expenditure defining bottom quintile of population (pre-transfer).

a. 61 provinces in 1999 and 63 in 2009

b. 614 districts in 1999 and 685 in 2009.

c. 10,474 communes in 1999 and 10,896 in 2009.

TABLE 4A.2 **Impact on FGT0 of targeting at different levels of geographic disaggregation: Optional targeting scheme, 1999 and 2009**

	1999	2009
Original FGT0	0.2000	0.2000
FGT0 after:		
i) Uniform transfer	0.1673	0.1724
ii) Province-level targeting[a] (61/63 Provinces)	0.1522	0.1555
iii) District-level targeting[b] (614/685 Districts)	0.1443	0.1465
iv) Commune-level targeting[c] (10474/10896 communes)	0.139	0.1372
Original FGT0	1.00	1.00
FGT0 after:		
i) Uniform transfer	0.84 (1.00)	0.86 (1.00)
ii) Province-level targeting[a] (61/63 Provinces)	0.76 (0.90)	0.78 (0.91)
iii) District-level targeting[b] (614/685 Districts)	0.72 (0.86)	0.73 (0.85)
iv) Commune-level targeting[c] (10474/10896 communes)	0.70 (0.83)	0.69 (0.80)

Note: Budget = 5 percent of (total population × 25th percentile per capita expenditure); poverty line = per capita expenditure defining bottom quintile of population (pre-transfer).

a. 61 provinces in 1999 and 63 in 2009.

b. 614 districts in 1999 and 685 in 2009.

c. 10,474 communes in 1999 and 10,896 in 2009.

ing FGT0 estimates from having applied the procedure to allocate our budget in such a way as to minimize the resulting FGT2 measure. Table 4A.2 indicates that the gains from geographic targeting for the FGT0 are far less marked than was observed when the FGT2 measure was our reference measure.

Discussion

The stylized analysis presented in this annex cannot be used to evaluate existing poverty reduction programs in Vietnam. One possible exercise that could inform policy makers' deliberations would be to compare the hypothetical "optimal" province- and district-level budgetary distribution deriving from an exercise as has been presented here with the actual province- and district-level distribution that is currently in place. There is no presumption that these two should line up exactly. But follow-up work would be justified if such an exercise were to reveal glaring inconsistencies.

Some important caveats are attached to the findings reported here. First, we assume that the government is willing to accept that households with equal pre-transfer per capita consumption levels might enjoy different post-transfer consumption levels. Second, we have assumed that the budget available for distribution is exogenously determined. We ignore the question of how the transfers are financed. Political economy considerations could influence the options for resource mobilization (see, for example, Gelbach and Pritchett 2002). Third, we do not address the very real possibility that the costs of administering a given transfer scheme might increase with the degree of disaggregation. Fourth, we do not allow for behavioral responses in the population. Fifth, we do not address the possibility that inequalities in power and influence that prevail in a community influence how transfers are allocated. All of these factors could result in an overestimation of the impact of spatial targeting on poverty reduction.

The findings presented here are illustrative only. At all times, the gains from targeting should be juxtaposed against potential costs and political-economy considerations and should be scrutinized against other possible policy objectives. In practice, a combination of geographic targeting among villages and means-tested targeting within villages may be the best way forward. Policy makers in Vietnam will need to assess such programs on a case-by-case basis to determine just how far to rely on fine geographic targeting as a central element in their social protection and poverty reduction strategies.

Notes

1. It is not feasible to produce reliable commune-level poverty estimates using the 15 percent sample of the 2009 Population and Housing Census (GSO 2009). This will be done at a later date if the GSO makes the unit record data available for the full 2009 census.
2. The mapping methodology may underestimate ethnic minority poverty, because it assumes that minorities receive the same returns on their endowments as the Kinh majority. Studies suggest that minorities not only have lower levels of assets, but also receive lower returns on their assets (Baulch and Vu 2012). Estimates presented here and in chapter 3 provide lower-bound estimates of geographically disaggregated poverty levels.
3. We build on an earlier analysis in Ravallion (1993), who finds that spatial disaggregation to the broad regional level in Indonesia, the lowest level at which household survey data provide reliable estimates of poverty, improves targeting, but only to a modest extent. In contrast, Elbers et al. (2004) find that fine geographic targeting offers significant benefits over broad targeting.
4. We focus on the squared poverty gap because of its appealing properties from both a conceptual and a technical point of view. The basic approach explored here would also work for other poverty measures, particularly Foster-Greer-Thorbecke measures with values of parameter α greater than 1. However, with the headcount measure (the FGT measure with α = 0) of welfare, "optimization" is not well defined, and the approach taken here is thus less obviously applicable (see, for example, Ray 1998, 254–55).
5. Following Foster, Greer, and Thorbecke (1984), the FGT class of poverty measures takes the following form: $FGT(a) = \left(\dfrac{1}{\sum w_i}\right) \sum w_i \left[1 - (x_i / z)\right]^a$, where x_i is per capita expenditure for those individuals with weight w_i who are below the

poverty line and zero for those above, z is the poverty line, and $\sum w_i$ is total population size. The superscript a takes a value of 0 for the headcount index, 1 for the poverty gap, and 2 for the squared poverty gap. For further discussion, see Ravallion (1994).

6. The consumption distribution is constructed on the basis of the average, across r replications, of household-level predicted per capita consumption in the Population Census.

7. Other interpolation schemes are possible. For instance, if the *poverty gap* is given at table values zk/n, an even simpler computation presents itself. Often, the poverty-mapping software will give percentiles of the expenditure distribution. These can also be used for interpolation, but the formulas are more cumbersome, since the percentiles are not spaced equally.

8. While targeting improves significantly as one is able to disaggregate progressively, for example, from the province, to the district, to the commune level, it is far from perfect. Simulating the impact of optimal targeting of our postulated budget to individual households would result in a further decline in the FGT2 from 0.0057 in 2009 (table 4A.1) to 0.0019. The fact that commune-level targeting is unable to reproduce what would be achieved with perfect, household-level targeting confirms the findings from earlier sections that inequality can be significant at the subnational level in Vietnam; even with commune-level targeting, there would be significant leakage of resources to non-poor households.

References

Baulch, Bob, and Hoang Dat Vu. 2012. "Exploring the Ethnic Dimensions of Poverty in Vietnam." Background paper for the 2012 Poverty Assessment, World Bank, Washington, DC.

Bedi, Tara, Aline Coudouel, and Kenneth Simler, eds. 2007. *More Than a Pretty Picture: Using Poverty Maps to Design Better Policies and Interventions.* Washington, DC: World Bank.

Elbers, Chris, Jean Lanjouw, and Peter Lanjouw. 2002. "Micro-Level Estimation of Welfare." Policy Research Working Paper WPS 2911, World Bank, Washington, DC.

———. 2003. "Micro-Level Estimation of Poverty and Inequality." *Econometrica* 71 (1): 355–64.

Elbers, Chris, Tomoki Fujii, Peter Lanjouw, Berk Özler, and Wesley Yin. 2004. "Poverty Alleviation through Geographic Targeting: How Much Does Disaggregation Help?" *Journal of Development Economics* 83 (1): 198–213.

Ferreira, Francisco, and Peter Lanjouw. 2001. "Rural Nonfarm Activities and Poverty in the Brazilian Northeast." *World Development* 29 (3): 509–28.

Foster, James, Joel Greer, and Eric Thorbecke. 1984. "A Class of Decomposable Poverty Measures." *Econometrics* 52 (3): 761–66.

Gelbach, Jonah, and Lant Pritchett. 2002. "Is More for the Poor Less for the Poor? The Politics of Means-Tested Targeting." *Topics in Economic Analysis and Policy* 2 (1, July): 6.

GSO (General Statistics Office of Vietnam). 2009. *Population and Housing Census Vietnam 2009*. Hanoi: GSO.

Hoang, Xuan Thanh, Phuong Thu Nguyen, Ngoc Van Vu, Quyen Thi Do, Hoa Thi Nguyen, Hoa Thanh Dang, and Giang Tam Nguyen. 2012. "Inequality Perception Study in Vietnam." Background paper for the 2012 Vietnam Poverty Assessment, Ageless Consultants, Hanoi.

Kanbur, Ravi. 1987. "Measurement and Alleviation of Poverty." *IMF Staff Papers* 34 (1, March): 60–85.

Lanjouw, Jean O., and Peter Lanjouw. 2000. "The Rural Non-Farm Sector: Issues and Evidence from Developing Countries." *Agricultural Economics* 26 (1): 1–23.

Lanjouw, Peter, and Marleen Marra. 2013. "Rural Poverty Reduction, Non-farm Employment, and Proximity to Cities." Background paper prepared for the 2012 Vietnam Poverty Assessment, Washington, DC.

Minot, Nicholas, Bob Baulch, and Michael Epprecht. 2003. "Poverty and Inequality in Vietnam: Spatial Patterns and Geographic Determinants." Final report of project Poverty Mapping and Market Access in Vietnam, conducted by the International Food Policy Research Institute and the Institute of Development Studies, Washington, DC.

MOLISA (Ministry of Labor, Invalids, and Social Affairs). 2014. "The Government Report on the Implementation of Policies and Laws on Poverty Reduction between 2005 and 2012." Report 63/BC-CP, MOLISA, Hanoi.

Nguyen, Viet Cuong. 2009. "Updating Poverty Maps without Panel Data: Evidence from Vietnam." *Asian Economic Journal* 253 (4): 397–418.

Nguyen, Viet Cuong, Truong Ngoc Tran, and Roy van der Weide. 2010. "Poverty and Inequality Maps in Rural Vietnam: An Application of Small Area Estimation." *Asian Economic Journal* 24 (4): 355–90.

Nguyen, Viet Cuong, Peter Lanjouw, and Marleen Marra. 2012. "Vietnam's Poverty Mapping using the 2009 Housing Population Census and 2010 Vietnam Living Standards Survey." Background paper prepared for the 2012 Poverty Assessment, World Bank, Hanoi.

Oseni, Gbemisola, and Paul Winters. 2009. "Rural Nonfarm Activities and Agricultural Crop Production in Nigeria." *Agricultural Economics* 40 (2, March): 189–201.

Ravallion, Martin. 1993. "Poverty Alleviation through Regional Targeting: A Case Study of Indonesia." In *The Economics of Rural Organization: Theory, Practice, and Policy,* edited by Avishay Braverman, Karla Hoff, and Joseph Stiglitz. New York: World Bank and Oxford University Press.

———. 1994. *Poverty Comparisons*. Chur, Switzerland: Harwood Academic Press.

Ravallion, Martin, Shaohua Chen, and Prem Sangraula. 2007. "New Evidence on the Urbanization of Global Poverty." Policy Research Working Paper 4199, World Bank, Washington, DC.

Ray, Debraj. 1998. *Development Economics*. Princeton, NJ: Princeton University Press.

CHAPTER 5

Reducing Poverty among Ethnic Minorities

Poverty among ethnic minority groups in Vietnam is analyzed using multiple dimensions of well-being, including not only income poverty but also measures such as access to education, water and sanitation, and public utilities. A combination of qualitative and quantitative methods shows the diversity of ethnic experiences, encompassing rural entrepreneurship, vulnerability to shocks, and ongoing stigma and disadvantage. While ethnic minorities' welfare has increased overall, poverty reduction has been uneven among ethnic groups and regions, resulting in a widening gap between most ethnic minorities and the Kinh majority.

Ethnic minority poverty presents a particular and persistent challenge for Vietnam. Vietnam is a multiethnic country with 54 officially recognized ethnic groups, including the Kinh majority and an additional 53 minority groups (box 5.1). Although minority groups have experienced rising living standards since 1998, they have not progressed as rapidly as the Kinh majority. As noted in chapter 1, per capita consumption grew at an annual rate of 7.4 percent for minorities between 1998 and 2010 compared to 9.4 percent over the same period for the Kinh. At the same time, ethnic minority households have become increasingly linked to the commercial market, while continuing to engage in some traditional activities that generate non-cash livelihoods such as semi-subsistence agriculture and livestock raising (McElwee 2011; Turner and Michaud 2011).

Ethnic minority poverty rates have fallen as a result of rising incomes and expenditures. From a rate of 75.2 percent in 1998, the level of ethnic poverty (excluding the Hoa Chinese) fell to 50.3 percent by 2008, using the original General Statistics Office–World Bank (GSO-WB) poverty lines and methodology. This rate remains much higher than that among the Kinh majority, however. The profile of ethnic minority poverty in chapter 3, based on the new 2010 poverty lines, suggests that disparities have risen; 47 percent of the poor in Vietnam are ethnic minorities, and the

BOX 5.1 Ethnicity in Vietnam

Vietnam is a multiethnic country with 54 officially recognized ethnic groups. The Kinh (ethnic Vietnamese) make up 85.7 percent of the national population of nearly 86 million, according to the 2009 census; the remaining 53 groups are classified as ethnic minorities (*dan toc thieu so,* literally "people lacking numbers").

As of 2009, the following are the eight largest ethnic minority groups:

- Tay, 1,626,000
- Thai, 1,550,000
- Muong, 1,269,000
- Khmer, 1,261,000
- Hmong, 1,068,000
- Nung, 969,000
- Hoa (Chinese), 823,000
- Dao, 751,000.

At the other end of the scale, 16 groups have fewer than 10,000 members; the smallest recorded in the 2009 census is the O Du, with 376 people. These very small ethnic groups are at risk of losing their language and culture.

Most ethnic minorities live in upland rural areas away from the coastal plains and major cities. The largest minority populations are found in the northern mountains and central highlands, with significant populations also found in the north-central, south-central, and Mekong Delta regions. Anthropologists classify Vietnamese ethnicities into five linguistic groups: the Hmong-Dao language family in the northwest, the Tibeto-Burman family along the Chinese border, the Mon-Khmer family including many central highland groups as well as Khmer, the Malay-related Austronesian family in the south-central region, and the Viet-Muong group, which includes the Kinh. Of these, 11 groups have written languages using either traditional scripts or the Latin alphabet.

Many ethnic minority groups are the indigenous inhabitants of mountainous areas of Vietnam. Others moved south from what is now China as recently as the eighteenth and nineteenth centuries or are descendants of the former Cham and Khmer empires in the central and southern regions. As a result, many ethnic minorities in Vietnam can also be found in neighboring countries. Upland Vietnam is a mosaic of diverse ethnic groups: while most villages have one or two dominant groups, it is rare to find an entire commune populated by a single ethnicity.

Ethnic minorities vary greatly in their level of economic and social development, both among groups and within any given group. Poverty and development statistics commonly group the Kinh and Hoa (Chinese) in one column and all remaining minority groups in a second, sometimes subdivided by region or language group. At this level of analysis, ethnic minorities appear somewhat poorer to much poorer than the Kinh-Hoa in terms of income. In fact, some ethnic groups (and some villages) have achieved more rapid reductions in poverty and improvements in socioeconomic status than others. Monetized measures of well-being

(Box continues next page)

BOX 5.1 **(continued)**

may also mask variation in noncash assets held by certain ethnic minority house-holds, such as livestock and access to forestland.

Many Kinh, particularly those living in urban areas, have little contact with or knowledge of ethnic minority cultures and tend to aggregate them together as "non-Kinh." Paternalistic attitudes and ethnocentric prejudice are common. However, all ethnic groups in Vietnam have full citizenship and legal rights. Ethnic minorities are represented in the National Assembly and at all levels of government: the highest-profile individual leader is former Communist Party general secretary, Nong Duc Manh, a member of the Tay ethnicity.

Sources: World Bank 2009; GSO 2009.

ethnic minority poverty rate is 66.3 percent. Although the well-being of minorities has increased in terms of income and consumption, for many households these improvements have not been enough to put them above the poverty line. Yet these same data also show that almost a quarter (24.9 percent) of ethnic minority households have escaped poverty since 1998.

The gap in reported poverty levels between Kinh and ethnic minorities increased rapidly during the earlier years of Vietnam's high economic growth and rapid poverty reduction. In 1993, a member of an ethnic minority group was only 1.6 times more likely to be poor than a Kinh person (see table 1.7). By 1998, this had risen to 2.4 times and by 2004 to 4.5 times. By 2010, minorities were, on average, 5.1 times more likely to be poor than the Kinh and, as documented in chapter 4, substantial gaps in living conditions are evident throughout Vietnam.

The causes of persistent ethnic minority poverty have been researched in depth (ADB 2003; DFID and UNDP 2003; Oxfam GB and ActionAid 2009; World Bank 2009). The World Bank's 2009 "Country Social Analysis: Ethnicity and Development" finds that minorities face disadvantages in access to education, mobility, credit, land, links to markets, and ethnic stereotyping by the Kinh majority (box 5.2). The reasons why some ethnic minorities have escaped poverty despite these barriers have received less attention, yet may reveal positive practices that can be incorporated into better-targeted and more innovative poverty reduction programs (Wells-Dang 2012).

The gap in living standards between minorities and Kinh can be explained by examining the structural disadvantages faced by minorities. Research shows that, although minority household assets have improved over time—in particular, higher levels of education and better access to basic infrastructure and services such as roads, clean water and sanitation, and electricity—there is still a substantial gap in returns to assets

BOX 5.2 **Six "pillars of disadvantage"**

The 2009 World Bank "Country Social Analysis: Ethnicity and Development" (World Bank 2009) identified three trends that account for different economic outcomes in minority and Kinh communities: differences in assets, differences in capacity, and differences in voice. Within each broad trend, there are numerous specific causal factors for ethnic minority poverty, summarized as six "pillars of disadvantage":

- Lower levels of education
- Less mobility
- Less access to financial services
- Less productive, lower-quality land
- Limited market access
- Stereotyping and other cultural barriers.

No single factor explains the difference in outcomes among ethnic minorities and Kinh, even among those living in the same area. Instead, differences in these six areas combine in a "vicious cycle" to influence ethnic minority livelihood outcomes and lead both directly and indirectly to persistent poverty. The country social analysis concludes that poverty reduction depends on taking a comprehensive approach to removing each of these pillars of disadvantage.

between minorities and the Kinh (Baulch and Vu 2012; Imai and Gaiha 2007; Kang 2009). A factor contributing to the ethnic poverty gap is the fact that minorities continue to work primarily in agriculture (chapter 3), which has grown more slowly than other sectors of the economy. The gap, however, may be overstated due to measurement errors, subjective linking of minorities and poverty by researchers and officials, and the likelihood that some minorities have unreported and noncash income sources that are not captured in the statistics.

This chapter draws on the broad framing of ethnic minority poverty in chapters 3 and 4, with the aim of looking in greater depth at the situation and challenges faced by diverse ethnic minority groups and at examples of successful development for specific groups and in various regions.

Poverty reduction across regions and among and within minority ethnic groups

Results from poverty mapping (presented in chapter 4; Nguyen, Lanjouw, and Marra 2012) demonstrate that ethnic minorities are not a homogeneous group. Figure 5.1 disaggregates changes in living standards among four broad categories of ethnic groups that share certain cultural, geographic, and social similarities. Among these four categories, the Khmer and Cham have achieved the largest increases in income and the lowest

FIGURE 5.1 **Changes in welfare levels (per capita consumption) for different ethnic groups in Vietnam, 1998–2010**

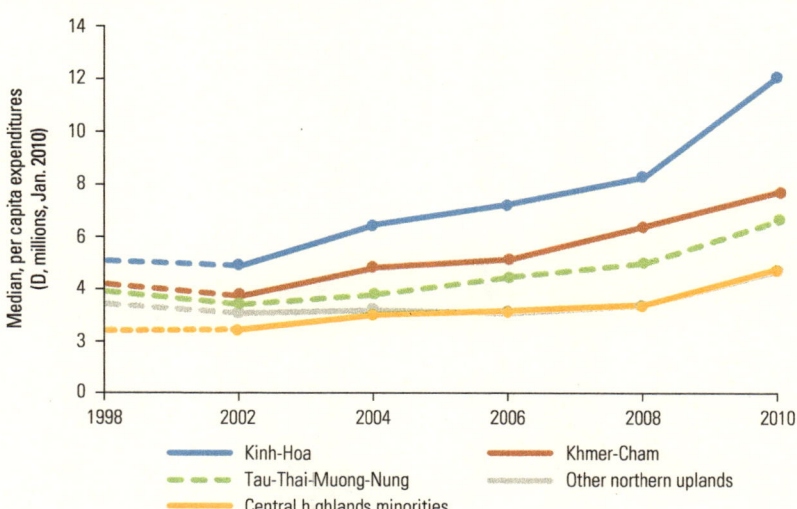

Source: Estimates based on various rounds of the Vietnam Household Living Standard Survey: comparable per capita consumption during 1998 and 2002; comprehensive per capita consumption during 2004–10.

overall poverty rates. From 1998 to 2008, poverty fell steadily for all groups except central highland minorities; however, there are some indications that progress is slowing. In 1998, minorities in the central highlands had the highest poverty and lowest expenditures, but by 2010, this distinction had passed to groups in the category "other northern uplands," including the Hmong and Dao and many smaller ethnicities.

Table 5.1 shows the predicted poverty headcount, poverty gap, and mean per capita expenditures in 2010 for the 20 largest ethnic groups in Vietnam (listed in order of population size), using the poverty-mapping methodology presented in chapter 4.[1] Attention is confined to rural areas since this is where the vast majority of ethnic minority people live (84.3 percent, according to the 2009 census). Of the largest ethnic minority groups, the Tay and Khmer have relatively low poverty rates and high per capita expenditures; the Hoa (Chinese) have lower poverty rates and higher per capita expenditures than the Kinh majority. Poverty rates can vary significantly among ethnic groups residing in the same region, as shown in the differences between the historically more prosperous Tay, Nung, Thai, and Muong and other northern minorities such as the Hmong and Dao. These latter groups, and many central highland minorities, have poverty rates higher than 75 percent and poverty gaps of more than 25 percent. Compared to the 1990s, however, the difference between central highland

TABLE 5.1 Poverty and median expenditures of major ethnic groups in rural areas of Vietnam, 2009

Ethnic group	Poverty headcount	Poverty gap	Mean Per capita expenditures	Primary region
1 Kinh	17.0	3.6	12,145,000	n.a.
2 Tay	46.5	13.0	9,918,800	Northern mountains
3 Thai	69.1	22.6	7,210,600	Northern mountains
4 Muong	56.3	16.8	8,603,800	Northern mountains
5 Khmer[a]	43.2	11.6	9,976,300	Mekong Delta
6 Hoa	13.4	3.1	19,727,500	Mekong Delta
7 Nung	56.0	17.5	8,611,600	Northern mountains
8 Hmong	93.3	45.3	4,455,100	Northern mountains
9 Dao	75.6	27.9	6,456,900	Northern mountains
10 Gia Rai	81.9	32.2	5,754,600	Central highlands
11 Ede	75.1	27.6	6,460,100	Central highlands
12 Ba Na	86.2	36.6	5,311,400	Central highlands
13 San Chay	57.2	17.0	8,263,300	Northern mountains
14 Cham	57.2	17.0	8,504,100	South-central
15 Co Ho	76.2	28.1	6,329,300	Central highlands
16 Xo-Dang	91.1	42.4	4,760,600	Central highlands
17 San Diu	37.5	10.2	11,132,400	Northern mountains
18 Hre	79.1	26.2	6,294,400	Central highlands
19 Ra Glai	84.9	31.1	5,716,200	South-Central
20 Mnong	80.9	32.9	5,828,000	Central highlands

Sources: Estimates based on poverty-mapping methods, described in chapter 4, using 2010 VHLSS and 2009 Housing and Population Census.
Note: n.a. = not available.
a. In Vietnamese, *Khóme*. The *H'Mông* and *Ê Đê* are also listed here by their common English names.

minorities and others has gradually decreased, continuing a trend that was noted in earlier rounds of the Vietnam Household Living Standards Survey (VHLSS; Baulch, Pham, and Reilly 2007).

Figure 5.2 shows the distribution of per capita expenditures in 2006 and 2010 (based on the VHLSS) for the five ethnic minority groupings. Both the mean and distribution of expenditures improved for all groups from 2006 to 2010, resulting in declining poverty rates. The peak of the distribution curve for the Kinh-Hoa is now far above the 2010 GSO-WB poverty line. For the Tay, Thai, Muong, and Nung and for the Khmer and Cham, the curve peaks near the poverty line. But for the other northern and central highland minorities, the vast majority of households still live well below the poverty line, despite improvements in the upper and middle ends of the expenditure distribution between 2006 and 2010.

Focusing on specific ethnic groups in distinct locations increases the diversity of results. In Lao Cai Province, for example, the Ministry of Labor, Invalids, and Social Affairs (MOLISA) reports an overall poverty rate of 43 percent. The Hmong (the most populous ethnicity in the province) have a reported rate of 83 percent; Nung, 75 percent; and Dao, 72

FIGURE 5.2 **Real per capita expenditures for five ethnic groupings in Vietnam, 2006–10**

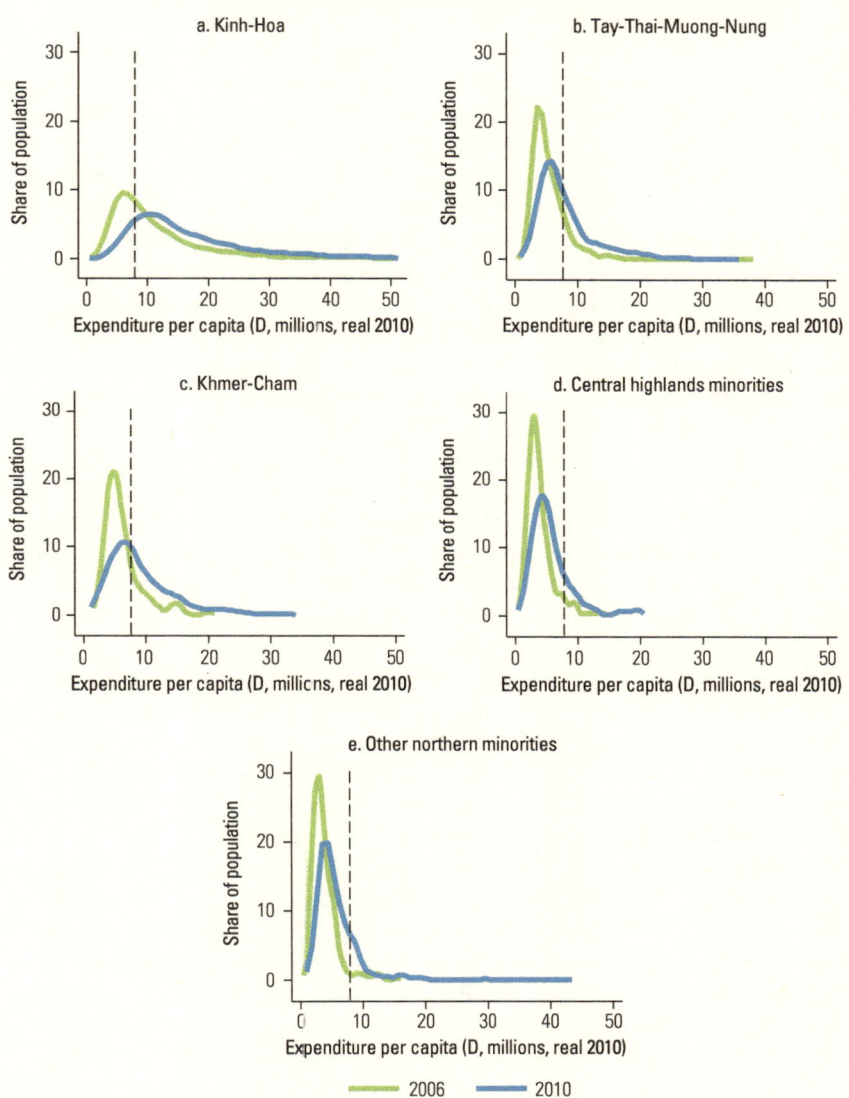

Sources: 2010, 2006 VHLSS.

percent (Lao Cai DOLISA 2012). One of the smaller ethnic groups, the Phu La, has the highest reported poverty rate in the province, at 84 percent. But not all very small groups are equally disadvantaged. The Tu Di, a subgroup of Bo Y, are involved in inter-commune and cross-border trade and have high reported educational attainment (Baulch and Vu 2012; Wells-Dang

2012). Central highland provinces such as Dak Nong are characterized by "complex patterns of interpenetration between ethnic groups"; Kinh make up a majority of the population, have a 20 percent poverty rate, but constitute 41 percent of poor people in the province. In-migrating northern ethnic minorities (Thai, Tay, Nung, Dao, Muong, and Hmong) make up 20 percent of the population and 37 percent of poor people, with a poverty rate of 56.8 percent; indigenous minorities (Ede, Mnong, Ma, and others) make up only 11 percent of the population and 21 percent of poor people, but their poverty rate is 63.8 percent (Shanks et al. 2012, 22–24).

Comparisons of 1999 and 2009 poverty maps (chapter 4) indicate that the fastest poverty reduction has taken place among ethnic minorities in the central highlands. Of districts with ethnic minority populations of at least 40 percent, 7 of the 10 with the highest rates of poverty reduction are located in this region (three in Dak Lak and two each in Gia Lai and Lam Dong). Two of the others, in Quang Nam and Binh Dinh provinces, border the central highlands. All of these districts started from a very low income level in 1999 and have now reached a low to moderate level.

As described earlier, poor ethnic minority households are still concentrated in mountainous and upland areas in the north of Vietnam and the central highlands. In contrast, the wealthiest ethnic minorities (defined as ethnic minorities with per capita expenditures in the top 15 percent of the national expenditure distribution) live primarily (57 percent) in the Mekong Delta and southeast regions. A third area with a concentration of wealthier minorities is in cities and towns in the northeast mountains. The lowest reported welfare levels for ethnic minorities are found in the northwest mountains and central coastal areas (Quang Binh and Quang Tri). In the central highlands, Dak Lak and Lam Dong report average income levels, while other provinces report below-average levels (map 5.1).

Among rural districts with more than 5,000 ethnic minority residents surveyed in the 2009 Population and Housing Census, 9 of the wealthiest 10 are located in the Mekong Delta, and all have predominantly Khmer and Cham inhabitants. This includes four districts in Tra Vinh Province and three in Soc Trang. Expanding the subsample to include urban districts, higher expenditure levels are found among ethnic minorities in the cities of Cao Bang and Lang Son and in two peri-urban districts of Ho Chi Minh City (Hoc Mon and Binh Chanh), home to many migrant workers. Ethnic minority residents of these areas are predominantly Tay-Nung and Khmer, respectively.

Disparities in access to education, infrastructure, and public services

Including noneconomic indicators of well-being adds further complexity to the picture of differential development outcomes among ethnic minorities. For instance, the relative gap in access to education between Kinh and

MAP 5.1 Regional patterns of poverty and wealth for ethnic minorities in Vietnam, 2009

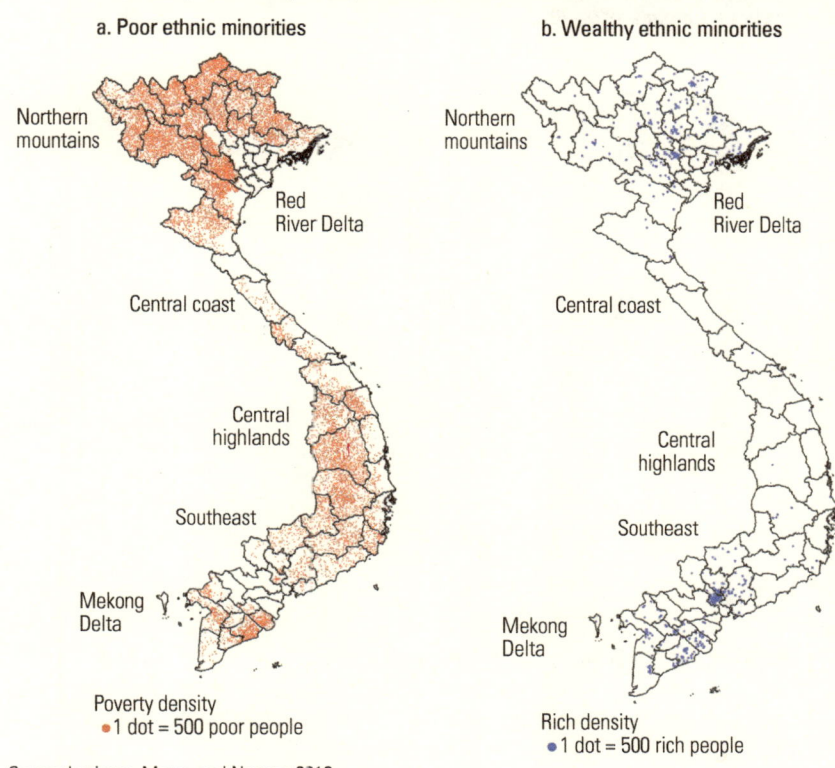

a. Poor ethnic minorities

Northern mountains

Red River Delta

Central coast

Central highlands

Southeast

Mekong Delta

Poverty density
• 1 dot = 500 poor people

b. Wealthy ethnic minorities

Northern mountains

Red River Delta

Central coast

Central highlands

Southeast

Mekong Delta

Rich density
• 1 dot = 500 rich people

Source: Lanjouw, Marra, and Nguyen 2012.

ethnic minorities is smaller due to the increase in the number of schools, improved roads, and higher incomes among minority households (Hoang et al. 2012). Particularly at the primary and lower-secondary level, ethnic minorities have higher levels of public school enrollment than they did in the late 1990s (figure 5.3). Primary school enrollments for ethnic minority groups are only a little lower than for Kinh but fall as children move through the school system. By the time they reach upper-secondary school, majority pupils are more than twice as likely to attend school as minority pupils. This is, in part, a question of access, because most upper-secondary schools are located far from rural villages, and, in part, one of formal and informal costs of secondary education. A focus group in Son La described these limitations:

> Education [in our community] is good, [and] dropout rates at primary and lower-secondary levels are low. We try to bring our children to school up the 12th grade. At upper-secondary level the children have to go to school in the district town, renting rooms, bringing rice and

FIGURE 5.3 **Changes in net school enrollment rates for Kinh and ethnic minorities in rural areas of Vietnam, 1998–2010**

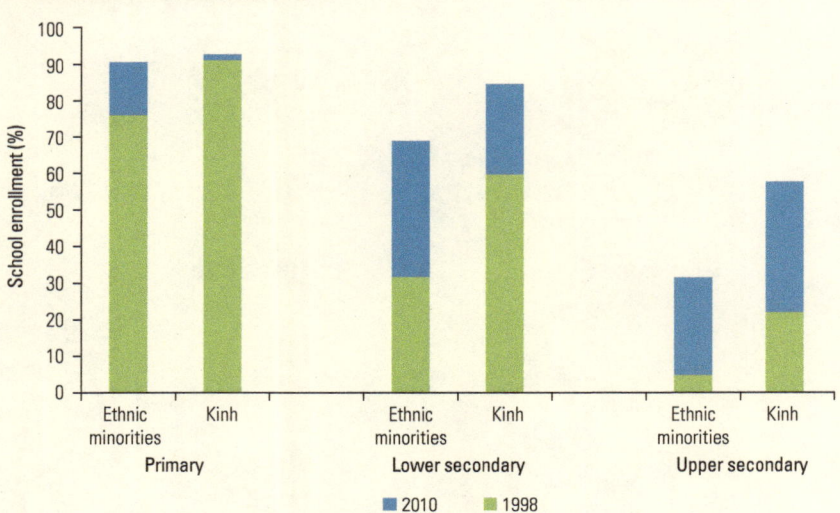

Sources: 1999 Vietnam Living Standards Survey; 2010 VHLSS.

vegetables from home, attending extra classes. Room rental is 150 thousand dong, pocket money 200–300 thousand dong per month at the lowest. But many households cannot afford such costs, their children have to drop out. (Hoang et al. 2012: 25)

As a result of increased access to public education and to television and roads, the Vietnamese language capabilities of many young minorities are greater than they were in the past. Without upper-secondary diplomas, however, employment options remain limited for many young people, due to both location and discrimination. Khmer and Cham have relatively high incomes and better than average nutritional outcomes for their children, but low secondary school completion rates in public Vietnamese-language schools affect subsequent job opportunities (Baulch et al. 2010). In the central highlands, local enterprises require upper-secondary diplomas for most industrial jobs, excluding indigenous minorities from a wide range of opportunities (Truong 2011).

Analysis of school enrollment rates from the 2009 Housing and Population Census shows that certain ethnic groups, including the Hoa, Nung, and Tay, have net primary and lower-secondary school enrollment rates that are equal to or slightly higher than those of the Kinh (figure 5.4). In contrast, 18 other ethnic groups have net primary enrollment rates of less than 85 percent and lower-secondary rates under 50 percent—notably, the Hmong, whose primary enrollment rate of 69.6 percent is nevertheless sub-

FIGURE 5.4 **Net school enrollment of selected ethnic minority groups in Vietnam, 2009**

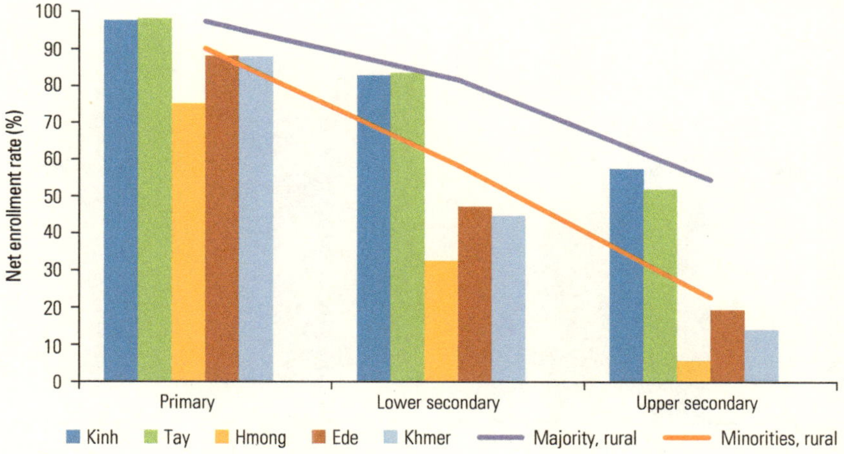

Source: 2009 Housing and Population Census

stantially higher than the 41.5 percent recorded in 1999. Primary school enrollment in the central highlands has also increased significantly since 1999. By the upper-secondary level, only the Kinh, Hoa, and Tay have net enrollment rates greater than 50 percent, with 21 groups enrolling less than 10 percent of children in upper-secondary school (Baulch and Vu 2012).

Improved services and remaining inequalities are also evident in access to public utilities. Coverage has improved since 2004 for both majority and minority groups in rural areas, but access to improved water and sanitation facilities and to electricity is still unequal for minorities. Differential access is particularly stark for sanitation: in 2010 around 7 out of 10 majority households had access to improved sanitation facilities compared to fewer than 2 out of 10 minority households. In contrast, more than two-thirds of ethnic minority households had access to an improved water source in 2010, with the Khmer and Cham having better access than the majority. This dramatic increase in access to improved water since 2004 may be attributed partly to Program 134, which, along with distributing land and building houses for ethnic minority households, had a clean water component.

Greater access to improved water and sanitation has contributed to better nutrition among children. Drawing on anthropometric data from the 1998 Vietnam Living Standards Survey (VLSS), the 2006 VHLSS, and the 2010 Multiple Indicator Cluster Survey (MICS), stunting (low height for age) has fallen rapidly and consistently among the rural Kinh, from 49.5 percent of children 0–5 years of age in 1998 to 23.3 percent in 2010 (GSO, UNICEF, and UNFPA 2011). Meanwhile, stunting among minority

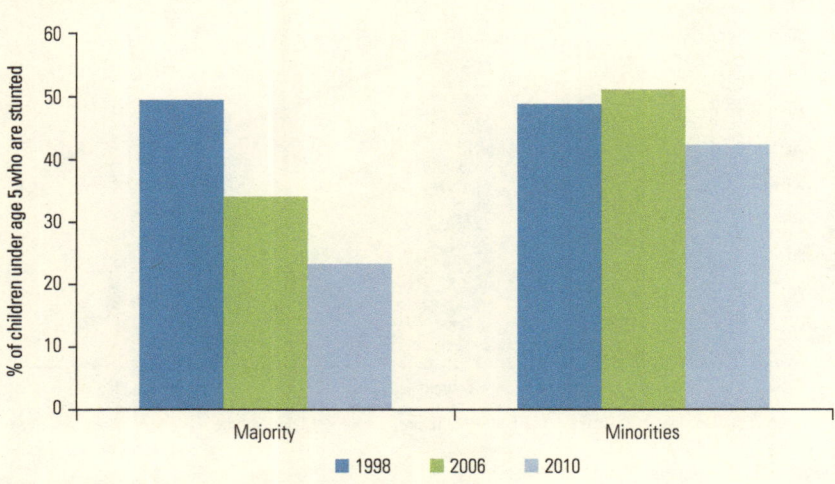

FIGURE 5.5 Stunting among children under age 5 in rural areas of Vietnam, by ethnicity, 1998–2010

Sources: 1998 VLSS; 2006 VHLSS; 2010 MICS.

children has fallen from essentially the same level as the Kinh in 1998 (48.7 percent) to 42.3 percent in 2010, with a slight rise in 2006 (figure 5.5).[2]

Wasting (low weight for height) is a short-term measure of nutritional status that is often seasonally dependent.[3] It also declined from 1998 to 2010, although with very small changes between 1998 and 2006. Children under five years of age from both the majority and minority started with similar levels of wasting (just under 12 percent) in 1998, with wasting declining to 3.9 percent among majority children compared to 5.5 percent among minority children by 2010. The statistics on stunting and wasting provide evidence of a widening gap in nutrition between majority and minority children.

Investment in rural electrification during the 2000s raised access to grid electricity to nearly universal levels for the majority, but more than a quarter of ethnic minorities rely on other sources of power for their main source of lighting (table 5.2). Access to electrification is greater in the central highlands than in the northern mountains, even though both are upland areas with significant hydropower resources.

In addition to intergroup and geographic differences, ethnicities are also internally heterogeneous. Hmong in one district of Lao Cai employ different livelihood strategies and cultural practices than Hmong in another, and the practices among Hmong within a single district overlap with the practices of other ethnic groups. Even within a single commune, poverty rates can vary significantly among villages. In light of this diversity, pov-

TABLE 5.2 Access to public utilities in rural areas of Vietnam, by ethnicity, 2004 and 2010
% of households with access

Ethnic category	Improved water		Improved sanitation facilities		Electricity grid	
	2004	2010	2004	2010	2004	2010
Kinh and Hoa	89.1	90.9	46.8	69.2	94.5	98.9
All ethnic minorities[a]	53.3	69.6	9.9	18.4	72.5	83.2
Khmer-Cham	35.9	93.6	5.5	13.8	69.0	84.2
Tay-Thai-Muong-Nung	52.0	68.8	13.4	23.6	74.0	87.4
Other northern mountains	37.1	64.2	8.2	12.0	56.0	61.5
Central highlands	51.3	67.0	4.6	13.7	80.5	91.9

Sources: 2004, 2010 VHLSS.
a. Excluding Hoa.

erty reduction and development programs that target "extremely difficult" geographic areas or all ethnic minorities as an undifferentiated group will inevitably benefit some populations more than others. Findings from the 2010 VHLSS indicate that this may be taking place. The mean ethnic expenditure gap is increasing at all levels of income except the highest sixth, where it has decreased slightly since 2004. Although some of the disparities are due to commune characteristics, much of the difference in returns to endowments faced by ethnic minorities is due to factors such as the quality of education or land combined with discrimination in access to employment and markets (Baulch and Vu 2012).

New research on "perceptions of inequality" carried out for this book suggests that ethnic inequality is one component of broader income and social inequalities (Hoang et al. 2012). Focus groups of ethnic minority youth, senior citizens, and local leaders emphasized livelihood-related modalities of inequality in terms of access to market, credit, and agricultural services. In rural areas such as Chieng Khoa Commune, Son La, there was perceived to be little inequality within ethnic minority communities, since agricultural production remains the key source of livelihood. However, the transition to a commodity-based economy was seen as a source of growing inequality.

Ethnic minority focus groups identified inequalities of opportunity when comparing their communities with better-off towns nearby. The disparities noted are related to the six "pillars of disadvantage" (box 5.2) and are perceived as linked; that is, poor infrastructure leads to poor education, poor employment, and then poor access to markets and services. Although some of these structural disadvantages can be corrected by policy measures, they continue to play an important role in keeping many ethnic minorities from earning a better living.

Agricultural land disparity is perceived as very important in determining outcome inequality in the rural mountainous ethnic minority areas of Son

La and Quang Nam provinces, where off-farm employment and migration are negligible (Hoang et al. 2012). In Son La, rice paddy land was equally allocated among Thai households in the early 1990s. Better-off households expanded their rice fields by reclaiming vacant land, but such land is no longer available. The more important source of land disparity is in sloping land for maize and tea farming. Well-established households have large holdings, while newly separated households and newcomers have little land and are often considered poor. In Quang Nam, by contrast, the Ve people (a branch of the Gie Trieng ethnic group) do not see land dispar-ity as a key driver of increased wealth disparity; instead they see livestock ownership and access to public sector employment as the key drivers of disparity. Ve households can still expand their cultivated area based on the availability of labor.

The perceptions of inequality study conducted for this book finds lit-tle concern about interethnic inequalities. Thai people in Son La noted that they are more advantaged than Hmong people in terms of access to infrastructure, education, and markets, but disadvantaged in terms of land quality and quantity. These differences appear to be decreasing over time, in part due to government investment in infrastructure. Similarly, com-mune officials in Quang Nam drew comparisons between the Ve people and the larger Co Tu group, who live in more central parts of the district and have better access to markets and employment.

However, many minority respondents raised concerns about unfair behavior of the Kinh toward ethnic minorities. Such behavior and related prejudice were widely perceived to have serious implications for social unity and ethnic cohesion. Minority youth living nearer provincial towns and cities experience ethnic discrimination in their schooling, employment, and social relations, as in the following example of a young Nung woman in Lao Cai:

> As we [people from the ethnic minorities] can be recognized by clothing, the way medical staff treat people from the ethnic minori-ties is different from the way they treat Kinh people. They [doctors] don't treat us well . . . In the market, Kinh people who are cleverer usually get good bargains . . . In a bus, their [Kinh] prejudice toward us is demonstrated through language and intonation, shouting with disrespectful words.

In Kinh focus groups, participants denied that they discriminate against ethnic minority groups, and many pointed out that minorities receive spe-cial benefits. A Kinh student in Quang Nam stated,

> We don't think we are superior to the ethnic [minority] classmates. They are receiving preferential treatments such as subsidies and scor-ing incentives. Perhaps they themselves feel inferiority; there is no discrimination from us.

Focusing on the experiences of successful ethnic households: Lessons for future policies and programs

The Vietnamese government, with World Bank and donor support, has implemented an array of economic policies since the 1990s, such as land reform, infrastructure investment, education and vocational training projects, and agricultural commercialization efforts. These policies have brought many Vietnamese into the growth process and have succeeded in reducing poverty among the Kinh more than twice as rapidly as among ethnic minorities (Pham 2009). The remaining poor are thought to be harder to help (DFID and UNDP 2003; Oxfam GB and ActionAid 2009). This situation has led to pessimism about the likely effectiveness of future development programs and reinforced the stereotypes of ethnic minorities as culturally "backward" (*lac hau*), uneducated, and unwilling to help themselves. Meanwhile, anthropologists and other external observers have criticized the Vietnamese government and donor agencies for pursuing assimilationist policies that lead to a decline in cultural identity among ethnic minority groups (McElwee 2004; Taylor 2004). Although government officials, donors, and academics may reach divergent conclusions, they all take a constraint-based approach to analysis, looking for what is wrong with a situation and how it can be fixed.

In background research conducted for this poverty assessment, Wells-Dang (2012) adopts a contrasting approach of identifying communities that are succeeding where others are not and seeking to understand the reasons behind their success. This approach, which bears some similarities to methodologies of "positive deviance" applied worldwide in health and business management sectors, aims to build confidence and social interactions among participants and points toward effective future project and policy interventions, something that an approach focusing on constraints is unlikely to do (Marsh et al. 2004; Ramalingam 2011). The research presumes that ethnic people are actively engaged in their own development as "innovative constructive agents . . . not as resistance to domination, but as a logical or obvious response to new opportunities" (Sowerwine 2011).

Based on an analysis of census data on poverty reduction and expenditures among ethnic minorities, the research team selected field visit sites in Dak Lak, Lao Cai, and Tra Vinh provinces and sought to identify villages or ethnic groups within a commune that show uncommonly positive results in ethnic minority development and poverty reduction. All three provinces have been included in previous studies of ethnic minority poverty. Dak Lak was one of four provinces visited in the country social analysis of the World Bank (2009). Tra Vinh and Lao Cai were both included in the 1999 participatory poverty assessments conducted by the World Bank and a group of international nongovernmental organizations (Oxfam GB 1999; World Bank 1999). It is also remarkable that both Lao Cai (ranked 2 of 63 provinces in 2010) and Tra Vinh (ranked 4) score highly on the provincial competitiveness index of business and investment criteria (USAID 2011).

Transforming agriculture from semi-subsistence to commercial production

Agriculture is the primary livelihood activity for ethnic minority communities in all three sites as well as generally across Vietnam (World Bank 2009). In most communes visited for this study, 80 to 90 percent of households were involved in agriculture. Thus any program of ethnic minority poverty reduction must include a strong agricultural component. Ethnic minority farmers have landholdings equivalent to or even higher than the average landholdings of Kinh, but their land is of variable quality (World Bank 2009, 113). In the central highlands, a coffee farmer with as little as 0.25 hectare of high-quality land can earn above the poverty line for a family of five. Vegetable and fruit growers in other provinces require approximately double this amount of land to reach the same income level.

Farmers with sufficient, good-quality land have multiple options to escape poverty. Farmers with less land can only do so by growing high-value cash crops, which may or may not be viable depending on local soil and weather conditions. Many households in the Mekong Delta have lost their land through indebtedness or sale. These families have mostly migrated or shifted to nonagricultural work, although some continue as agricultural wage laborers. Landlessness is no longer viewed as the crisis it was in the 1990s, given the increased availability of nonagricultural work and the possibility of migration.

Cash crop farmers are highly dependent on local and world market prices for their commodities. In this sense, they are already connected to the global economy and not at all "remote" (*vung sau vung xa*), despite the perceptions of many urban Vietnamese (Taylor 2007). Coffee and other commodity farmers sell their crop to dealers (who are mostly Kinh), who then resell it to export-processing facilities in provincial cities. Ethnic minority farmers do not know where their crops are exported, but they do follow market prices, which are broadcast on television and radio, printed in newspapers, and posted at local offices. Cash crop farmers in border areas export their products directly or via ethnic and Kinh middlemen (box 5.3).

Since previous research on ethnic minority development was conducted (ADB 2003; Oxfam GB 1999; Oxfam GB and ActionAid 2009; World Bank 2009), certain key features of the agricultural economy have improved. One of these aspects is *price information*, mentioned above. Another is *better access to credit*, via the Social Policy Bank (*Ngan hang Chinh sach*) and the Vietnam Bank for Agriculture (*Ngan hang Nong nghiep*). According to data from the 2010 VHLSS, 32.6 percent of all rural ethnic minority households and 52.0 percent of poor ethnic minority households have access to preferential loans from the Vietnam Social Policy Bank and other sources

BOX 5.3 An Ede coffee "hotspot"

Ede are the largest indigenous ethnic group in Dak Lak, although they make up less than 20 percent of the total population. Before waves of migration after the Vietnam War, Ede were the only residents of Ea Khal Commune, extending 20 kilometers westward from the provincial town of Ea Drang. Now there are 16 villages in the commune, of which only 2 are indigenous Ede. One of these is Buon Dung, about 2 kilometers from the commune center, an Ede village with high income from coffee and other crops. According to commune statistics, overall poverty rates in 2011 were 23 percent for Ede, 34 percent for other ethnic minority in-migrants, and 16 percent for Kinh. In Dak Lak Province overall, 50 percent of ethnic minorities are considered poor. Thus Ede in Ea Khal are less than half as poor as average ethnic communities in the province.

Young Ede coffee-farming families in Buon Dung have between 1 and 4 hectares of good-quality fields and are accessing large, high-interest loans from the Vietnam Bank for Agriculture. They have taken part in technical training on coffee production organized by agricultural extension services or the Farmer's Union. Cognizant of the risks in coffee production, they monitor prices carefully to get the best return for their crop. The village also has storage and drying facilities, so farmers can wait until prices are high before selling.

After several years of good harvests, families are investing their profits in purchasing additional land in neighboring villages and in constructing new houses in a mixture of traditional Ede and Kinh styles. The reasons for their relative prosperity include access to land, social cohesion, and preferential treatment of indigenous minorities by local authorities.

compared to 10.4 percent of all rural Kinh and 35.2 percent of poor Kinh. In communes visited during background research for the poverty assessment, 80 percent of ethnic minority households had access to loans, which were often channeled through local mass organizations. Loan amounts had increased to a maximum of D 30 million (US$1,500), compared with between D 3 million and D 5 million, as noted in the country social analysis (World Bank 2009, 148).

Most respondents reported using loans to purchase seeds, raise animals, or conduct small business activities, such as purchasing goods for a market stall. Borrowers through mass organizations receive some instruction and support for their stated use of the loan, such as agricultural extension or animal raising. Formal and informal farmers' groups play a significant role in agricultural production, particularly among Khmer in Tra Vinh. These cooperative groups (*to hop tac*) exchange price and technical information, produce cash crops cooperatively for fixed-price contracts, and link poor and better-off farmers in a community.

Ethnic minority farmers are skilled at producing crops, raising animals, and engaging in other agricultural activities. However, their relative position in the market has weakened over time; many of the benefits of economic growth have accrued to better-off households and those working in industrial and commercial activities (chapter 6). Few ethnic minorities are represented in these groups. The lower relative returns to agriculture are, in part, a result of policy decisions that have a disproportionate effect on ethnic minorities. Future growth in agricultural livelihoods is also threatened by risks and vulnerabilities such as changes in commodity market prices, natural disasters, climate change, and environmental degradation.

Diversifying into nonagricultural employment

Diversification is a key, though not universal, feature of ethnic minority livelihood strategies, moving from subsistence production to a multiplicity of activities and income sources (Minot et al. 2006; Shanks et al. 2012). Agricultural work remains the norm for the majority of ethnic minority families, but most respondents plant multiple crops—grain in the wet season and vegetables in the dry season, a combination of hybrid and traditional rice and maize seeds, or a mixture of export cash crops. Almost all ethnic households raise some animals for household use or sale. Of families pursuing nonagricultural livelihoods, such as factory work, trading, or tourism, nearly 100 percent maintain some tie to agriculture, at a minimum through usufruct rights to leased land. With the exception of a few large export dealers, ethnic minorities view handicrafts, tourism, trading, and other service employment as a complement to agriculture. This strategy of "selective diversification" simultaneously allows for cultural preservation and higher incomes (Turner and Michaud 2011).

The involvement of ethnic minorities in nonagricultural work varies from very little in Dak Lak and modest in Lao Cai to significant in Tra Vinh, where Khmer are involved in all kinds of trading, services, and industrial jobs. Factory work has become available in Tra Vinh since 2007 and now employs 30,000 workers provincewide, primarily women under age 35. Base salaries in such factories are substantially lower than in Ho Chi Minh City, but living costs are also lower by a factor of a third or more. For some Khmer families, industrial work offers a stable income and a way out of poverty even for a family with little (or no) land. Respondents said they prefer to stay in their own community rather than migrate for industrial work, even though local salaries are lower.

Local ethnic minority traders in Muong Khuong, Lao Cai, use their comparative advantages of a location on the Chinese border, relationships with relatives and others of the same ethnic group across the border, and knowledge of the regional Chinese dialect Quan Hoa. One young Hmong man who had spent several years as a laborer in China is now trading mineral ore and other products across the border, earning enough to purchase a private car. A Phu La-Nung couple in another village began by trading rice and corn in local markets and then took advantage of available loan

BOX 5.4 **Pineapples along the border**

Na Loc, a cluster of seven villages in Ban Lau Commune, Muong Khuong District, Lao Cai, extends through a narrow valley on one side of a small stream: the Chinese border. Hmong farmers in Na Loc have long had close links to the Chinese market. In the 1990s, three men crossed into China to work as wage laborers and brought back techniques of pineapple cultivation that they introduced to other villagers. One of the first pineapple growers later became a village chief.

Na Loc villagers have earned high profits from pineapple for more than 15 years, earning incomes of D 150 million (US$7,500) per year or more. Since around 2005, cash crop production has spread from Na Loc to other villages in Ban Lau Commune. Almost all land in the commune, including steep hillsides, has been converted to pineapple, banana, and tea production. Returns were high until 2012, when Chinese buyers suddenly stopped purchasing pineapple and Vietnamese market prices plunged to as low as D 1,000 (US$0.05) per kilogram. Farmers in Na Loc are now struggling to break even, but most are sufficiently diversified and have accumulated enough savings that they believe they can ride out the downturn.

This experience, like that of coffee in the central highlands, shows that long-term poverty reduction cannot depend on a single commodity.

capital and switched to growing pineapples in 2009 (box 5.4). In these cases, ethnic minorities are no longer clients only of Kinh private traders, as was the case a decade ago (DFID and UNDP 2003). Their involvement in business contributes to a leveling of opportunities and information, as shown by a decline in complaints by ethnic minorities about being cheated or treated unfairly in market transactions with the Kinh. Near border areas, ethnic minorities may have more trading connections than Kinh do. Ethnic business owners are also more likely to employ minority staff, creating some job opportunities in the local private sector.

Figure 5.6 describes the sources of income of Kinh and minorities in rural areas based on the 2010 VHLSS. Apart from the substantial difference in overall household incomes, the figure reveals three outstanding factors (Baulch and Vu 2012). First, nonagricultural wages make up a much smaller part of income for ethnic minorities than for Kinh. This is true even controlling for income; poor Kinh have more diversified earnings and income portfolios than poor minorities (chapter 3). Second, minority households earn very little from nonfarm enterprises, consistent with the dominance of Kinh traders found especially in the northern mountains (Wells-Dang 2012; World Bank 2009). Finally, income transfers, including private remittances and public programs, are considerably lower among minority households, a result of less domestic migration and lower access to public services (Baulch et al. 2010).

FIGURE 5.6 **Sources of income for majority and minority households in rural areas of Vietnam, 2010**

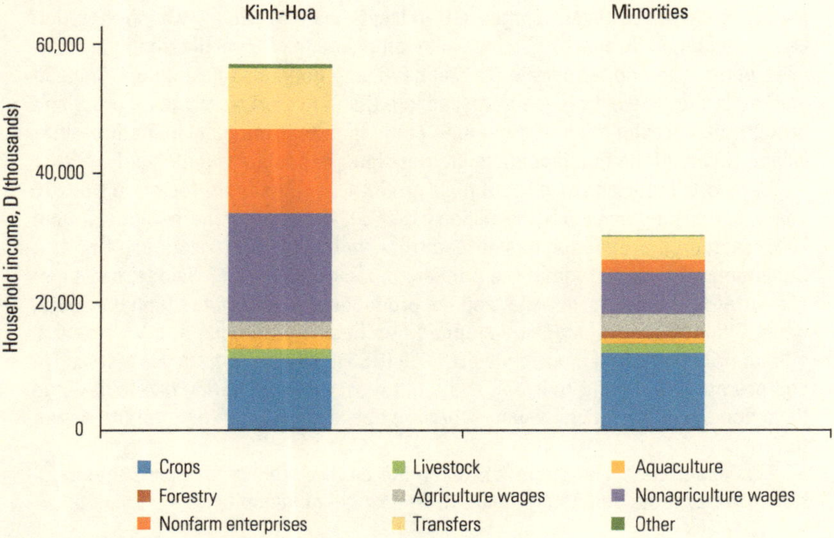

Source: 2010 VHLSS.

Income sources vary across the distribution for minority households (figure 5.7). Crop incomes almost double from the poorest to the richest quintile, while nonagricultural wages increase by a factor of 10. Income from forestry, aquaculture, and agricultural wages remains roughly constant across quintiles and does not contribute significantly to income gains. Income from nonfarm enterprises is negligible for quintiles 1 and 2 and then expands rapidly in the top three quintiles. These patterns are broadly consistent with the patterns of diversification identified in qualitative research, showing that rural households generate a surplus from agriculture before investing in a nonfarm enterprise. For the richest quintile, transfers (in particular, remittances) are also important, since households at this income level often have family members working in cities, government jobs, or other nonagricultural positions.

The data on sources of income and diversification suggest that minority households generally earn a relatively small share of their income from nonagricultural wage employment. This is principally because ethnic minority workers find it more difficult to obtain wage jobs than the majority, but differences in wage rates also play a role. In 2010, 28.8 percent of ethnic minority households had wage workers compared to 60.5 percent of majority households, and ethnic minority wage workers in rural areas earned, on average, 13.8 percent less than Kinh workers. Gaps remain even

FIGURE 5.7 Sources of income for minority households in rural areas of Vietnam, by quintile, 2010

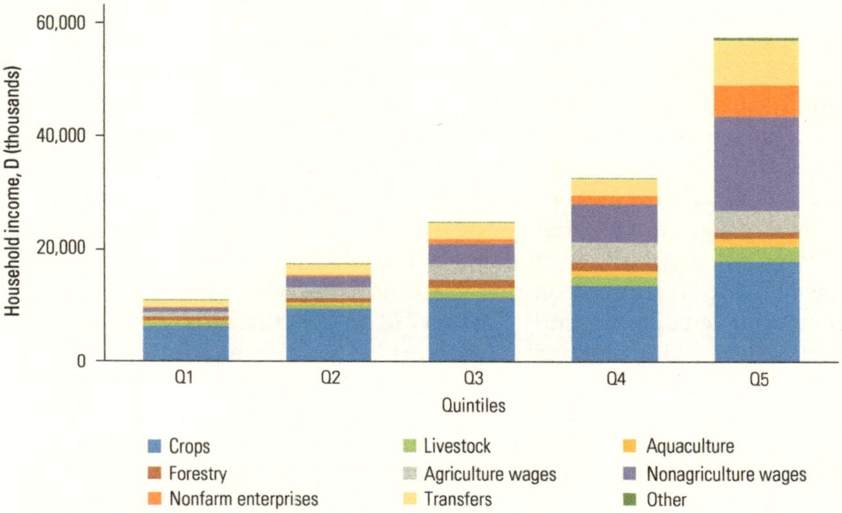

Legend:
- Crops
- Forestry
- Nonfarm enterprises
- Livestock
- Agriculture wages
- Transfers
- Aquaculture
- Nonagriculture wages
- Other

Source: 2010 VHLSS.

after controlling for education and sector of employment. While some of this differential can be attributed to differences in education and experience, wage differentials are also substantial for workers with secondary education or university qualifications.

Migrating for work

In the central highlands and northern mountains, there are few cases of young indigenous minorities migrating to cities for industrial work. Migration from the north to the central highlands has also slowed. Provincial officials stated that a majority of ethnic migrants who had gone to work in urban factories in the past five years had returned home for a combination of economic and cultural reasons. In most instances, the available wages were relatively low. Ethnic minority informants, including some returned migrants, stated that they prefer to stay in their community and do not feel confident or comfortable in large cities. The reasons given for the low levels of out-migration are that agricultural work is available locally, net returns from work in cities are not much higher, and living far from home is not culturally comfortable. If more industrial and service jobs were available locally, informants indicated that they would be willing to work in these sectors.

Out-migration of ethnic minorities is a significant pattern only in the Mekong Delta. According to Tra Vinh officials, 80,000 workers from the province are living in and around Ho Chi Minh City, about half of them Khmer. Both poorer and better-off Khmer practice migration as a strategy, but for different purposes. Those with large landholdings (or established nonagricultural businesses) send their children to urban areas for education and subsequent entry into white-collar professions such as teaching, business management, and public sector employment. The land-poor and landless, by contrast, migrate for employment and survival, acquiring skills and knowledge in the process that raise their incomes over the poverty line, but at a social cost of distance from their home community.

Many poor and landless young people, especially women, move to the city to look for work when they reach adulthood. The pace of migration has remained relatively constant in recent years, with few migrants returning to the delta permanently (Oxfam GB and ActionAid 2009). Given the high cost of living in the city, few workers are able to send much money back to their families. Migration is thus more an employment strategy than a source of remittances. Without the safety valve of migration, landholdings would be divided into smaller pieces, and there would be more competition for nearby nonagricultural work. Local officials do not view migration as a problem, but rather as one of various livelihood strategies practiced by local households.

Steps for development in ethnic minority communities

Despite regional and cultural diversity, ethnic minorities in Vietnam share certain important characteristics. They all reside in the same nation-state, with the same national policies and structures; they all largely practice agriculture; and all must define and maintain their identities in relation to a much larger ethnic majority group that controls most of the important political, economic, and social institutions. To escape poverty in these conditions, ethnic minorities first shift from semi-subsistence agriculture to a market orientation, then make efforts to maintain their cultural identity while building financial and social capital. This process, outlined in figure 5.8, has four main steps toward success, with agricultural and nonagricultural branches.

In step 1, poor households with average landholdings and land quality shift part of their available land (or one planting season) away from semi-subsistence grain production and begin planting a cash crop. In Dak Lak, this is usually coffee or sometimes pepper; in other locations, vegetables and fruit are common cash crops. The key requirements for cash crop production are capital to purchase fertilizers, water for irrigation, and technical knowledge to achieve a decent yield. Many households meet part of the initial capital outlay through a loan from the Social Policy Bank, supplemented by no-interest loans from relatives and community members, as well as support from other government programs. However, fluctuating

FIGURE 5.8 **Paths to successful ethnic minority development in Vietnam**

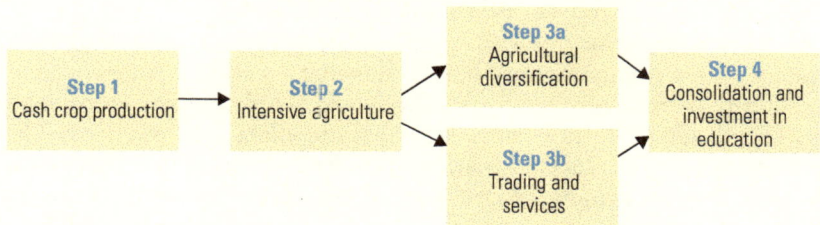

Source: Wells-Dang 2012.

prices and climate conditions pose serious risks to getting started in cash crop production. Many families who are no longer classified as poor are still not confident of staying out of poverty in future years. According to a Jarai village chief in Ea H'leo District, Dak Lak, it takes a family about five years of small-scale cash crop production to achieve the confidence.

Once households amass some savings and experience in producing cash crops, they take the greater risk of concentrating their effort on a single product. This step requires a quantum leap into a fully marketized economy. These farmers have bought or leased small amounts of additional land, where possible, even if it is far from their home. Using this land as collateral, they begin to access higher-interest loans from the Vietnam Bank for Agriculture, although some continue to renew their loans from the Social Policy Bank (some of which are open to ethnic minority borrowers regardless of poverty). They take part in technical training organized by agricultural extension services or the Farmer's Union. Compared to the farmers at step 1, they monitor prices carefully to get the best return for their crops and are highly conscious of price risks; the costs of failure are extremely high.

In the agricultural variation of step 3, farmers who have achieved higher incomes from cash crop production—around D 100 million per year for a family of five or a per capita income near the national average of US$1,000—then take steps to reduce risk by diversifying into other crops or into larger-scale animal raising. Aquaculture, forestry, or tree plantations such as rubber are additional options for diversification in some areas for those with enough capital to purchase larger tracts of land and the ability to wait five or more years for returns. Households at this level have above-average landholdings and are eligible for larger loans from the Bank for Agriculture, although some have enough savings to avoid taking out loans. As experienced, successful farmers, they are well-known and respected members of their community and have good connections with commune- and district-level authorities.

Relatively few ethnic minorities have pursued step 3b in the diversification strategy model: moving into trading and services; those with significant nonagricultural income are typically located in the top income quintile (figure 5.7). Of ethnic minority households that do select nonagricultural diversification strategies, most are already successful commercial farmers first. They begin off-farm business activities by selling their own or neighbors' agricultural products at markets and then investing in a truck or a small shop. After gaining experience and confidence, some traders and shop owners drop their involvement in agriculture entirely and concentrate fully on their new business. Others continue to be involved in both sectors. Once trading or service business becomes the primary livelihood of the household, fields are typically leased out or workers are hired to grow rice or corn rather than more intensive cash crops. Families at this level receive (and require) little support from government programs.

The few ethnic minority households that reach step 4 in figure 5.8 have resources and savings above the national average. As their children approach adulthood, older farmers consolidate their status and further reduce risk by sending children for secondary and higher education in provincial cities or beyond. After graduation, children are then expected to get nonagricultural jobs and contribute to the family income. In most of the cases observed, children had not yet begun sending funds back to their parents, but the presence of nonagricultural work balances the risk to the family farm or small business. Even among the most prosperous minorities, researchers did not see strong evidence of cultural assimilation at the village level; ethnic minority communities remain as distinct villages, with local languages spoken and social structures persisting. These results concur with findings from research in the northern mountains that identify "some models of development based on local knowledge that have reduced poverty and even made some people rich, while still preserving the value of traditional culture and the local environment" (Mai, Le, and Le 2011, 55–56). However, an unanswered question is how the lives of youth who access education in the cities will change in the future—whether it will be toward absorption into mainstream Kinh society or toward a renewed sense of ethnic identity.

Government programs are particularly important for households below or slightly above the poverty line, as a source of capital and livelihood inputs. No single program has been most effective at poverty reduction; instead, ethnic minority respondents pointed to the role of several programs providing low-interest credit, infrastructure, housing, and cash transfers and to the role of farmers' cooperatives. Existing credit and extension services are targeted mainly to households with agricultural land; animal-raising training is an important exception. Land is held as collateral for interest-bearing loans. Most households that have benefited from Decree 167, which allocates land to the landless, have received residential land only; very few have received agricultural land. Many of the changes brought about by these programs have taken effect since 2006, due to improved targeting of programs, greater availability of funds, and the benefits of higher market prices for agricultural products, among other possible factors.

Interview respondents said that other government programs, including forestry, labor export, and vocational training, contribute less to ethnic minority development and poverty reduction. The vocational training courses available from the local government are not yet well matched with market demand; as many as half of trainees have difficulty using skills after completing training. Training in local languages is available in only a few locations, such as the Women's Union in Bac Ha District, Lao Cai, which uses Hmong staff in majority Hmong areas to reach its membership.

When asked about dreams for their children's careers, parents across all ethnic minority groups said that they hoped that their children would get an upper-secondary or higher education and then a job in the state sector as a teacher or public official. No one expressed a desire for children to work in industry or business, with the exception of Khmer families already involved in trading in Tra Vinh. In Dak Lak and Lao Cai, some industrial jobs are available near the provincial cities, but few minorities work in these companies. In part, this is because many do not meet the required educational qualifications, but even if they do, they may be labeled as "lacking knowledge," part of the vicious circle of ethnic disadvantage. Since there are few private sector jobs in many mountainous areas, the thinking that "jobs are public sector jobs" persists. However, the number of government jobs available is also limited, so few young ethnic minorities who have completed secondary or higher education are assigned to government positions. According to a youth focus group of Ve people in Dak Pree Commune, Quang Nam,

> We have many graduates, but few of them find jobs. I have seen many students who had no choice but came back to farming work. The year 2011 alone saw eight graduates from pedagogic schools, but only one of them could work on a fixed-term contract basis at the commune. The remaining seven students came back to farming work. It is not possible to apply for jobs in other districts, as they also have enough staff. (Hoang et al. 2012, 30)

Narratives of ethnic minority livelihoods, cultures, and gender relations

Interview respondents, both community members and local officials, spoke of changing attitudes toward ethnic minority capacities and cultures. In this narrative, Ede, Khmer, Hmong, and other ethnic minorities are hardworking and serious, with high levels of intra-village cooperation. In some cases, having a critical mass of a minority population, including adequate representation in local leadership, was seen to promote greater equity (box 5.5). In Dak Lak and Tra Vinh, Kinh officials at the district and commune levels said that they have seen a shift in ethnic minority work, savings

BOX 5.5 **Equity in the Khmer heartland**

Luong Hoa A Commune in Chau Thanh District, Tra Vinh, is a majority Khmer community with poverty levels that are average overall, but relatively equal between the two main ethnic groups. Both Kinh and Khmer officials spoke of equality, respect, and tolerance among ethnic groups. At the provincial and district levels, this came across as the party line, but in the three communes, relative equality is backed up by observations and data. In Luong Hoa A and other Khmer majority communes, Khmer appear to be doing as well as Kinh, even though this is not true at the provincial and district levels.

Among the factors leading to this success is, first of all, a cohesive Khmer majority population that is well represented in local leadership. In other words, the difference between Kinh and ethnic minorities is smaller in areas with a greater concentration of ethnic minority residents. If poverty is considered an "ethnic problem," then this finding is counterintuitive. Conversely, Khmer are relatively worse off in areas where Kinh are the majority. Where it is "normal" to be Khmer, then Khmer and Kinh appear to have relatively equal access to information and leadership positions.

habits, and lifestyles over the past decade (although these characteristics might have been true previously). Ethnic stereotyping was rarely heard of and then most often in the past tense, sometimes from ethnic minorities themselves, as in "we used to be backward." In Tra Vinh, for example, respondents said that Khmer previously planted only rice and did not work in the dry season, but when more opportunities became available, they adapted to cash crops and nonagricultural work. The local explanations offered for this change were the opportunity to become better off through cash crop production and the positive influence of education. The younger generation is becoming more literate in Vietnamese than their parents. Yet given the prevailing cultural stereotypes, will formal education lead to more employment opportunities in the future?

A shift in gender patterns has accompanied the perceived cultural shift in work habits. Families that have transitioned to market-based livelihoods appear to have adopted a more equitable working style between husbands and wives. Women in trading families play important roles in managing finances and interacting with customers. Men used to be the primary participants in agricultural extension training and community meetings, but officials and nongovernmental organizations now report greater participation of women; only when women are actively involved do livelihood habits change. Women's Union representatives mentioned the positive impacts of credit and savings programs in fostering participation and a model of better-off women in a village cooperating to help one or more poor women out of poverty.

The shift in ethnic minority livelihood patterns captured in the process of diversification and consolidation has cultural and economic aspects. Embodied in the leap from semi-subsistence to commercial agriculture, this transformation is a consequence of the marketization and commodification of upland products, land, and labor in a capitalist direction (Sikor 2011). At the same time, it reflects a conscious attempt by ethnic minority people to reimagine themselves as modern individuals, in charge of their destiny and not conforming to old stereotypes.

The experience of ethnic minorities in poverty reduction is not fundamentally different from that of Kinh in certain respects. Kinh have also entered into market relations and international markets, although without some of the additional barriers and obstacles facing ethnic minorities. The fact that minority groups encounter commodity markets and transnational social identities in distinct places at different times means that the outcomes of their transformations will be distinct and not merely repeat the Kinh experience. No single ethnic group (in Vietnam or elsewhere) has a monopoly on a particular livelihood strategy. To suggest that minorities who engage in trading or other nonagricultural businesses are "acting like Kinh" or "following a Kinh path to development" is simply another form of ethnocentric prejudice. Although pressures for cultural and linguistic assimilation are real, especially for some of the smallest minority groups, some ethnic minority communities have begun to prosper without losing their identity. In fact, cohesive communities of people who are not poor have a better chance of maintaining their language, religion, and other cultural traditions than those who are struggling to make a living.

This chapter has presented a mixed picture of ethnic minority development and poverty reduction. Expenditure and income gaps between Kinh and minorities continue to increase, as do gaps in important noneconomic measurements of welfare such as child nutrition. Yet evidence also indicates that some of the "pillars of disadvantage" identified in World Bank (2009) may be shrinking. Ethnic minorities have increasing access to education, credit, mobility, and markets, which may take time to translate into higher incomes. Although it is beyond the scope of this report to evaluate specific Vietnamese government and donor-funded programs, it is clear that without investments in schools, rural infrastructure, and financial services, some of these changes would not have been possible. At the same time, findings discussed in previous chapters suggest that better targeting and, more important, better coverage of poverty reduction policies and programs would go further to reduce the poverty gap between the Kinh and ethnic minority groups. Design is important as well. Effective programs for reducing ethnic minority poverty must be targeted to address specific factors of marginality and build on positive examples of what ethnic households are already doing to improve their lives.

Conclusions: Emerging policy recommendations for reducing ethnic minority poverty

Recent research on ethnic minority development and poverty reduction in Vietnam, including background papers for this poverty assessment, stresses the need for nuanced and targeted policies, programs, and projects that address the specific needs of ethnic communities (Shanks et al. 2012; Wells-Dang 2012; World Bank 2009). Rather than a standardized national approach to poverty reduction that may have been appropriate in the past, current recommendations favor taking a provincial or regional focus with components aimed at disadvantaged groups in the population, such as youth, migrants, older women, or members of one or more particular ethnicity. Activities should be based on evidence of success in one ethnic minority area or more.

The methodology is as important as the content. Policies and programs should respect cultural norms while seeking to integrate ethnic minority communities with local governance and social programs. Activities should be conducted bilingually where possible and include local ethnic minorities as trainers and facilitators as well as beneficiaries.

The following are some of the possible approaches to consider for future initiatives:

- *Offer business training for ethnic women* (and men), such as training offered in the Start and Improve Your Business Program initiated in Vietnam by the International Labour Organization in 1998 and later integrated into the mainstream activities supported by the Vietnam Chamber of Commerce and Industry.
- *Expand vocational training for youth,* with an emphasis on skills with an identified local market in the agriculture and nonagriculture sectors
- *Provide credit, agricultural extension training, and market information to formal and informal farmers' groups,* on a demand basis, that respond to locally identified needs
- *Scale up bilingual education* in larger ethnic minority languages, following the pilot conducted by the Ministry of Education and Training and the United Nations Children's Fund (UNICEF) in Lao Cai, Gia Lai, and Tra Vinh
- *Offer incentives for responsible industrial development and local enterprise investment* in ethnic minority areas, providing diversified employment options without the social costs of migration
- *Recruit and develop the capacity of leaders from local ethnic groups,* in both formal governance structures such as commune and district people's committees and traditional village leaders
- *Involve local and international nongovernmental organizations to a greater extent* in cooperation with government and the private sector, such as through provincial innovation funds for local social projects.

Notes

1. The sample size in the VHLSS is too small to permit disaggregation by specific minority groups; hence, we use mapping methods based on the 2009 Housing and Population Census.
2. Due to sample size considerations and less detailed ethnic codes in the 2010 MICS, it is not possible to disaggregate these nutritional results into the five broad ethnic categories used earlier. However, stunting (and wasting) is generally lower among the (better-off) Tay, Thai, Muong, and Nung group.
3. Defined as weight for height z-scores less than two standard deviations from the 2006 World Health Organization standards for child growth.

References

ADB (Asian Development Bank). 2003. "Participatory Poverty and Governance Assessment: Central Coast and Highlands Region." ADB, Manila, October.

Baulch, Bob, Hoa Thi Minh Nguyen, Phuong Thi Thu Phuong, and Hung Thai Pham. 2010. "Ethnic Poverty in Vietnam." Working Paper 169, Chronic Poverty Research Centre, Manchester, U.K., February.

Baulch, Bob, T. P. Pham, and Barry Reilly. 2007, "Ethnicity and Household Welfare in Vietnam: Empirical Evidence from 1993 to 2004." Mimeo, University of Sussex, Institute of Development Studies.

Baulch, Bob, and Hoang Dat Vu. 2012. "Exploring the Ethnic Dimensions of Poverty in Vietnam." Background paper for the 2012 Poverty Assessment, World Bank, Washington, DC, May.

DFID (Department for International Development) and UNDP (United Nations Development Programme). 2003. "Poverty Reduction in the Northern Mountains: A Synthesis of Participatory Poverty Assessments in Lao Cai and Ha Giang Province and Regional VHLSS Data." DFID and UNDP, Hanoi, September.

GSO (General Statistics Office of Vietnam). 2009. *Population and Housing Census Vietnam 2009*. General Statistics Office of Vietnam, Hanoi.

GSO, UNICEF (United Nations Children's Program), and UNFPA (United Nations Population Fund). 2011. "Vietnam: Multiple Indicator Cluster Survey, 2010–2011: Final Report." GSO, UNICEF, and UNFPA, Hanoi, December.

Hoang, Xuan Thanh, Thu Phuong Nguyen, Van Ngoc Vu, Thi Quyen Do, Thi Hoa Nguyen, Thanh Hoa Dang, and Tam Giang Nguyen. 2012. "Inequality Perception Study in Vietnam." Background paper for the 2012 Vietnam Poverty Assessment, Ageless Consultants, Hanoi, May.

Imai, Katshushi, and Raghav Gaiha. 2007. *Poverty, Inequality, and Ethnic Minorities in Vietnam*. Discussion Paper EDP-0708. Manchester, U.K.: University of Manchester.

Kang, Woojin. 2009. *Pro-Poor Growth, Poverty, and Inequality in Rural Vietnam: The Welfare Gap between the Ethnic Majority and Minority*. Discussion Paper EDP-0906. Manchester, U.K.: University of Manchester.

Lanjouw, Peter, Marianne Marra, and Cuong Viet Nguyen. 2012. "Spatial Poverty and Its Evolution in Vietnam: Insights and Lessons for Policy from the 1999 and

2009 Vietnam Poverty Maps." Background paper for the 2012 Poverty Assessment, World Bank, Washington, DC, June.

Loa Cai DOLISA (Lao Cai Department of Labor, Invalids, and Social Affairs). 2012. "Tinh hinh giam ngheo doi voi nguoi dan toc thieu so [Situation of Poverty Reduction for Ethnic Minorities]." Report prepared for World Bank delegation visit, Hanoi, February.

Mai, Thanh Son, Dinh Phung Le, and Duc Thinh Le. 2011. "Bien doi khi hau: Tac dong, Kha nang ung pho va mot so van de ve chinh sach: Nghien cuu truong hop Dong bao cac dan toc thieu so vung nui phia bac) [Climate Change: Effects, Response Capacity, and Some Policy Issues: Research on Ethnic Minorities in the Northern Mountains]." Climate Change Working Group and Ethnic Minority Working Group, Vietnam Union of Friendship Organizations–NGO Resource Center, Hanoi. http://www.ngocentre.org.vn/content/comingo-vufo-and-paccom.

Marsh, David, Dirk Schroeder, Kirk Dearden, Jerry Sternin, and Monique Sternin. 2004. "The Power of Positive Deviance." *British Medical Journal* 329 (7475): 1177–79.

McElwee, Pamela. 2004. "Becoming Socialist or Becoming Kinh? Government Policies for Ethnic Minorities in the Socialist Republic of Vietnam." In *Civilizing the Margins: Southeast Asian Government Policies for the Development of Minorities*, edited by Christopher Duncan, 182–213. Ithaca, NY: Cornell University Press.

———. 2011. "'Blood Relatives' or Uneasy Neighbors? Kinh Migrant and Ethnic Minority Relations in the Truong Son Mountains." In *Minorities at Large: New Approaches to Minority Ethnicity in Vietnam*, edited by Philip Taylor, 81–116. Singapore: Institute of Southeast Asian Studies.

Minot, Nicholas, Michael Epprecht, Thi Tram Anh Tran, and Quang Trung Le. 2006. "Income Diversification and Poverty in the Northern Uplands of Vietnam." IFPRI Research Report Abstract 145, International Food Policy Research Institute, Washington, DC.

Nguyen, Viet Cuong, Peter Lanjouw, and Marleen Marra. 2012. "Vietnam's Evolving Poverty Map: Patterns and Implications for Policy." Background paper prepared for the 2012 Poverty Assessment, Hanoi.

Oxfam GB (Great Britain). 1999. "Participatory Poverty Assessment in Tra Vinh Province." Background paper for the 2000 Vietnam Poverty Assessment, Oxfam Great Britain, Hanoi.

Oxfam GB and ActionAid. 2009. "The Impacts of the Global Financial Crisis on Socio-economic Groups in Vietnam." Monitoring report, Oxfam Great Britain and ActionAid Vietnam. Hanoi, August.

Pham, Anh Tuan. 2009. "Viet Nam Country Case Study: Background Paper for the Chronic Poverty Report 2008–09." Manchester, U.K.: Chronic Poverty Research Centre.

Ramalingam, Ben. 2011. "A Q&A on Positive Deviance, Innovation, and Complexity." Aid on the Edge, February 8. http://aidontheedge.info/2011/02/08/a-qa-on-positive-deviance-innovation-and-complexity/.

Shanks, Edwin, Quoc Hung Duong, Ngoc Nga Dao, Thi Ly Cao, and Huy Bao. 2012. "Central Highlands of Viet Nam: Ethnic Minority Livelihoods, Local Governance Context, and Lesson-Learning Study." Report prepared for the World Bank, Mandala Consulting, Hanoi, April.

Sikor, Thomas. 2011. "Introduction: Opening Boundaries." In *Upland Transformations in Vietnam*, edited by Thomas Sikor, Nghiem Phuong Tuyen, Jennifer Sowerwine, and Jeff Romm, 1–24. Singapore: National University of Singapore Press.

Sowerwine, Jennifer. 2011. "The Politics of Highland Landscapes in Vietnamese Statecraft: (Re)Framing the Dominant Environmental Imaginary." In *Upland Transformations in Vietnam*, edited by Thomas Sikor, Nghiem Phuong Tuyen, Jenniver Sowerwine, and Jeff Romm, 51–72. Singapore: National University of Singapore Press.

Taylor, Philip. 2004. "Introduction: Social Inequality in a Socialist State." In *Social Inequality in Vietnam and the Challenges to Reform*, edited by Philip Taylor, 1–40. Singapore: Institute of Southeast Asian Studies.

———. 2007. "Poor Policies, Wealthy Peasants: Alternative Trajectories of Rural Development in Vietnam." *Journal of Vietnamese Studies* 2 (2): 3–56.

Truong, Huyen Chi. 2011. "'They Think We Don't Value Schooling': Paradoxes of Education in the Multi-Ethnic Central Highlands of Vietnam." In *Education in Vietnam*, edited by Jonathan London, 171–211. Singapore: Institute of Southeast Asian Studies.

Turner, Sarah, and Jean Michaud. 2011. "Imaginative and Adaptive Economic Strategies for Hmong Livelihoods in Lao Cai Province, Northern Vietnam." In *Minorities at Large: New Approaches to Minority Ethnicity in Vietnam*, edited by Philip Taylor, 158–90. Singapore: Institute of Southeast Asian Studies.

USAID (U.S. Agency for International Development). 2011. "The 2010 Vietnam Provincial Competitiveness Index: Promoting Economic Governance and Sustainable Investment." Policy Paper 15, USAID/VNCI Hanoi.

Wells-Dang, Andrew. 2012. "Ethnic Minority Development in Vietnam: What Leads to Success?" Background paper prepared for the 2012 Poverty Assessment, Hanoi, April.

World Bank. 1999. "A Synthesis of Participatory Poverty Assessments from Four Sites in Viet Nam: Lao Cai, Ha Tinh, Tra Vinh, and Ho Chi Minh City." World Bank, Hanoi, July.

———. 2009. "Country Social Analysis: Ethnicity and Development in Vietnam." World Bank, Washington, DC.

CHAPTER 6

Is Inequality Rising in Vietnam? Perceptions and Empirics

Inequality is examined through two lenses—a qualitative study of perceptions of inequality and a quantitative analysis. The chapter documents widespread concerns across the population about rising inequality. The qualitative study draws on rich focus group discussions that describe which inequalities are viewed as unacceptable in the eyes of Vietnamese people and captures less easily measured inequalities, such as inequalities in connections, voice, and influence. The quantitative analysis examines the factors driving the rise in inequality, including geographic variations in growth processes, growth in the nonagriculture sector, and disparities in education and ethnic identity. Rising inequality is linked to growth processes in the service sector and industry that have left some groups and regions behind.

Over the last two decades, Vietnam has undergone rapid growth, substantial poverty reduction, and economic transformation. Unlike other fast-growing economies, such as China and Indonesia, past empirical work suggests that Vietnam's extraordinary economic transformation has been one of growth without an appreciable rise in inequality, a path similar to that of the Republic of Korea and Taiwan, China, during their early stages of development (ADB 2012; McCaig, Benjamin, and Brandt 2009; VASS 2011; World Bank 2009). Commonly used measures of inequality suggest that inequality in Vietnam rose modestly during the 1990s and stabilized during the 2000s.

Recent studies, including a major report on poverty prepared in 2010 by the Vietnamese Academy of Social Sciences, note that relatively modest changes in empirical measures of inequality based on household surveys stand in sharp contrast to the widely shared perception among Vietnamese people that inequality in incomes and wealth is rising (VASS 2011). The perception of rising inequality is also notable in the press, among policy makers, and among academics in Vietnam.

This chapter examines inequality through two lenses: a qualitative study of "perceptions of inequality" (Hoang et al. 2012) and a quantitative analysis that builds on lessons from the qualitative assessment. Examining inequality using both quantitative and qualitative tools gives a richer picture of the inequalities in outcomes, opportunities, and social and political capital among Vietnamese people. Inequality in outcomes refers to inequalities in income, consumption, and wealth, while inequality in opportunities refers to differences in human capital driven by circumstances such as gender, ethnicity, location, or parental characteristics. Inequality in social and political capital refers to differences among individuals measured in terms of connections, voice, and influence.

The perceptions study helps to identify which types of inequalities are tolerated and which are viewed as unacceptable in the eyes of Vietnamese people; it also captures inequalities that are difficult to measure in quantitative analysis, such as inequalities in connections, voice, and influence. The quantitative assessment focuses on measuring changes in the distribution of outcomes and opportunities over time and on understanding the drivers of these changes using data from household surveys, including various rounds of the Vietnam Household Living Standards Survey (VHLSS).

The perceptions study suggests that Vietnamese people from all backgrounds—rural and urban, rich and poor—think that inequality has risen substantially over the last five years. Focus group participants rarely discussed income or expenditure inequality in isolation, but instead linked it to determinants—notably inequalities in education, access to good employment opportunities, access to land, and connections, power, and influence. As such, inequality in access to employment was seen as a consequence of inequality in access to education, and inequality in employment was then linked to inequalities in income, expenditures, and wealth. Inequalities in power and connections were perceived as increasingly important in determining access to jobs (transforming education into employment) or maintaining land rights. Despite the perception that inequalities in income and wealth are rising, the majority of respondents considered inequality in outcomes to be acceptable as long as it is generated through fair and legitimate means. The tolerance for income inequality is a major shift in public attitudes from Vietnam's prereform period.

Empirical evidence on inequality from the 2010 round of the VHLSS suggests a modest rise in income inequality, driven primarily by growth in rural areas, where income from higher-value sideline activities and sources of nonagricultural income has been rising among better-off households. The rise in income inequality reflects, in part, growth processes that have altered the relative return to assets such as education and productive capital in the economy. As such, the empirical analysis suggests that growth has interacted with existing inequalities in opportunities—inequalities in education, patterns of social exclusion between ethnic minorities and the majority, access to good jobs, and geographic disparities—to increase income inequality and income gaps between rich and poor households.

Why are we concerned about inequality?

Should policy makers be concerned about rising inequality in income or expenditures? Whether inequality in outcomes is likely to be a concern depends, in part, on the drivers and processes that generate the inequality. It is useful to distinguish between "good" and "bad" processes and the subsequent inequality created. "Good" processes and inequalities are those that reward effort and hard work, reflect incentives to innovate, stimulate entrepreneurship, and provide the impetus for economic growth.[1] "Bad" processes and inequalities are those that prevent certain segments of the population from benefiting from growth processes and from transitioning out of poverty and low-income-generating activities.[2] These inequalities often reflect unequal opportunities for children born into certain circumstances, such as ethnicity, location, income or education level of the parents, or gender (Roemer 2011). They also reflect inequalities in connections, voice, and influence, where people from different backgrounds face different chances of getting into a good university, acquiring a well-paying job, or of converting land because of their background or circumstances. It is these second drivers of inequality—linked to inequalities in opportunity and process—that are most likely to damage growth, foster social exclusion, and breed societal tolerance for inequality in income and wealth (World Bank 2006).

The evidence suggests that the rise in income inequality in Vietnam since the mid-2000s is the result of both "good" and "bad" processes. While a substantial fraction of the population has contributed to the growth processes and has benefited from growth, inequalities in opportunities continue to repeat themselves across generations, and there is a growing sense of unfairness in processes such as how access to public services is gained, how jobs are acquired in the public sector, and how land conversions occur.

The perceptions study provides us with a unique depiction of "good" and "bad" types of inequality as seen through the eyes of Vietnamese people from a variety of backgrounds, including young and old, rural migrants and long-term urban residents, workers in the informal sector and higher-paid employees in the formal sector, and minority populations and poorer individuals more generally, particularly living in rural areas. In the perceptions study, focus group participants were asked to categorize which forms of inequality they considered more or less acceptable and to explain their views.

Study respondents largely viewed rising income inequality as acceptable if it is associated with market-orientated growth-generating processes that reward education, skills, hard work, and talent. The acceptability of inequality of incomes generated through legitimate means across all demographic and socioeconomic groups constitutes a major shift in public attitudes toward inequality, away from the previous focus on egalitarianism and toward market-based mechanisms and incentives. As two interviewees explained,

> Disparity and competition are natural in a market-orientated economy. If you are talented, you can be rich. (Group of elder persons, Me Tri Commune, Hanoi)

> Those who have talent and luck are conditioned to succeed. Those who have none just suffer. I heard no complaint about inequalities. Such is reasonable. (Village officials group, Cam Hung Commune, Hai Duong)

The empirical evidence also suggests that inequalities generated by reforms and structural transformation partly reflect "good" processes that are associated with economic momentum and enhanced economic incentives. Since the *Doi Moi* reforms began in 1986, Vietnam has witnessed a rapid economic transformation that has harnessed the power of market incentives to foster rapid economic growth alongside strong poverty reduction. The rise in income inequality partly reflects the process of structural transformation that has occurred since the reforms, which have shifted labor away from agriculture and into the manufacturing and service sectors where value added per worker is higher.[3] The inequalities generated through these growth processes are inevitable in the sense that they are associated with a positive momentum in the economy and are likely to encourage growth.

However, not all of the forces driving income inequality are perceived as "fair." For example, inequalities in connections, voice, and influence are perceived to be unfair and to be rising. Whether inequality in outcomes is viewed as acceptable or not depends more on the process by which the inequality is generated than on the level of disparity. Study participants widely accepted inequality in outcomes if the income or expenditure was generated through processes or sources that were perceived to be fair, while they considered inequalities generated through illegitimate practices to be unacceptable. For example, inequalities arising from differences in education, capital, hard work, honest business practices, and luck were seen as acceptable, while those generated through the illegitimate use of power or influence were not. As some respondents explained,

> There are types of illegitimate richness, and we do not accept these types, we see them as being an injustice. For example, some traders sell seedlings to us at extremely high prices. And corruption happens at all levels. (Youth group, Chieng Khoa Commune, Son La)

> Without [unfair] power and connections the directors just differ from the workers by some coefficient of basic salary. Because they

have power and information, holding important positions, doing businesses, they have used this to become much richer. (Long-term migrant group, An Son Ward, Tam Ky City, Quang Nam)

Inequalities in opportunities imply that current differences in incomes will be perpetuated in future generations unless the intergenerational links are broken. Therefore, the inequalities currently seen in labor markets are likely to replicate themselves in the children of those who are unable to take advantage of growth processes and may result in groups that are already disproportionately poor falling even further behind. Although inequalities in educational attainment have narrowed in recent years, particularly at the primary level, the educational attainment of children from poor rural households remains low, particularly in some regions of the country (chapter 3), and the characteristics of the family a child is born into continue to be a strong predictor of whether a child acquires secondary education and beyond. Therefore, the inequalities currently seen in income and wealth are likely to replicate themselves in the children of those who are unable to take advantage of growth processes, resulting in the intergenerational transmission of poverty and well-being.

Is inequality of outcomes rising?

Past empirical work suggests that Vietnam's two-decade period of rapid growth has not been accompanied by an appreciable rise in inequality. The Gini coefficient of income inequality remained fairly stable in the early 2000s (McCaig, Benjamin, and Brandt 2009), and expenditure inequality did not rise appreciably at the national level (VASS 2011). According to a 2010 study led by a team from the Vietnamese Academy of Social Sciences (VASS), the Gini coefficient of expenditure inequality increased from 0.33 to 0.35 between 1993 and 2002, but remained fairly stable between 2002 and 2008 (VASS 2011).

Based on several commonly used measures of inequality, empirical work done for this study suggests that income inequality has risen modestly since 2004, while inequality in expenditures remained stable between 2004 and 2010. Findings from the perceptions study are, however, somewhat at odds with the empirical picture of inequality emerging from the 2010 VHLSS. The perceptions study finds that inequality in outcomes is widely perceived to have risen over the last five years in both urban and rural areas. This section looks briefly at the source of some of these discrepancies.

Focus group respondents in both urban and rural areas reported that they perceive inequality in outcomes—typically defined using income, but also including spending on consumer durables and assets—to have risen and significantly in urban areas since 2005.

Perceptions of inequality were often, but not always, rooted in direct life experiences and varied across groups according to socioeconomic characteristics. Individuals tended first to compare themselves with others in their community and then to compare themselves with slightly better-off individuals or places. For example, low-skilled workers in Hai Duong and Ho Chi Minh City compared themselves with higher-skilled workers, and individuals living in peri-urban areas in Hai Duong, Hanoi, and Da Nang compared themselves with people living in inner-city areas. Those living in urban environments tended to have broader frames of reference, and in these areas disparities relating to conspicuous consumption (automobiles, high-end cell phones, large houses) were noted, in particular.

Some focus groups in more remote and difficult rural areas were less comfortable discussing inequality of outcomes within their own community than inequality within society, potentially due to unease in singling out differences in closely knit communities sharing common disadvantages of location, agricultural livelihoods, social and political capital, and other ethnic specifications. Participants in these focus groups appeared to be more at ease, however, when discussing inequalities beyond their community and, in particular, inequalities in connections, voice, and influence.

Focus groups consisting of less educated individuals from poorer households considered disparities related to substantially wealthier groups as being less important for their lives and showed limited interest in comparing their situation with others in more favorable circumstances. For example, one member of the migrant focus group in Da Nang said,

> I feel it is okay. I do not spend much, and my earning is sufficient for my living. My life might not be as good as theirs, but I spend to my liking and do not want to compare myself with others.

The empirical evidence suggests that income inequality has been rising at the national level in Vietnam, albeit modestly. Figure 6.1 shows the ratio of mean per capita income of the top and bottom quintile, decile, and vigntile of the income distribution. Although all groups saw substantial growth between 2004 and 2010, the unevenness of growth implies that the ratio of mean per capita income of the top 20 percent relative to the bottom 20 percent (referred to recently by the General Statistics Office as the "rich-poor gap") increased from just over 7.0 to 8.5. Similar tendencies are seen across other income quintiles, and the disparities grow as one narrows in on the very poorest and very richest households.

Ethnic minorities are being increasingly left behind in these growth processes. The last three groups of bars on figure 6.1 show that average income and growth of the bottom 20 and 10 percent of the ethnic minority distribution were lower than those of the majority population in 2004–10. Moreover, the top 20 percent of the majority population earned 11.4 times what was earned by the bottom 20 percent of minorities in 2004 and 17.5 times what was earned in 2010. In comparison, when we look at the entire population, the ratio of incomes among the top to bottom 20 percent rose

FIGURE 6.1 **Ratio of mean per capita income in Vietnam, by percentile, 2004–10**

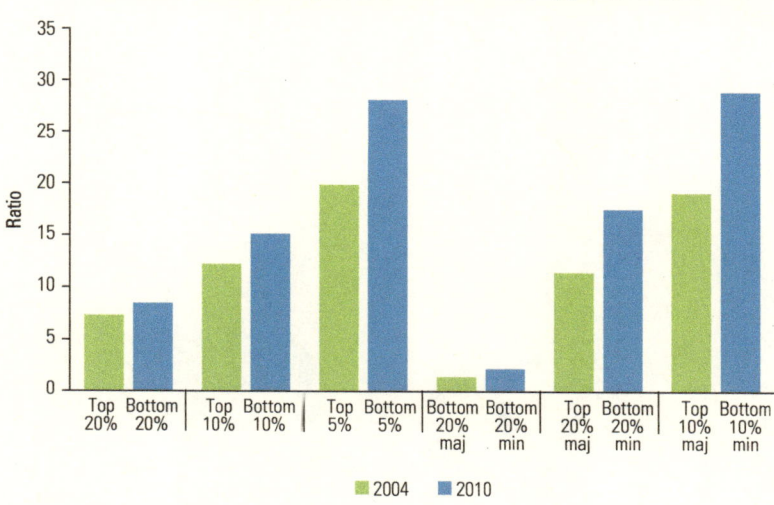

Sources: 2004, 2010 VHLSS.
Note: maj = majority; min = minority.

from 7.2 in 2004 to 8.4 in 2010. This confirms that ethnic minorities are increasingly overrepresented among the poor. The gap between minorities and the rest of the population is rising. The ratio of income earned by the bottom 20 percent of majorities relative to the bottom 20 percent of the minority population also increased during this period, from 1.4 to 2.1. This may reflect, in part, the predominance of agriculture as a major source of income among minorities and poorer households (see chapter 5).

The rural sector has been the driving force behind the recent rise in income inequality. Figure 6.2 shows the growth incidence curve for income by per capita income decile in rural areas. Growth in rural areas has been far higher among richer households than among poorer households; growth in the poorest 10 percent of households was less than half that seen in the richest 10 percent of households, and the ratio of income consumed by the top income decile to that consumed by the bottom income decile increased 25 percent between 2004 and 2010. For the first time since VHLSS data started being collected, the Gini coefficient of income inequality is now of a similar magnitude in urban and rural areas. The Gini coefficient of income inequality in rural areas rose from 0.365 in 2004 to 0.413 in 2010, while it remained stable in urban areas over the same period, at approximately 0.381.[4]

The contribution of differences in mean income between rural and urban areas and between provinces to explaining overall inequality has declined over time. The Theil index of inequality can be decomposed into five components: (a) differences in mean income between rural and urban

FIGURE 6.2 **Mean per capita annual income in rural areas of Vietnam, by rural income decile, 2004–10**

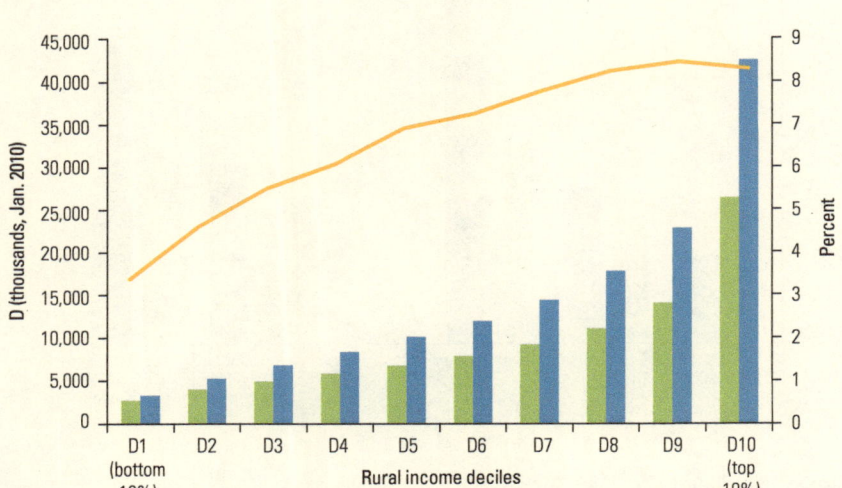

Sources: 2004, 2010 VHLSS.

areas nationally, (b) differences in mean income between rural areas of different provinces, (c) inequality within rural areas within each province, (d) differences in mean incomes between urban areas of different provinces, and (e) inequality within urban areas within each province.[5]

Figure 6.3 shows the fraction of income inequality attributable to these various components in 2004 and 2010. Between 2004 and 2010, the fraction of income and expenditure inequality attributable to differences in income between rural and urban areas declined. This reflects the faster average rate of growth in rural areas, with the result that mean income and expenditures in rural areas have been catching up with those in urban areas. The ratio of income in urban areas to income in rural areas declined from 1.87 in 2004 to 1.70 in 2010. Similar patterns are evident in consumption; the ratio of mean consumption in urban areas to rural areas declined from 2.26 in 2004 to 2.01 in 2010.[6] This appears to be driven by the top end of the rural income distribution; the income of households in the top 40 percent of income in rural areas has grown faster than that of households in the top 40 percent of income in urban areas, while the income of the bottom 20 percent of rural households has grown slower than that of their urban counterparts. The decline in differences between rural and urban welfare over time in Vietnam is in contrast to the development patterns of China, where a rapid expansion of the rural-urban gap has been an important source and driver of inequality (World Bank 2009).[7]

FIGURE 6.3 **Theil decomposition of the level and changes in income inequality in Vietnam, 2004–10**

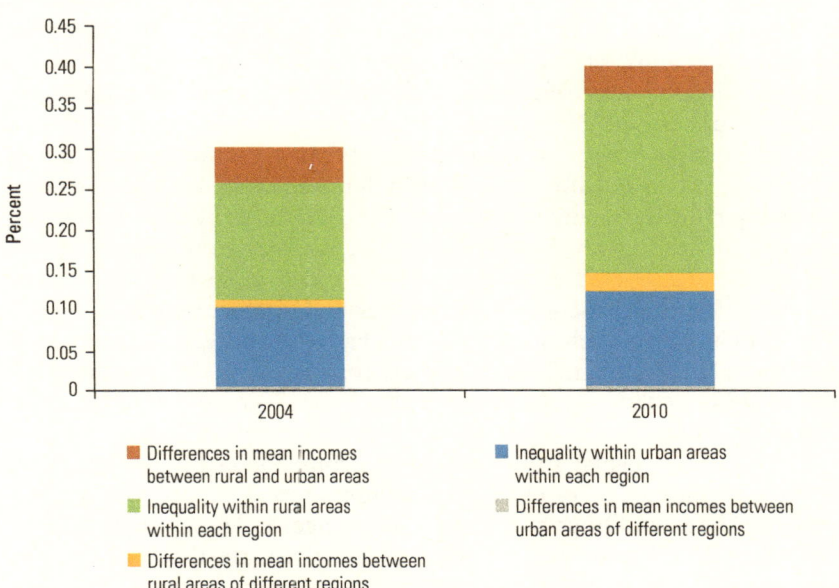

Differences in mean incomes between rural and urban areas

Inequality within rural areas within each region

Differences in mean incomes between rural areas of different regions

Inequality within urban areas within each region

Differences in mean incomes between urban areas of different regions

Sources: 2004, 2010 VHLSS.

Despite rising income inequality, inequality in consumption at a national level has not been increasing. The difference between patterns of income and consumption inequality warrants further analysis. Income is a flow measure, while consumption (as defined for this book) has been smoothed over time; for example, consumption also includes imputations for housing and durables. In addition, the way in which consumption was measured changed in 2010, raising issues of comparability with earlier rounds. Therefore, income is deemed a more suitable candidate for over-time comparisons of inequality.

Perceptions of inequality as captured in the qualitative study appear to capture different concepts than are reflected in empirical measures of inequality; as such, they provide a complementary facet of inequality. For example, the perception of rising inequality in urban and rural areas is at odds with the empirical evidence, which suggests that the rise in income inequality at the national level is driven mostly by rising inequality in rural areas. Furthermore, inequality in expenditures at the national level remained stable in the 2000s, in contrast to perceptions that it was rising. The annex to this chapter discusses how to reconcile differences between empirical measures of inequality and perceptions of inequality.

Why has income inequality increased?

Disparities in income across Vietnam and rising income inequality can be attributed to multiple and interrelated factors.[8] First, as discussed elsewhere in this book, ethnic minority groups have progressed less rapidly than the Kinh majority. Second, and closely related, geographic variations in growth patterns are likely to contribute to the rise in inequality—that is, differences in the drivers of agricultural and nonagricultural growth across regions contribute to differences in growth rates. Third, the rise in income inequality reflects changes in the pattern of production away from agriculture and toward the nonagriculture sector and away from low-skill work and toward higher-skill work outside the agriculture sector. The changes in production vary in scope across regions and interact with existing disparities in human and physical capital to change the distribution of income over time. Finally, the misuse of power, corruption, and connections are likely to be linked to inequality, although it is not clear to what degree these factors have contributed to the rise in income inequality.

The first three explanations for rising income inequality are examined in this section; inequality in power, corruption, and connections are discussed in the next. Other factors such as changes in landholding patterns and regional variations in agricultural productivity are also likely to play an important role and are left for future exploration.

The rise in income inequality reflects the increasing economic polarization of many ethnic minority groups. The evidence suggests that differences in growth rates between ethnic minorities and the majority population have contributed to rising inequality particularly within rural areas. Since ethnic minorities have lower educational outcomes and lower access to productive capital, differences in these other assets contribute to and substantially reinforce differences in income across ethnicities. As the nonagriculture sector has grown in Vietnam and more educated individuals have profited from this growth, the predominance of minorities in the slower-growing agriculture sector has resulted in a widening gap, on average, between minorities and the Kinh majority.

Figure 6.4 shows growth by income source among ethnic minorities and the majority, by quintile, between 2004 and 2010. The majority of income growth among poorer ethnic minority households has come from agriculture and sideline activities. Income among all minority quintiles apart from the richest is growing at a slower rate than that of the majority, and even the fastest-growing minority households experience lower income growth than the average majority households. The divergence in growth rates is strongly related to the income-generating activities of households. The fraction of income and growth from wage income and nonagricultural sources rises as one moves up the income quintiles. Only the richest 20 percent of minority households experience substantial growth in income arising from nonagricultural business activities.

FIGURE 6.4 Income growth in Vietnam, by ethnicity and income source, 2004–10

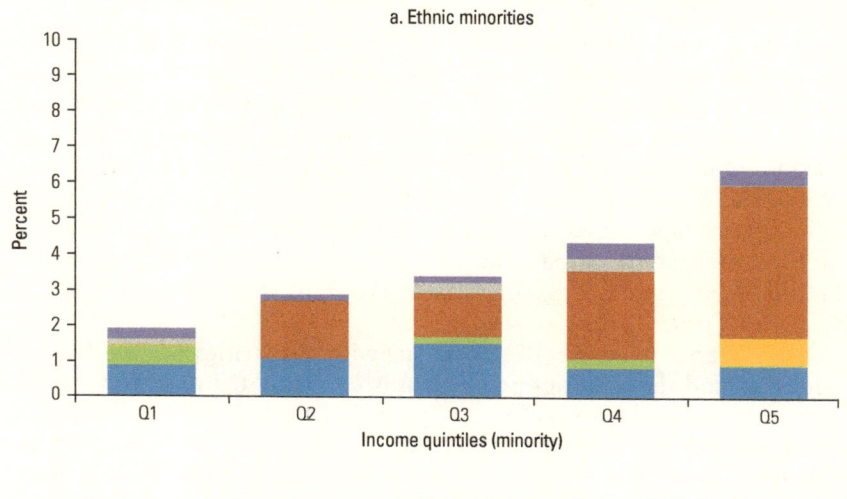

a. Ethnic minorities

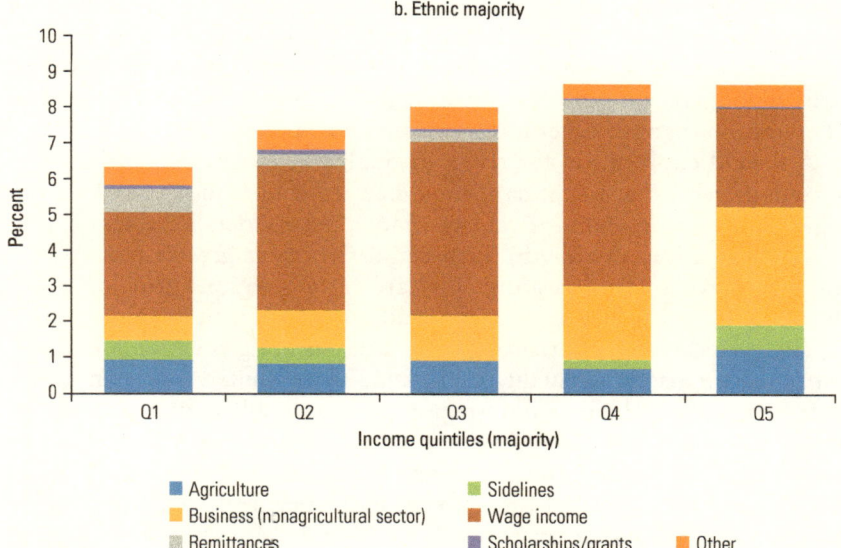

b. Ethnic majority

■ Agriculture	■ Sidelines	
■ Business (nonagricultural sector)	■ Wage income	
■ Remittances	■ Scholarships/grants	■ Other

Sources: 2004, 2010 VHLSS.

The fraction of inequality attributable to differences in mean income between the majority and minority has risen over time, from 9 percent of total inequality to 14 percent, and approximately one-quarter of the rise in income inequality over time in rural areas can be attributed to differences between the majority and ethnic minorities. Therefore, differences in growth rates between minorities and the majority have contributed to the rise in inequality over time, particularly in rural areas where ethnic minorities are concentrated.

Alongside an increase in the differences in mean income between minorities and the majority, the uneven pattern of growth across income quintiles suggests that inequality has risen within both the majority and the minority group. Income among the poorest 20 percent of minorities grew at an average annual rate of only 2 percent, substantially slower than the growth rate for the wealthiest 20 percent of minorities.

The percentage rise in the Gini coefficient of income inequality among the Kinh majority (in urban and rural areas) is greater than that seen in the combined sample, suggesting that the overall rise in income inequality is driven by other factors as well.

The evidence from the VHLSS of growing disparities between ethnic minorities and the majority population is corroborated in a study tracking rural households over time using the Vietnam Access to Resources Household Survey (McKay and Tarp 2012). This study finds that income grew more slowly, on average, between 2006 and 2010 for ethnic minorities than for the rest of the rural population, and this was the case even among minority and majority households with similar observable productive assets and education. Of interest, the study also documents substantially higher growth rates for ethnic minority households with high levels of education than for other minority households.

A second explanation for rising inequality is geographic variation in growth patterns that might have caused an increase in inequality between regions, provinces, and districts (see chapter 4 for a detailed discussion of regional variations in growth). Regional variations in growth patterns do, however, prompt the question: Why are certain regions growing faster than others, and what is driving these differences in growth?

The evidence suggests that regional variations in growth patterns contribute to the rise in inequality, but play a more limited role than differences across households within regions. There is substantial evidence of variations in growth across regions, with some poorer regions such as the northeast, north-central coast, and northwest growing substantially more slowly than the Red River Delta and the central highlands. Figure 6.5 shows mean income and growth between 2004 and 2010 by region. Income growth was uneven across regions; it was lower in the northeast than in other parts of the country and higher in the Red River Delta and the central highlands than the average growth rates of 8 percent. The southeast region had the highest income per capita. These growth patterns differ somewhat from patterns in the 1990s; between 1993 and 1998, the northern uplands and central highlands grew the least, while the southeast grew the most (World Bank 1999).

The fraction of income variation attributable to differences across regions and provinces has risen over time in rural areas, in part due to

FIGURE 6.5 **Mean annual per capita income in rural areas of Vietnam, by region, 2004–10**

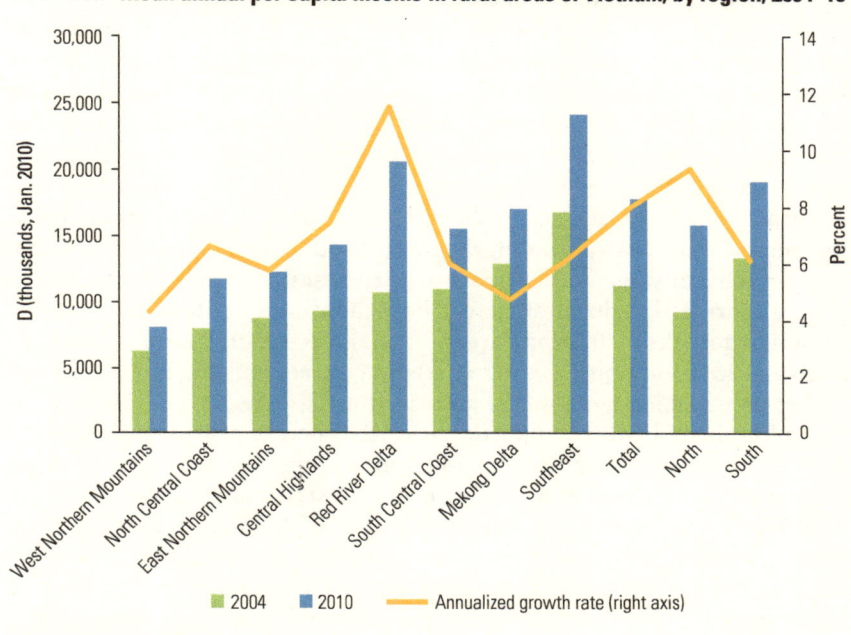

Sources: 2004, 2010 VHLSS.

uneven growth in agriculture and in part due to geographic variation in opportunities in the nonagriculture sector. In contrast, China saw a reduction in the variation in incomes attributable to location over the 1990s and early 2000s (Benjamin and Brandt 2002b; Benjamin, Brandt, and Giles 2005; Benjamin et al. 2007). An important caveat is that migration and remittances are likely to play a mediating role in reducing variations in income and growth across regions, and the extent of this role is not fully captured in the data.[9] This area deserves further attention in future analysis of inequality.

Differences in incomes and expenditures are increasingly related to differences in household characteristics rather than to where households live, although location continues to be an important correlate of household welfare. Education is one of the most important characteristics explaining differences in income and expenditure across households in 2010. Controlling for the average education of working-age adults explains more of the variation in household income in rural areas than region of residence. The fraction of variation in income explained by education increased between 2004 and 2010, suggesting that education is becoming an increasingly important correlate of income. The amount of variation in household income attributable to differences between regions of residence has also increased over time, but this increase has been from a lower base. Between 2004 and 2010, 65 percent of the increase in the Theil index can be attributed to an increase in inequality between household education levels, where household education is defined using the education of the household head.

The third explanation for rising inequality relates to shifts in production away from agriculture and into the nonagriculture sector. Nonagricultural opportunities and employment are strongly identified in the perceptions study as factors contributing to the rise in inequality. The factors discussed included a move away from agricultural production and toward greater nonagricultural wage and business opportunities, rising returns to education, disparities in education across households, and differences in initial capital endowments. In urban areas, discussions centered around access to good employment opportunities and land conversion, while in rural areas higher value-added agricultural and sideline activities and access to nonagricultural employment opportunities were cited as prime candidates for rising inequalities. Respondents noted increasing difficulties in accessing good jobs, particularly with respect to public sector employment.

The composition of household income and employment has moved away from agriculture and toward manufacturing and services. Figure 6.6 shows the share of workers in the primary, secondary, and tertiary sectors and indicates the fraction of workers in each sector in rural and urban areas. Between 1998 and 2010, the share of the working population employed in agriculture declined from 68 to 45 percent, while the share employed in manufacturing rose from 12 to 24 percent and that in services rose from 20 to 31 percent. In both rural and urban areas, wage income grew quickly and at above-average rates over the period, while income from agricultural and allied activities grew relatively slowly. Although agricultural and allied activities continue to be an important source of income for rural households, their contribution declined from an estimated 55 percent of rural income in 1998 (McCaig, Benjamin, and Brandt 2009) to only 35 percent in 2010.

There is substantial regional variation in both the speed at which economic activity has moved away from agriculture in rural areas and the intensity with which nonagricultural activities are conducted at the household level. In rural areas, diversification into nonagricultural employment has occurred at both the household and individual level, constituting a powerful force for poverty reduction over the past decade. Variation in the speed at which this is occurring is likely related to the variation in living standards and growth rates across regions.

The expansion of nonagricultural wage and salaried work in urban and rural areas continues a trend seen in the 1990s. In rural areas in 1998, wages and salaried work contributed only 14 percent of total income overall (McCaig, Benjamin, and Brandt 2009). Wages became a more significant source of income throughout the 2000s; by 2010, wages accounted

FIGURE 6.6 **Sector of employment of the working-age population in Vietnam, 1998, 2004, and 2010**

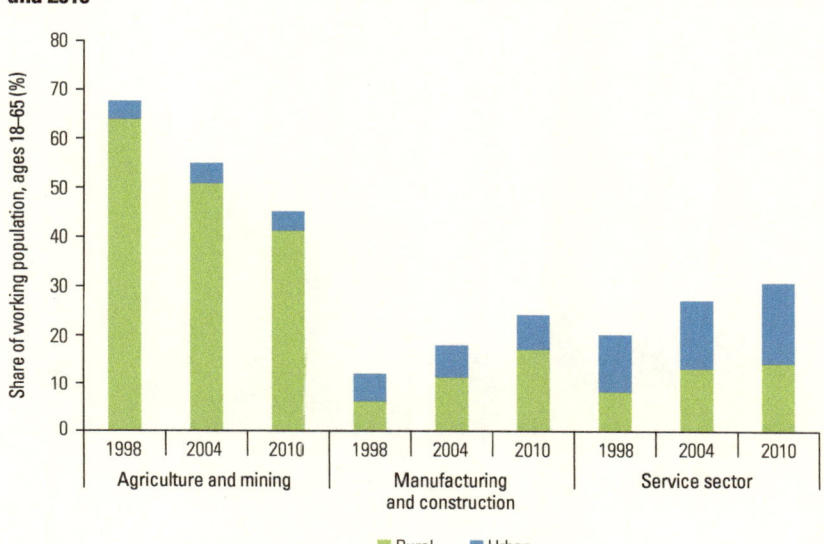

Sources: 1998 VLSS; 2004, 2010 VHLSS.
Note: Classifications are based on occupation codes. Agriculture includes high- and low-skilled agricultural work. Nonagricultural occupations are separated into lower- and higher-skilled work: higher-skilled work consists of all professional and office-based categories; lower-skilled work includes machine operators, service and sales, and unskilled work. The broad classification is due to changes in occupation codes over time.

for 32 and 52 percent of income in rural and urban areas, up from 26 and 44 percent, respectively, in 2004.[10] Although 19 percent of individuals receiving wages in rural areas in 2010 worked for wages in the agriculture sector, the vast majority of rural wage work was outside of agriculture.[11]

Employment patterns in the nonagriculture sector are very different in rural and urban areas. In rural areas, the move out of agriculture has been accompanied by a sharp rise in employment in manufacturing and construction. In 2010, nearly 70 percent of individuals in the secondary sector were found in rural areas, and this sector accounted for nearly 20 percent of overall employment in these areas. By contrast, urban areas have seen a decline in the fraction of individuals employed in the manufacturing sector and a corresponding expansion in services.

Occupations in the nonagriculture sector differ in their demand for skills, and the composition of nonagricultural growth by type of occupation differs across rural and urban areas. Figure 6.7 shows the split of workers between agriculture and lower- and higher-skilled nonagricultural work (blue- and white-collar work) in rural and urban areas. Although the fraction of workers conducting high-skilled (white-collar) work has

FIGURE 6.7 **Type of occupation of the working-age population in Vietnam, 1998, 2004, and 2010**

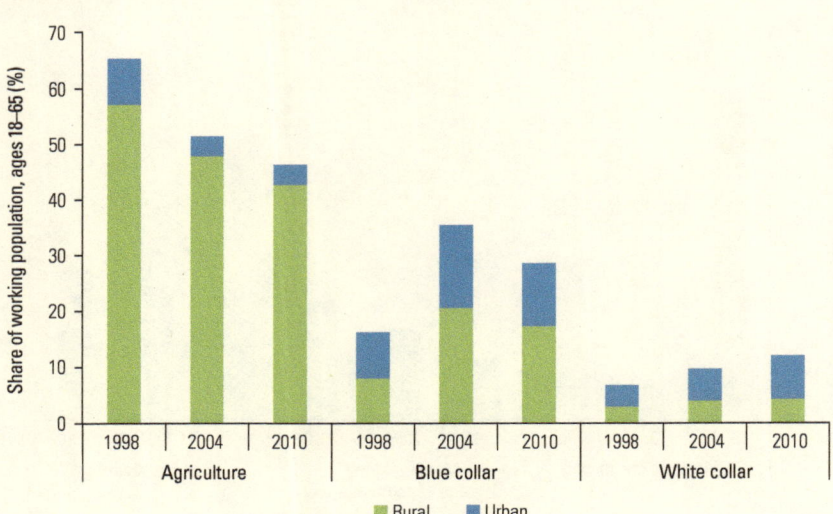

Sources: 1998 VLSS; 2004, 2010 VHLSS.
Note: Classifications are based on occupation codes. Agriculture includes high- and low-skilled agricultural work. Nonagricultural occupations are separated into lower- and higher-skilled work: higher-skilled work consists of all professional and office-based categories, lower-skilled work includes machine operators, service and sales, and unskilled work. The blunt classification is due to changes in occupation codes over time.

risen over time, the majority of the increase has been in urban areas.[12] By contrast, rural areas have seen growth in lower-skilled, blue-collar nonagricultural employment, reflecting a substantial increase in manufacturing work in rural areas over time.

The pattern of nonagricultural growth—more growth in manufacturing and blue-collar employment in rural areas and more growth in service sector and white-collar employment in urban areas—is perceived as a source of disparity among focus group respondents in rural areas and in small urban towns. For example, in rural areas with industrial parks, such as Hai Duong, factory employment is the primary source of labor demand in the nonagriculture sector. While it is possible to find low-skilled and relatively low-paid work in a factory, it is perceived that there are far fewer higher-skilled and higher-paid employment opportunities than in big cities such as Hanoi.

Figure 6.8 shows the composition and growth of income across income quintiles in urban and rural areas, respectively. The share of income from agriculture and allied activities has declined over time but continues to be the major source of income for the poorest 40 percent of the rural population. The share of income coming from sideline activities related to agricul-

FIGURE 6.8 Composition of income in urban and rural areas of Vietnam, 2010

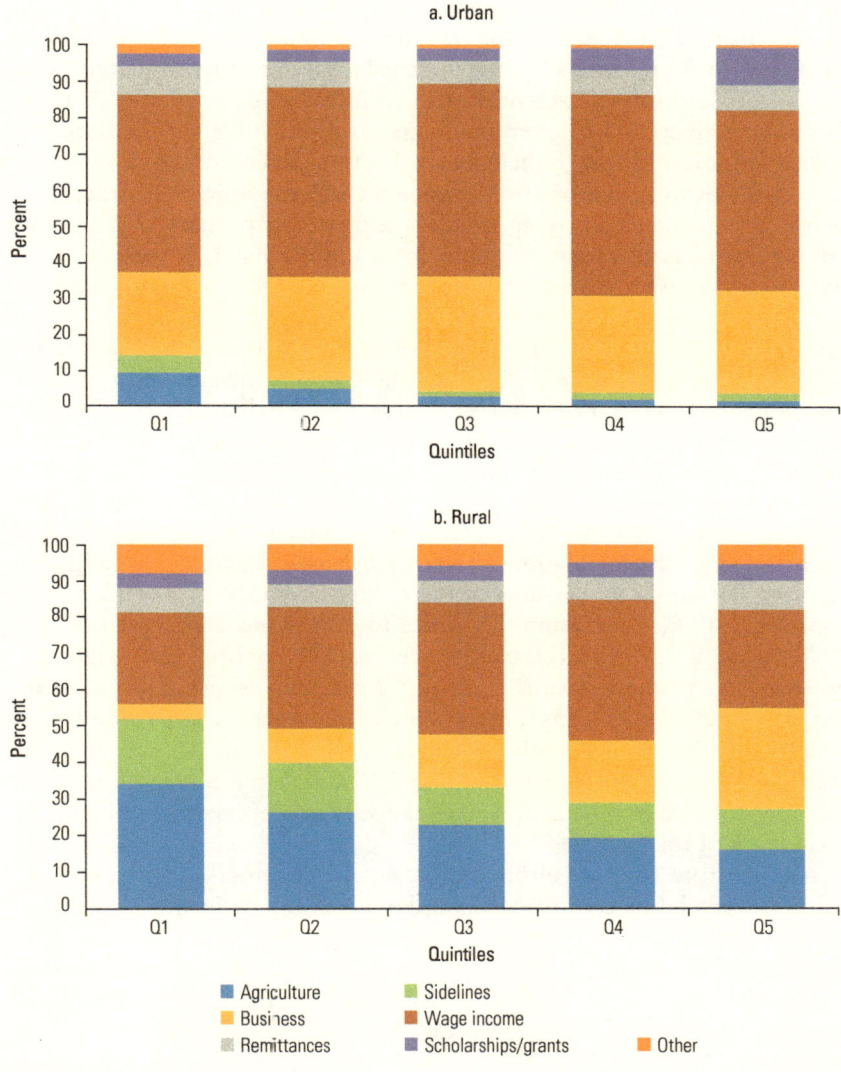

Source: 2010 VHLSS.

ture has remained substantial among poorer households and has grown as a share of income for the poorest quintiles since 1993 (McCaig, Benjamin, and Brandt 2009). The majority of income from this component across all income quintiles is from livestock farming and aquaculture.

Figure 6.8 shows the rising share of wage income across the income distribution. In urban areas, wages are the most important source of income across all income groups, accounting for more than half of income. This is in stark contrast to the income profile in 1993, when the majority of income from the top half of the income distribution came from business income.[13] In rural areas, all groups earned a greater share of income from agriculture and sideline activities than from wages in 1993 and 2004. By 2010, wage income had overtaken agricultural income for the third and fourth quintiles. Although their share of wages increased, the richest quintile continues to earn more from business and agriculture. The fraction of working individuals receiving wages as either their primary or secondary employment has also risen over time, from approximately 17 percent of the workforce 18 to 65 years of age in 1998 to 40 percent in 2010, and from 13 to 37 percent, respectively, in rural areas.[14]

To explore more formally the contribution of different income sources to income inequality, we decompose the Gini coefficient into its source components (Adams 1994; Stark, Taylor, and Yitzhaki 1986). The Gini coefficient of total income can be written as the sum of the contributions of each income source. The effect of a source on total income can then be broken down into three components: (a) the source of income as a share of total income; (b) the inequality within the sample of income from a given source; and (c) the correlation between a given source of income and total income. The larger the product of these three components, the greater the contribution of income from the source to overall income inequality.

Figure 6.9 presents relative concentration coefficients, indicating whether an income source is inequality increasing or inequality decreasing. If the relative concentration coefficient is greater than 1, the source is inequality increasing, while if it takes a value less than 1, the source of income is inequality decreasing. Figure 6.10 shows the contribution of the different sources of income to the Gini coefficient of inequality, including their share of total income.

Income from the agriculture sector, notably from crop activities, agricultural wage labor, and livestock and aquaculture, is inequality decreasing. Agricultural wage labor and cropping activities are among the most equalizing components of income.[15] A rise in the relative concentration coefficient of agriculture between 2004 and 2010 implies that the extent to which agriculture is equalizing has declined over time. Relative to its share of income, however, the contribution of the agriculture sector to overall inequality is low; the agriculture sector (including agricultural wages) contributed approximately 29 percent of total income but accounted for only 15 percent of inequality. In rural areas, agricultural sideline activities were a relatively equalizing source of income in 2004; in 2010 they had become mildly disequalizing, a change that reflects the faster growth in these sources of income among richer rural households.

The distribution of remittance income has become more equalizing over time in both rural and urban areas. In 2004, the share from remittances

FIGURE 6.9 **Relative concentration coefficients of different sources of income in Vietnam, 2004 and 2010**

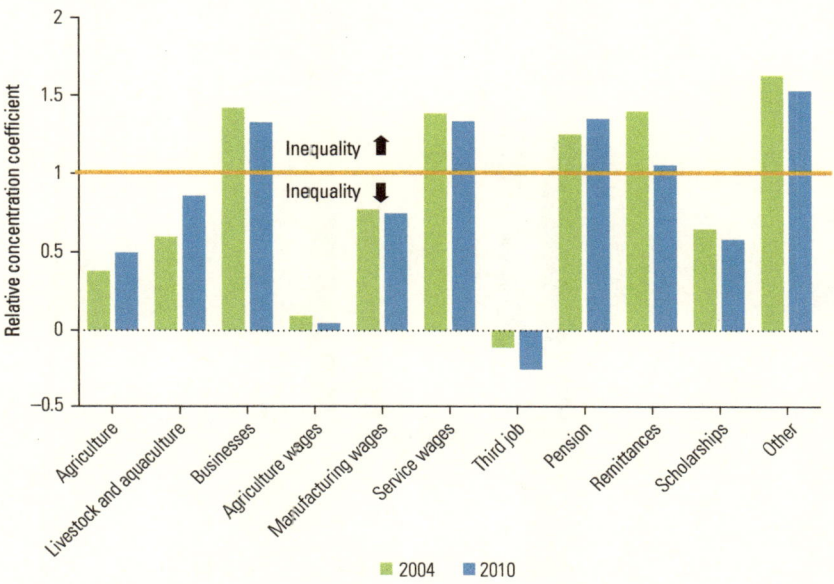

Sources: 2004, 2010 VHLSS.
Note: Based on a Shorrock's decomposition by income source. A relative concentration coefficient greater than 1 suggests that the income source is inequality increasing, and a value less than 1 suggests that it is inequality decreasing (that is, it is not concentrated disproportionately among richer households).

in the richest quintile was double that in the poorest quintile; by 2010 the share from remittances was similar. The change in the distributional impact on remittances was driven predominantly by changes in the migration patterns of richer households. The quantitative and perceptions studies both suggest a declining role for higher-paid international migration among richer households; the share of remittances coming from international migration declined from 35 percent of remittances to 30 percent over time. Income from remittances dropped in absolute terms in the top quintile, and the share of international remittances declined from 47 percent of remittance income to 42 percent among the richest 20 percent of the population.

Households working in the nonagriculture sector earn more than those working in the agriculture sector, and their incomes have grown at a faster pace. Figure 6.11 shows per capita income conditional on the sector of employment of the household head. The income of households with a household head employed in a white-collar occupation in the nonagriculture sector is highest in both urban and rural areas, followed by the income

FIGURE 6.10 Contribution of different income sources to the Gini coefficient in Vietnam, 2004 and 2010

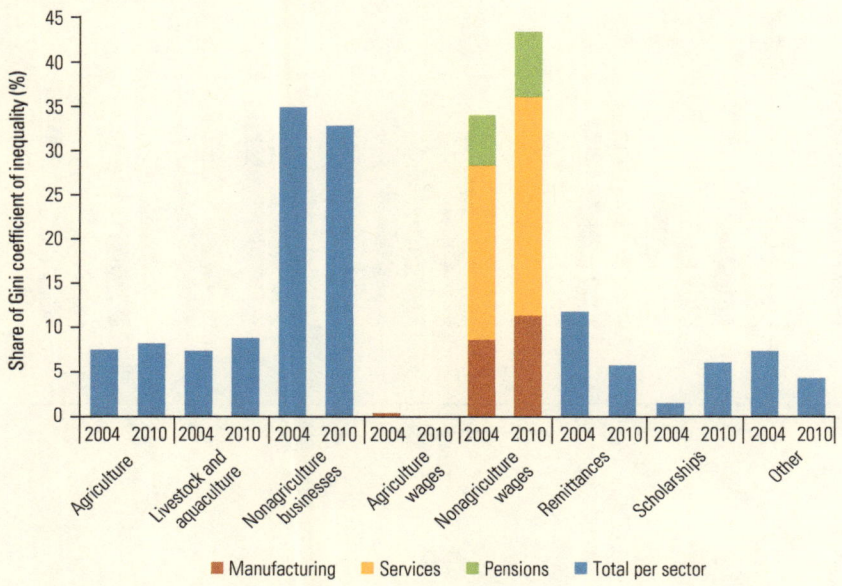

Source: 2010 VHLSS.

FIGURE 6.11 Per capita annual income in rural and urban areas of Vietnam, by occupation of the household head, 2004 and 2010

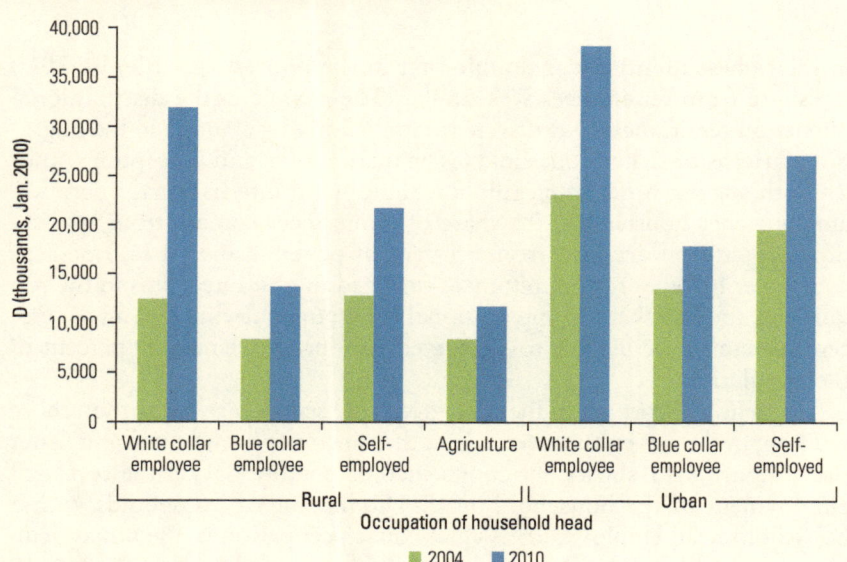

Sources: 2004, 2010 VHLSS.

of self-employed nonagricultural workers. In rural areas, households whose head works in agriculture have the lowest income in both periods and the lowest average growth. The difference between these households and agricultural households was relatively small in 2004 but has grown over time.

Education is an important determinant of whether an individual works in the agriculture or nonagriculture sector and the type of nonagricultural work conducted. The relationship between education and type of employment is evident for relatively recent labor market entrants who have completed their schooling. Figure 6.12 shows the structure of employment for workers 25 to 30 years of age in 1998 and 2010. Having an upper-secondary education or above is a significant determinant of having nonagricultural employment, and individuals with a college education are the most likely to be found in more attractive, higher-skilled employment.[16]

Returns to education increased during the 2000s, with substantially larger increases for workers in urban areas (figure 6.13). Empirical work carried out for this chapter finds evidence of rising returns to education in the wage labor market during the 2000s; for nonagricultural jobs, the hourly wage return to a year of schooling increased from 5.3 percent in 2004 to 5.8 percent in 2010. The labor income return to education (based on total earnings) is greater than the wage return to education (based on hourly earnings) since individuals with more education work longer hours in the wage labor market than individuals with less education. An additional year of education raised labor incomes an estimated 9.7 percent in

FIGURE 6.12 **Workers ages 25–30 in Vietnam, by education level and type of job, 1998–2010**

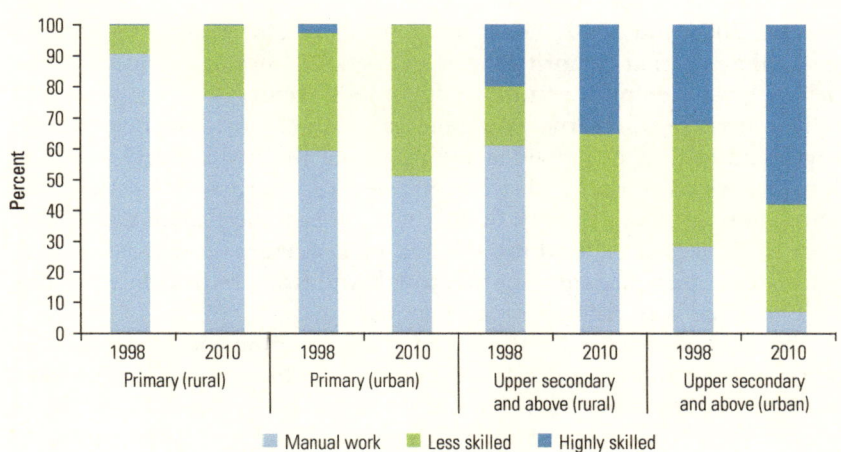

Source: 2010 VHLSS.

Note: High-skilled workers are professional or office workers. These positions are usually classified as white-collar work. Lower-skilled workers are employed in the service sector, in sales, as machine operators, or as skilled manual or handicraft workers. Manual workers include agricultural laborers and unskilled manual workers.

FIGURE 6.13 Hourly wage and labor income returns to schooling in Vietnam, 2004–10

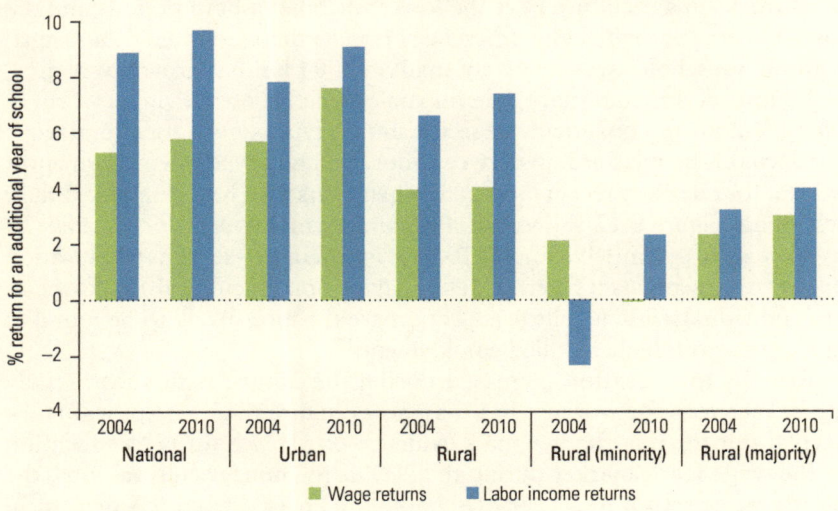

Sources: 2004, 2010 VHLSS.

2010 compared to 8.9 percent in 2004. Returns to education are higher for workers in urban than in rural areas and have risen faster over time. In urban areas, an additional year of schooling was associated with a 7.6 percent increase in hourly wages, while in rural areas it was associated with a 4.1 percent increase. Within rural areas, returns to education are lower for ethnic minorities than for the majority and appear to have declined between 2004 and 2010. The lower returns for ethnic minority workers reflect the fact that minorities tend to work in lower-paid occupations, including wage employment in the agriculture sector.

The increase in returns over time has widened the gap between the wages and income of individuals with higher and lower levels of education.[17] Since education is distributed unequally across the working-age population and adjusts only slowly over time, some people will benefit more from nonagricultural growth and higher returns to education than others. Therefore, nonagricultural growth and rising returns to education are associated with rising inequality in income.

The link between education and rising income inequality can be explored by examining the relative gap between the incomes of more and less educated households, which rose between 2004 and 2010. In 2004, households with at least one working-age individual with a college education earned 1.3 times more income than those with an upper-secondary education and 2.5 times more than households with no education. By 2010, college-educated households earned 1.7 and 3.0 times more, respec-

FIGURE 6.14 **Per capita annual income of urban and rural households in Vietnam, by education of the most educated working-age household member, 2004 and 2010**

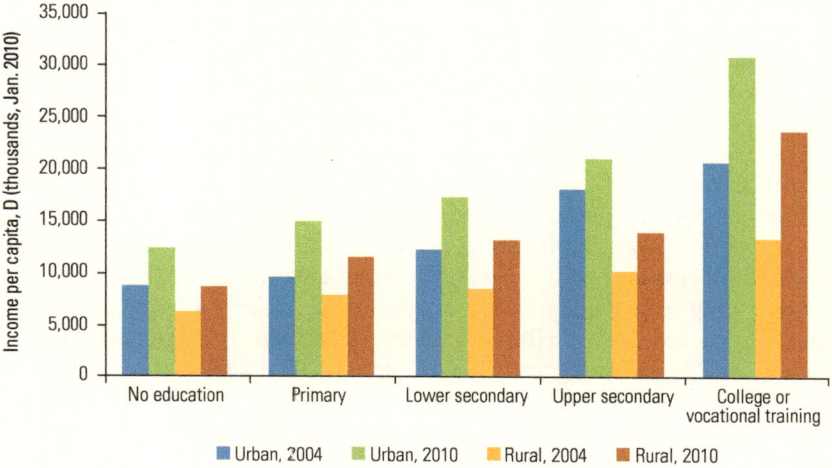

Source: 2010 VHLSS.

tively. Figure 6.14 shows income in urban and rural households, by level of education. Between 2004 and 2010, households with more education earned more than households with less education, and the income of the most educated households grew faster than that of all other education categories in both rural and urban areas. Although urban households continued to earn more in every education category in 2010 than in 2004, the ratio of the income of rural households to that of urban households at education levels above lower secondary fell over time. This suggests that the decline in mean income between rural and urban areas is due to the relatively richer, more educated individuals in rural areas catching up to their urban peers, rather than to catch-up at the bottom end of the income distributions.

Inequalities in opportunities and income differences across generations

The analysis of opportunities focuses predominantly on education. This choice of focus was driven in part by the perceptions study, as education and employment were central concerns in many focus groups. It was also motivated by the empirical evidence, which suggests an increasingly important role of education as a determinant of income inequality. It is recognized that the focus on education comes at the exclusion of other important factors that drive inequality, however—in particular, access to health care and basic public services.[18]

Growth in the demand for educated labor and in the return to education in urban areas implies that education is an increasingly important—and dividing—asset in Vietnam. Education levels in the labor market and in households are rising as more educated younger cohorts join the labor market and less educated older cohorts retire. However, the stock of education among the working-age population changes slowly in response to changing returns; therefore, initial differences in education endowments can translate into large differences in income as the return to education rises and the demand for skilled labor in the nonagriculture sector grows.

Whether income inequality and disparities are perpetuated across generations depends on whether investments in human capital among younger generations respond to changes in income generation opportunities or whether they reflect inequalities in opportunities linked to younger persons' circumstances of birth, such as the birthplace, characteristics of the parents, or ethnicity. The evidence suggests that inequalities in education are likely to be transmitted to future generations, implying that deprivations continue to be perpetuated across generations and require decisive action.

The transmission of deprivation across generations was reflected in multiple focus group discussions, with groups commenting that children born to poorer households are likely to drop out of school earlier than those born to richer households and to work in less-skilled occupations. Many participants recognized that gaps in educational enrollment have narrowed between better-off and worse-off households at lower levels of education. However, gaps remain at higher levels of education, and quality gaps arise at all ages, implying that poverty perpetuates across generations. As one member of a lower-educated migrant group expressed it,

> Education is an important cause of inequality. Without education, I work as an unskilled worker and send my children to lower-quality schools. With a good education and income, I could send my children to good schools. It is a vicious cycle. (Lower-educated migrant group, Ho Chi Minh City)

Substantial progress has been made in equalizing enrollment and completion rates at the primary level. Between 1998 and 2010, differences in enrollment at the primary and secondary level narrowed across the rich and the poor and in rural and urban areas, as shown in figure 6.15. At the primary level, educational enrollment is close to universal for all groups, although important differences remain between ethnic minorities and the majority and across minority groups, as discussed in chapter 5.

Educational investment continues to be distributed unequally at higher levels, and this inequality will feed into inequalities in outcomes later in life. Gaps in enrollment at an upper-secondary level were still high in 2010, and a child's background continues to play a large role in determining his

FIGURE 6.15 **Ratio of enrollment in primary, lower-secondary, and upper-secondary school in Vietnam, by various groups, 1998 and 2010**

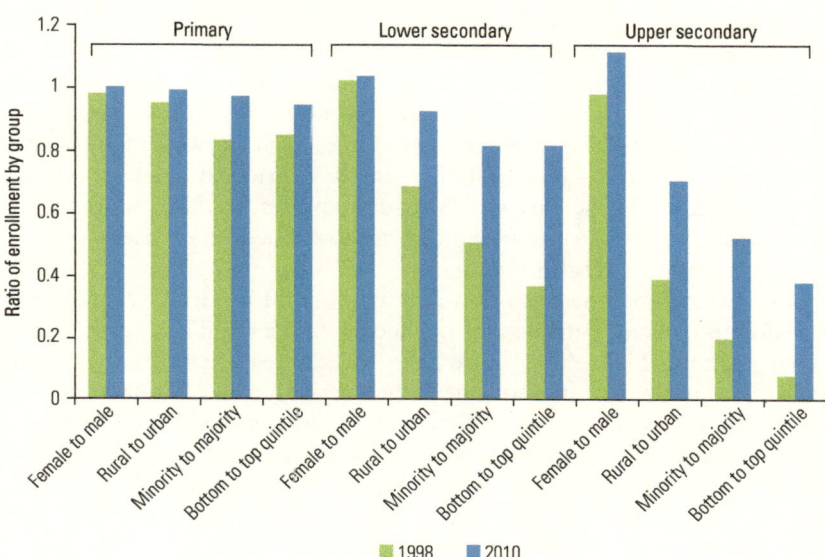

Sources: 1998 VLSS; 2010 VHLSS.

or her educational attainment at a higher level. Upper-secondary enrollment for children in rural areas is still only 70 percent of enrollment rates for children in urban areas, and ethnic minority enrollment is only half that of the majority. Only four poor students are enrolled in upper-secondary school for every 10 richer students enrolled. Since many of those richer students will continue on to college or university, the final educational difference between students residing in the top and bottom income quintiles will be wider than it is for upper-secondary education.

The characteristics of a child's parents and household wealth continue to be significant predictors of whether a child is enrolled in lower-secondary or upper-secondary school, although their impact on enrollment diminished between 1998 and 2010. Educational enrollment at the secondary level is affected by income, which can be considered a short-term liquidity constraint and is linked to longer-term, or permanent, factors such as parental education (World Bank 2011).[19] The evidence also suggests that the impact of income on educational decisions is twice as large for ethnic minorities as for the Kinh-Hoa majority (World Bank 2011).

Beyond family background, the quality of schooling also influences the skills that a child acquires in school. At the primary level, the characteristics of teachers, schools, and classrooms are statistically significantly related to student achievement in math and science, and these inputs are distributed unequally across schools in Vietnam (World Bank 2011).

Evidence from the Young Lives data suggests that children from poorer households perform worse on math tests prior to entering primary school and continue to perform worse than children from richer households throughout primary and lower-secondary school. Figure 6.16 shows the average rank of children on math tests at ages 5, 8, 12, and 15 by household wealth quantile. For children at age five, prior to entering school, average math scores increase with wealth quantiles, so that children from the poorest 25 percent of households have lower scores, on average, than children from other wealth quantiles.

Most worrisome, the circumstances that a child is born into appear to be a more important determinant of success than a child's potential when entering school. Figure 6.17 shows the trajectories of children who had math scores in the top and bottom 20 percent at age five. Trajectories are divided by the wealth status of their household at age eight. We can see that high-scoring children from poor households perform poorly relative to their high-scoring peers from rich households. Similarly, low-scoring children from rich households improve their scores over time more than low-scoring children from poorer households.

The perceptions study indicates that parents perceive significant variations in the quality of education across rural and urban areas at all levels of education. A frequently raised concern is that teachers in rural areas at

FIGURE 6.16 **Average rank on the math test in Vietnam, by wealth quartile, at ages 5, 8, and 15**

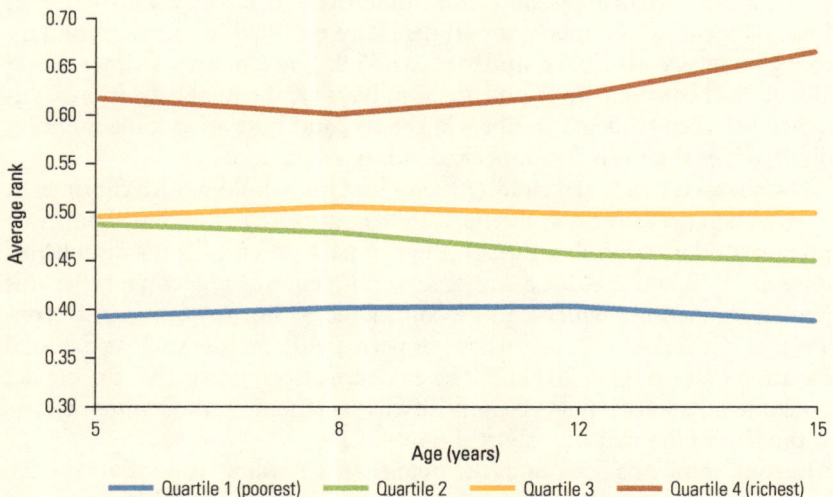

Source: Estimates based on Young Lives data, rounds 1–3: 2002, 2006, and 2009.

FIGURE 6.17 **Average rank on the math test in Vietnam, by initial test score and wealth**

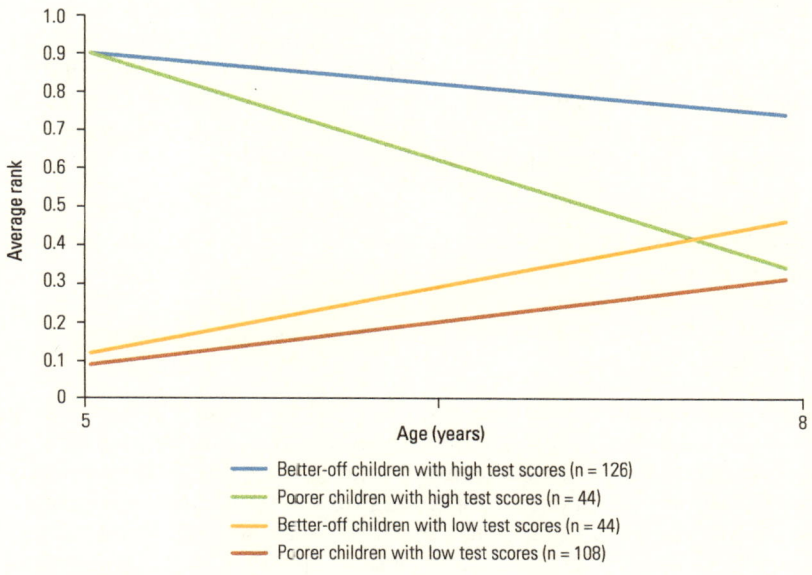

Source: Estimates based on Young Lives data, rounds 1–3: 2002, 2006, and 2009.

higher levels of education are less qualified than teachers in urban areas and that the poor are unable to afford to send their children to the same-quality schools as the rich.

The inequality in education quality is striking between richer and poorer households in urban areas, where rich children go to high-quality schools, attend extra classes, and pay private tuition, including for English and computer courses. Meanwhile, poor children attend average schools with few extra classes. In the past, there was little differentiation in the quality of education services, but now such differentiation is perceived to be very large in urban areas, and the rich are viewed as having the capability to invest in better-quality education for their children. For example, a student from Ward 26 in Ho Chi Minh City reported,

> As early as the child is still in preschool, the rich families will start to seek their way into good primary schools; the poorer families just want their children to be literate, so they don't care about which school their children are going to. Previously, there was a small number of international schools for the rich families to choose from, [and] both rich and poor students would attend the same school; now there are more schools providing a wider range of services, [and] the rich-poor gap also gets widened.

Unequal quality of education is perceived to start from an early age, with children from poorer households sending their children to lower-quality kindergartens. Some poorer households in An San Ward, Tam Ky City, Quang Nam, reported not being able to afford to send their children to kindergarten. Others who were able to do so expressed concerns about quality differences between the preschools attended by their children and those attended by children from wealthier backgrounds:

> The disparity can be found right from the preschool level. The poor households, who try their best, can send their kids to school[s] that cost D 500,000 per month. The better-off households, on the contrary, send their kids to key schools that ask for fees of D 700,000 to D 900,000 per month. The diet and care services among these schools are different.

Although empirical evidence on quality differences at higher levels of education is limited, looking at the composition of education expenditures across households can give insight into why quality differences may emerge. As noted in chapter 1, spending on inputs like extra courses is substantially higher among richer and urban households at the lower- and upper-secondary level, and the amount spent on these courses has increased over time among the richest households. These trends are strongest in urban areas, but are also evident in rural areas. If children from richer households can benefit from extracurricular activities and additional training through tutoring and foreign language studies, they are likely to receive a higher-quality and more rounded education than children from poorer households.

There is evidence of inequality of opportunities in Vietnam beyond education, and circumstances beyond the control of an individual contribute substantially to the inequality in access to basic services. Attitudes toward inequality, and whether it is perceived as unjust, unnecessary, and undesirable, depend on the processes that form it. An important factor is whether inequalities are perceived to be driven by differences in factors for which the individual can be held accountable ("efforts") or are due to circumstances beyond an individual's responsibility ("circumstances"; Roemer 1998). Factors beyond an individual's control that lead people to have different levels of well-being can thus be considered inequalities of opportunity (Paes de Barros et al. 2009).

The human opportunity index (HOI), developed by Paes de Barros et al. (2009), captures inequality of opportunity by examining the extent to which the circumstances that children are born into, such as gender, parental education, and ethnicity, affect the likelihood of their access to the basic building blocks of human capital, such as education and health services. The index captures two moments of access to basic services. It captures absolute levels of access and then calculates differences in the access rate across gender, location, parental background, income, and other indicators of circumstances. The degree of inequality is measured by the D-index, which captures the dissimilarity in access rates due to differences in circumstance. Differences in the degree of inequality of opportunity can be interpreted as the fraction of a given inequality that needs to be redistributed in order to achieve equality. The D-index measure of inequality of opportunity is used to scale down the average national access rate of a service to the given HOI.

The HOI in Vietnam is examined for 2004 and 2010 in a background paper for the poverty assessment led by researchers from the Vietnamese Academy of Social Sciences, with inputs from the World Bank (VASS 2012). Opportunities for access to basic building blocks were examined in three domains—education, health, and housing infrastructure—and the paper investigates whether access to these basic foundational blocks is spread evenly across children in the population or is circumscribed by inherent characteristics beyond an individual's control. The circumstances examined include both individual and household characteristics, including gender, parental education and well-being (expenditures), location, and ethnicity.

In international comparisons with countries in Africa and in Latin America and the Caribbean, Vietnam fares well on some dimensions, such as access to electricity and school attendance, and less well on others, such as access to piped water and flush toilets. Specifically, the HOI for school attendance is higher in Vietnam than in most African countries and several countries in Latin America and the Caribbean, while the HOI for access to electricity is higher than that in all African countries and only slightly lower than that in most Latin American and Caribbean countries. The international comparison is, however, less favorable in other dimensions. Vietnam's HOI for access to piped water is higher than that in only some African countries, and it is lower than that in all Latin American and Caribbean countries. The HOI for flush toilets is in the middle of the whole range in African and Latin American and Caribbean countries. However, Vietnam falls considerably behind top-performing countries in both of these basic services.

Although equality of access is high for education "quantity" in 2010, the HOI suggests that the quality of education is more divergent across the population. Among children 7 to 11 years old, both the coverage rate and the HOI are high, suggesting low inequalities in accessing primary education. At the lower-secondary level, however, although the coverage rate is high, there are some inequalities in access. The education of the household head is the most important characteristic determining whether a child attends lower-secondary school between ages 12 and 15, followed by household well-being (expenditure). These two circumstances account for more than 50 percent of the dissimilarity. Although ethnic minorities have lower educational outcomes, ethnicity alone plays a smaller role than well-being and education of the household head, which suggests that differences in other circumstances contribute substantially to and reinforce inequalities across ethnicities.

The quality of schooling received by a child is measured by his or her ability to advance independently to lower-secondary school without help when he or she is in the last grade of primary school. Only 62 percent of pupils in grade five would be able to advance to lower-secondary school without help. The considerable difference between the HOI for the quantity and quality dimensions of education suggests that greater emphasis needs to be placed on raising the quality of the education system, in general, and primary school, in particular. Household well-being and education are the two most important circumstances determining the quality of education received.

Although the HOI for access to electricity and improved water sources is high, the coverage of access to improved sanitation facilities is lower and distributed less evenly than the other infrastructure measures. Although there was significant progress during 2002–08 and further improvement in 2010, the coverage rate was approximately 64 percent in 2010, suggesting that more could be done to improve access to this basic service.[20] Furthermore, a substantial gap between the coverage rate and the HOI indicates a remarkable inequality in access to this service. The region where a household is located plays the biggest role in determining access to clean water and sanitation, followed by a household's well-being, ethnicity, and education of the household head.

The HOI is high for some indicators of health and low for others. Notably, the index suggests that Vietnam is doing well on the fraction of women receiving prenatal care, assistance at delivery, and child immunization against measles—92 percent of children one to five years of age were vaccinated against measles in 2010— but that immunization against polio is lower.

Household well-being is a leading determinant of opportunities in the health domain. Figure 6.18 shows the relative importance of circumstances for key health indicators in 2010, decomposed into the fraction attributable to different circumstances. Ethnicity is the most important circumstance for access to care for mothers, accounting for one-quarter of dissimilarities in receiving prenatal care and assistance at delivery. Among children, household well-being, region of residence, and education of the household head account for 65 percent or more of the dissimilarity in opportunities.

An analysis of the HOI at the region level suggests that there is substantial heterogeneity across regions with regard to access to improved sanitation facilities in both the initial year examined (2002) and in 2010. The southeast had the largest and most stable increase in access, while the

FIGURE 6.18 Relative importance of circumstances for access to health care in Vietnam, 2010

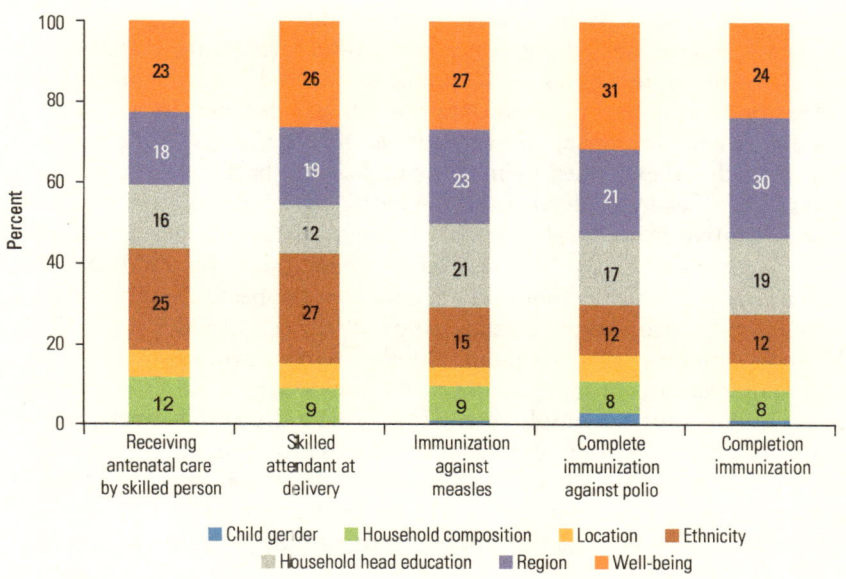

Source: VASS 2012.

northwest had a very low HOI in 2002, which improved in a slow and unstable manner.

Inequalities in connections, voice, and influence

Qualitative and quantitative evidence suggests that inequality in Vietnam reflects processes that may be more socially and economically damaging, such as inequalities in social and political capital, which manifest themselves through inequalities driven by influence, connections, and uneven voice. Inequalities of these forms were raised in many focus groups, urban and rural, rich and poor alike—as being important drivers of inequality and as having risen in recent years.[21]

Corruption is a systemic problem in Vietnam, and the qualitative evidence reflects many of the issues raised in previous analyses of corruption and transparency in the country (Anderson et al. 2009; CECODES et al. 2012; World Bank 2010; World Bank, Embassy of Sweden, and Embassy of Denmark 2011), but it does so through the lens of rich-poor differences and inequality, shedding light on how inequalities in socioeconomic outcomes interact with, are magnified by, and are perpetuated by inequalities in power and connections. Inequality of treatment by public authorities was raised with respect to several factors, including land conversion practices that favor investors over landholders and uneven quality of public service delivery in hospitals and public notaries that lead to frustration among poorer and less-well-connected individuals.

Rural respondents were concerned about increasing disparities in employment opportunities in the public sector and cited the need to pay bribes or have connections to obtain a job as a teacher, as a doctor, in a state-owned enterprise, and as a public official.[22] These concerns were widespread and expressed by individuals from all backgrounds, including commune officials. Evidence from the nationally representative provincial administrative procedural index study suggests that 29 percent of individuals agree that bribes are required to obtain a job in the public sector, and nearly half of all respondents believe that connections are important in obtaining various types of state employment (CECODES et al. 2012). Moreover, these views are shared in both urban and rural areas.

Unfair recruitment mechanisms in the public sector are linked to concerns about youth unemployment following substantial investment in higher levels of education. Participants in focus groups of youth, in particular, voiced frustration with procedural inequalities that affect their ability to translate their education into good jobs, such as the unfair role of power and relationships in obtaining public sector employment. In their words,

> Money is not enough. Money without connections can't get you a job in the public sector. I know some cases where the workers quit their job in pursuit of higher education but after graduation, they returned to work in the previous position as if they had never attended such courses. (Better-off group, Cam Hung Commune, Hai Duong)

> In my place, there are some guys who have to work as simple workers after completing university just because their families do not have D 50 million to D 70 million to bribe their way into an agency just to work as an administrative assistant. Many with poor academic performance somehow passed university entrance exams and were placed [in] a job after graduation. This is irrational but unlikely to abate in the future. (Senior citizen, Cam Hung Commune, Hai Duong)

In peri-urban areas where agricultural land is being converted to non-agricultural land for industrial zones, inequalities in outcomes related to land were seen as an unfair source of disparities, whereby people with connections and information gain from land speculation while those without are unable to convert their land into income. Focus group participants perceived that the current land conversion policies and processes favor commercial investors and that local landowners do not secure their rights to proper compensation and resettlement, effective vocational training, occupational replacement, and employment generation. As one group expressed it,

> Many owners of bogus projects have exploited loopholes under Decree 64 to appropriate land from local farmers with false claims of using it [the land] for public utilities. (Poor group, Me Tri, Ha Noi)

Focus group participants raised concerns suggesting that corruption in land management is regressive since it involves a transfer of land at lower-than-market prices from poorer households to relatively well-off investors. People with connections and access to information were reported to have made substantial profits from land speculation and trade, while those who lost land in the process have to struggle for their basic necessities after land conversion. A key concern here is speculative behavior, wherein land is bought at a low price and resold shortly after at a higher price, as reported by youth in Me Tri, Ha Noi:

> People in [the] land sector, they know in advance the information so that they can advise others to buy land when the price is low and then sell it at much higher prices.

Unequal access to public services was another major source of concern across focus groups, with differences in treatment noted between those who "do politics" and ordinary people. Concerns about access to quality public services are widespread and cover multiple forms of public services, from lengthy administrative procedures such as registering a marriage to the length of wait and quality of treatment given by doctors and hospital staff in public hospitals. In addition, concerns were raised in multiple settings regarding who receives the benefits from public social assistance programs targeted at the poor.

It is perceived that those who have been officials of government agencies are often given priority when they go through administrative procedures. In particular, a commonly voiced concern was that richer people use bribes to access better education or health care services. Participants expressed concern over the predominance of valuing money over traditional ethical values on the part of employees in public services as outcome inequalities widen. As one person put it,

> For example, when it comes to doing paperwork at the ward people's committee, if you had been with the state before you retired, you will still be given priority over other ordinary people. Even if you have to queue up, you will still be quicker to have the paperwork done than the others. Likewise in hospital, if you are an average person, you will not get the same treatment as the privileged. (Youth group, Ho Chi Minh City)

Many focus groups considered the use of power, connections, and corrupt means to get ahead in life and acquire better public services and employment opportunities as unacceptable and a key source of frustration. The evidence suggests that whether inequality in outcomes is viewed as acceptable or not depends more on the process by which the inequality is generated than on the level of disparity. A key concern among focus group participants in both urban and rural areas was whether existing inequalities in outcomes were generated through fair or unfair means, such as corruption, misuse of power, and dishonest business practices. Unfair use of political capital and corruption were perceived to affect well-being through multiple routes, from employment opportunities and land conversion to the ability to access high-quality public services and education.

If left uncurbed, inequalities in voice and connections that manifest themselves in myriad forms, from uneven land conversion practices to poor public service delivery, are likely to damage social cohesion, economic progress, and growth. In the perceptions study, these inequalities provoked the most concern and frustration among participants and were the focus of lengthy discussions. Inequalities in voice and connections are likely to play a role in determining whether individuals tolerate rising inequality in the future, directly through a sense of injustice and indirectly through their revised expectations of growth. This may already be occurring through a reduction in the perceived return to education in rural areas, where focus group participants suggested that their inability to translate education into employment opportunities, in part due to a lack of transparent recruitment mechanisms, has diminished their perception of the value of education for future generations.

Emerging policy recommendations

Three key messages emerge for policy makers in Vietnam.

First, income inequality has risen in Vietnam, indicating that growth processes have been less favorable to poorer households and that poorer households are being left behind. Ethnic minority households have experienced slower growth on average than Kinh majority households, although there is substantial variation among minority households depending on endowments and sources of income. There is evidence of regional variation in growth rates, which has contributed to the rise in inequality. In addition, households characterized by lower average education levels are less likely to benefit from growth processes and to transition into the nonagriculture sector than more educated households. These patterns suggest an active role for policy to help poor households to overcome the structural constraints that limit their growth potential.

Second, inequality of outcomes affects the opportunity of children to fulfill their potential, and circumstances overtake potential early in life in

Vietnam. Evidence presented in this chapter suggests that children who show promise at age five are unable to sustain that promise by age eight to the same degree as children from better-off households. Inequality in opportunities of this form are likely to dampen growth and progress in Vietnam, since they imply that the full potential and talent of Vietnamese children are not being fully achieved. It also contributes to social tensions. Closing the gap in early childhood development and education quality in Vietnam is, therefore, desirable for both equity and efficiency.

Finally, there is widespread concern that inequality in connections, influence, and voice is affecting many aspects of Vietnamese peoples' lives, including the ability of individuals to obtain public sector employment and to access good-quality public services. Vietnamese citizens from all backgrounds view these inequalities in political and social capital as unacceptable; they tolerate inequality in income and spending that is due to unfair processes less than inequality that arises through talent and hard work. Promoting transparent processes in Vietnam is necessary to ensure equitable growth—growth that is viewed as fair by all its population.

Annex 6A Why do "perceptions of inequality" diverge from empirical measures of inequality?

The empirical measure of inequality includes four components (Cowell 2011). Perceptions of inequality may differ from empirical measures of inequality due to the following considerations: (a) the factor examined, (b) the unit of analysis—that is, whether a household or individual; (c) the reference group—that is, the universe of comparison, such as inequality at the national, regional, rural, or urban level, and (d) the inequality thermometer or the tool used to capture changes in inequality, such as the Gini or Theil index. Annex 6A examines why perceptions may be different from empirical measures of inequality.

First, our measures of inequality may focus disproportionately on easily measured dimensions of inequality, such as outcomes, while Vietnamese people focus on other dimensions of inequality, such as the quality of education they receive or whether there is perceived unfairness in society. Chapter 6 discusses modalities of inequality as seen through the eyes of Vietnamese people. Not all modalities of inequality were discussed in each focus group, and the emphasis on different modalities of inequality varied substantially by group. For example, young working people often discussed employment inequalities in greater detail; ethnic minorities paid more attention to livelihood-related modalities of inequality in terms of access to market, credit, and technical services; and students and senior groups talked more about education and the unfair roles of power and connections in employment.[23]

Second, perceptions may differ from empirical measures because the frame of reference used in empirical analysis differs from that used by individuals when thinking about inequality. In contrast to most empirical measures of inequality, which capture inequalities at the national, regional, rural, or urban level, perceptions of inequality are often rooted in direct life experiences and have a narrower focus. Groups often discussed disparities within their community and then conceptualized a step up from their income level to compare themselves with people in more favorable places or higher positions. For example, in contrast to the decline in inequality attributable to differences between rural and urban areas, rural respondents perceive inequality between rural and urban areas to have risen. However, in contrast to the empirical measure of inequality that compares the average level of welfare within urban areas to the average level of welfare within rural areas, participants in the focus groups compared their own rural community to nearby urban centers in the region. Since the empirical measures of inequality and perceptions of inequality are taking place at different levels of aggregation, perceptions of inequality and measures of inequality may converge at a more local level.[24]

FIGURE 6A.1 **District-level expenditure inequality in Vietnam, 1999 and 2009**

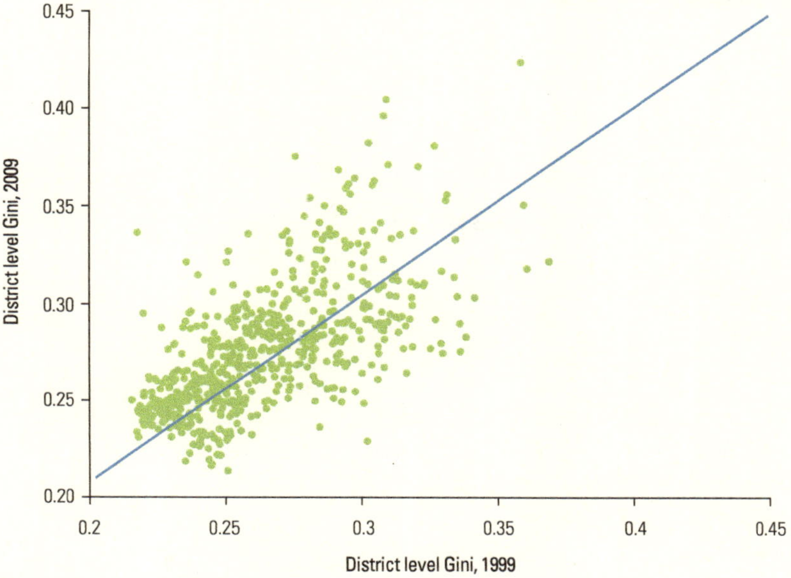

Source: Nguyen, Lanjouw, and Marra 2012.

An empirical examination of inequality at a lower level of aggregation than normally used in a quantitative assessment may help to bridge the gap between empirical measures and perceptions of inequality. Figure 6A.1 shows inequality at a district level in 1999 and 2009, where a district is a lower unit of analysis than normally used when empirically examining inequality.[25] District-level inequality rose in previously low-inequality districts and fell in higher-inequality districts. While this gets closer to the unit of analysis used by our focus group participants, since the frame of reference used appears to vary substantially across individuals, it remains an approximation.

The most commonly used measures of inequality—the Gini coefficient, the class of generalized entropy measures including the Theil index, and the ratios of outcomes for people at different percentiles of the outcome distribution—capture inequality in relative terms. However, individuals may view inequality in absolute terms (Amiel and Cowell 1999; Ravallion 2004). For example, if everyone's income rises 7 percent, then relative measures of inequality will not register a rise in inequality even though the absolute gap has grown. Evidence from a developed-country setting suggests that approximately 40 percent of individuals in a study on concepts

FIGURE 6A.2 District-level expenditure inequality in Vietnam, 1999 and 2009: Absolute Gini coefficients

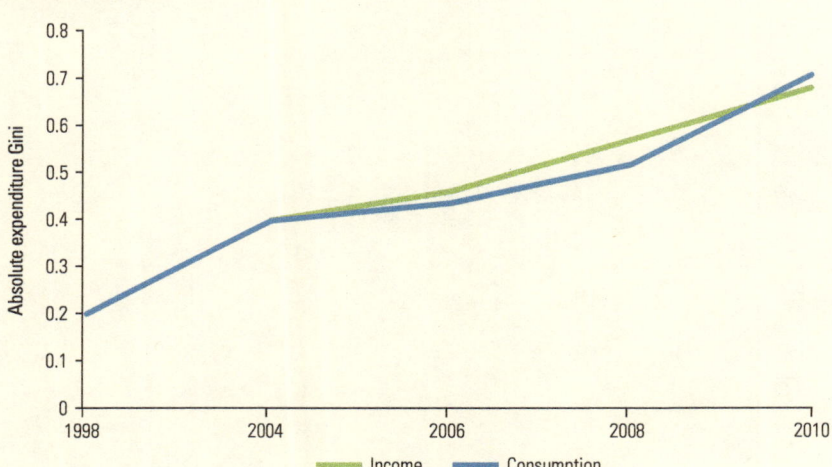

Source: Nguyen, Lanjouw, and Marra 2012.

of inequality thought of inequality in absolute rather than relative terms (Amiel and Cowell 1999). As shown in figure 6A.2, absolute inequality has been rising in Vietnam since 1998.

Whether individuals view inequality in relative or absolute terms is very difficult to capture, and there are only hints of this in the qualitative assessment. The suggestive evidence indicates that, in Vietnam, some individuals are likely to think about inequality in an absolute sense, while others are likely to think of it in a relative sense. Therefore, even if relative measures of inequality remain constant, some individuals will perceive inequality to be rising. For example, the following comments suggest that one focus group was discussing inequality in absolute terms, while the second was discussing it in relative terms. Whether Vietnamese people conceptualize inequality in absolute or relative terms will be examined further in follow-up work that is under way.

> The group claimed that the government's move to increase the salary base at times of inflation only broadened the income gap between the better-off and the poor. Justifying the irrationality of raising the salary base in percentage terms, they cited an example where the increase is 20 percent and the poor with the lower salary will get just some dozens of thousand dong, while the better-incomed with the often higher salary base will receive additional millions of dong to their pay. (Site report, better-off residents, Phuc Xa Ward, Hanoi)

The students claimed that the rich-poor gap over the past five years has been increasingly widened due to the increasing relative gap: the rich develop faster than the poor. (Site report, student group, Linh Xuan Ward, Ho Chi Minh City)

Notes

1. We may also be concerned about rising inequality if there is a causal relationship between inequality and growth. While many theoretical models postulate a negative (and positive) relationship between inequality and growth, a comprehensive assessment of the literature suggests that the empirical evidence is inconclusive (Banerjee and Duflo 2003; Bourguignon 2004; World Bank 2006).

2. These inequalities are linked to "pockets of poverty," whereby certain groups in the population continue to remain in poverty and poverty continues to perpetuate across generations, despite high average growth rates in the economy (VASS 2008).

3. Vietnamese poverty reduction in the 1990s and early 2000s was driven in part by strong growth in the agriculture sector, linked to the opening of agricultural markets from 1993 onward. The equitable distribution of land across the population meant that this period of growth was broad based and accompanied by a substantial rise in income in poor rural areas (Benjamin and Brandt 2002a; Ravallion and van de Walle 2008). In 2010, value added per worker was five times higher in the manufacturing and service sectors than in agriculture (calculations based on information from the *Statistical Yearbook of 2012*, GSO 2012).

4. Trimming for measurement error and then removing the bottom and top 1 percent of the income distribution reduce the magnitude of the Gini coefficients, but the trends over time remain the same; the Gini coefficient of inequality in urban areas remains fairly stable, while the Gini coefficient of inequality is higher in rural than in urban areas.

5. Since the fraction of the population in urban and rural areas, and by region, is changing over time, changes in the component of inequality may also be attributable to changes in the relative share of the population living in urban areas.

6. These figures reflect spatially deflated income and consumption aggregates. The patterns for nonspatially adjusted figures reflect a similar decline, from a ratio of 2.15 to 1.98 for income and from 2.72 to 2.57 for consumption. The higher nonspatially adjusted ratio reflects price differences between urban and rural areas.

7. The rural-urban income gap and trends in the gap vary substantially between provinces, and more recent analyses find that the gap has declined, in part, due to rural-to-urban migration. Between-group inequality consists of three factors: differences between groups in mean incomes, the number of groups, and

their relative size. Therefore, changes in the underlying population structure can make it difficult to compare decompositions over time. We therefore compare the standard measures of between inequality with the maximum possible between inequality for groups of the same size and number using the method of Elbers et al. (2008). We find that the conventional measure of inequality between regions accounts for a declining share of maximum inequality between 2004 and 2010. However, although declining, inequality attributable to differences between rural and urban areas, and between regions, continues to be an important characteristic correlated with inequality.

8. The factors discussed in the most detail in the text are those that are considered to be key factors related to rising inequality, as identified through empirical analysis and emerging from the qualitative study.

9. Among rural households, 4 percent declared having a household member who stayed away from home for more than six months over the previous year. This number appears low relative to evidence from the Population and Housing Census (GSO 2009) and misses patterns in shorter-term, longer-term, and household migration.

10. Wages are likely to include income remitted by members of the household who work in another region. Since many migrants move from rural to urban areas, the fraction of rural income coming from wages is likely to overstate the amount of wage work actually being conducted in rural areas.

11. There is substantial regional variation in the prevalence of agricultural wage work in rural areas. In the north, only 8 percent of individuals working for wages in rural areas are in the agriculture sector. In the south, nearly 29 percent of wage workers in rural areas are in agriculture.

12. High-skilled work has become disproportionately urbanized over time. In 1998, 56 percent of professional jobs were in urban areas compared to approximately 20 percent of the population; by 2010, 64 percent of professional jobs and 30 percent of the population were in urban areas.

13. The income structure of the richest quintile of the urban population has converged on the structure of the poorer groups over time. In 1993 and 2004, the income composition of the top 20 percent was quite different from that of the rest of the population; business incomes were a much larger share of income for the top quintile and the share of income from wage sources was the smallest. By 2010, the top quintile looked more similar to other groups; their share of wage income rose from 38 to 49 percent of income between 1998 and 2010, while the share of income from business sources declined from 37 to 28 percent. These trends continue patterns seen in the 1990s; in 1993, the upper quartile of the income distribution earned nearly 60 percent of their income from a home business and only 10 percent from wages (Benjamin, Brandt, and McCaig 2009).

14. Labor market participation also changed over this period. In 1998, 90 percent of individuals between 18 and 65 years of age reported working compared to 84 percent in 2010, while the fraction of the working-age population rose over

time, from 54 to 64 percent between 1998 and 2010 (calculated from the 1998 VLSS and 2010 VHLSS).

15. Agricultural sideline activities, notably livestock, aquaculture, and agricultural services, are the least equalizing of all agricultural sources and contribute more to income inequality than crop income. This is corroborated by the structure of income across income quintiles: sideline activities continue to be an important source of income for both rich and poor households.

16. Persons with upper-secondary education and above are still likely to be found doing unskilled work in rural areas, either in the agriculture sector or as an unskilled manual laborer in the nonagriculture sector. In the qualitative assessment, focus groups in rural areas discussed instances where individuals who had obtained some higher education were unable to find skilled work (either lower- or higher-skilled work) and hence returned to farming. They attributed this worrying observation to differences in the quality of education between urban and rural areas and to students choosing fields of study, such as pedagogy, for which labor market demand is limited.

17. The returns to education have risen substantially over time, driven largely by urban areas. Assessments of the average wage earned by individuals with different levels of education find low rates of return to education in the early 1990s. In 1993, the return to education using a basic Mincerian earnings equation was approximately 4 percent (Gallup 2002; Glewwe and Patrinos 1999). Although low by international standards, they were similar to rates of returns found in China in the early 1990s (Psacharopoulos 1994).

18. For an excellent discussion of inequalities in these other important dimensions, see VASS 2011).

19. Income is also likely to be related to unobserved correlates such as local returns to education, which are likely to have a positive influence on educational decisions. Furthermore, income is unlikely to reflect a true liquidity constraint since households also have access to savings and formal and informal credit institutions.

20. Due to changes in the sampling frame between 2008 and 2010, it is not possible to compare the progress achieved between 2002 and 2008 to that achieved between 2008 and 2010. Therefore, access to improved sanitation facilities is analyzed separately for 2010.

21. Quantitative evidence suggests mixed trends in reported corruption, as would be expected (World Bank 2010). Surveys of firms suggest that corruption is less of an obstacle for their operations, but the magnitude of bribes, as a percentage of revenues, has not declined. Individual reports from household surveys suggest that, while citizens do not find that corruption has worsened, neither has it improved (World Bank 2010).

22. In 2010, the public sector (including state-owned enterprises and civil servants) accounted for only 4 percent of nonagricultural work and 15 percent of wage or salaried jobs, but 52 percent of high-skilled jobs in rural areas. In urban areas, public sector jobs accounted for 9 percent of all nonagricultural work,

28 percent of wage or salaried jobs, and 42 percent of high-skilled jobs. Ho Chi Minh City has the highest private sector opportunities in the nonagriculture sector, while the northwest mountains region has the lowest private sector opportunities for highly skilled wage or salaried work.

23. Another concern is that the incomes or expenditures of the rich are underreported and undercaptured in household surveys. Therefore, empirical measures of inequality may be downward biased (Cowell 2011; VASS 2011).

24. People may not compare mean levels of welfare, but instead compare the richest people in urban areas with the richest, or poorest, in rural areas.

25. District-level inequality was computed using small-area estimation techniques. See Benjamin, Brandt, and McCaig (2009) for more details.

References

Adams, Richard H. 1994. "Non-Farm Income and Inequality in Rural Pakistan: A Decomposition Analysis." *Journal of Development Studies* 31 (1): 110–33.

ADB (Asian Development Bank). 2012. "Outlook 2012: Confronting Rising Inequality in Asia." Asian Development Bank, Manila.

Amiel, Yoran, and Frank Cowell. 1999. *Thinking about Inequality*. Cambridge, U.K.: Cambridge University Press.

Anderson, James H., Alcaide Garrido, Maria Delfina, and Tuyet Thi Phung. 2009. *Vietnam Development Report 2010: Modern Institutions*. Washington, DC: World Bank.

Banerjee, Abhijit V., and Esther Duflo. 2003. "Inequality and Growth: What Can the Data Say?" *Journal of Economic Growth* 8 (3, September): 267–99.

Benjamin, Dwayne, and Loren Brandt. 2002a. "Agriculture Income Distribution in Rural Vietnam under Economic Reforms: A Tale of Two Regions." William Davidson Working Paper 519, University of Toronto.

———. 2002b. "Property Rights, Labour Markets, and Efficiency in a Transition Economy: The Case of Rural China." *Canadian Journal of Economics* 35 (4, November): 689–716.

Benjamin, Dwayne, Loren Brandt, and John Giles. 2005. "The Evolution of Income Inequality in Rural China." *Economic Development and Cultural Change* 53 (4, July): 769–824.

Benjamin, Dwayne, Loren Brandt, John Giles, and Sangui Wang. 2007. "Inequality and Poverty in China during Reform." Working Paper 2007-7, Partnership for Economic Policy–Poverty Monitoring, Measurement, and Analysis.

Benjamin, Dwayne, Loren Brandt, and Brian McCaig. 2009. "The Evolution of Income Inequality in Vietnam between 1993 and 2006." University of Toronto.

Bourguignon, Francois. 2004. "The Poverty-Growth-Inequality Triangle." World Bank, Washington, DC.

CECODES (Centre for Community Support and Development Studies), FR (Front Review of the Central Committee for the Viet Nam Fatherland Front), CPP (Commission on People's Petitions of the Standing Committee for the National Assembly of Viet Nam), and UNDP (United Nations Development Programme).

2012. "The Viet Nam Governance and Public Administration Performance Index (PAPI): Measuring Citizens' Experiences." Joint Policy Research Paper, CECODES, FR, CPP, and UNDP, Hanoi.

Cowell, F. A. 2011. *Measuring Inequality,* 3d ed. Oxford: Oxford University Press.

Elbers, Chris, Peter Lanjouw, Johan Mistiaen, and Berk Özler. 2008. "Reinterpreting Between-Group Inequality." *Journal of Economic Inequality* (3, September): 231–45.

Gallup, John. 2002. "The Wage Labour Market and Inequality in Vietnam in the 1990s." World Bank, Washington, DC.

Glewwe, Paul, and Harry Patrinos. 1999. "The Role of the Private Sector in Education in Vietnam: Evidence from the Vietnam Living Standards Survey." *World Development* 27 (5): 887–902.

GSO (General Statistics Office of Vietnam). 2009. "Vietnam Population and Housing Census 2009: Migration and Urbanization in Vietnam; Patterns, Trends, and Differentials." Ministry of Planning and Investment, General Statistics Office, Government of Vietnam, Hanoi.

———. 2012. *Statistical Yearbook of 2012.* Hanoi: Government Printing Office.

Hoang, Xuan Thanh, Thu Phuong Nguyen, Van Ngoc Vu, Quyen Thi Do, Hoa Thi Nguyen, Thanh Hoa Dang, and Tam Giang Nguyen 2012. "Perceptions of Inequality in Vietnam: A Qualitative Study." Background paper for the 2012 Vietnam Poverty Assessment, Hanoi.

McCaig, Brian, Dwayne Benjamin, and Loren Brandt. 2009. "The Evolution of Income Inequality in Vietnam between 1993 and 2006." University of Toronto, Toronto.

McKay, Andy, and Finn Tarp. 2012. "Welfare Dynamics in Rural Vietnam, 2006 to 2010." Policy Brief 3 of 2012, Central Institute for Economic Management, Hanoi.

Nguyen, Viet Cuong, Peter Lanjouw, and Marleen Marra. 2012. "Vietnam's Poverty Mapping using the 2009 Housing Population Census and 2010 Vietnam Living Standards Survey." Background paper prepared for the 2012 Poverty Assessment, World Bank, Hanoi.

Paes de Barros, Ricardo, Francisco Ferreira, Jose Molinas Vega, and Jaime Saavedra Chanduvi. 2009. "Measuring Inequality of Opportunities in Latin America and the Caribbean." World Bank, Washington, DC.

Psacharopoulos, George. 1994. "Returns to Investment in Education: A Global Update Further Update." *World Development* 22 (9): 1325–43.

Ravallion, Martin. 2004. "Competing Concepts of Inequality in the Globalization Debate." In *Brookings Trade Forum 2004,* edited by Susan Collins and Carol Graham, 1–38. Washington, DC: Brookings Institution Press.

Ravallion, Martin, and Dominique van de Walle. 2008. "Does Rising Landlessness Signal Success or Failure for Vietnam's Agrarian Transition?" *Journal of Development Economics* 87 (2, October): 191–209.

Roemer, John. 1998. *Equality of Opportunity.* Cambridge, MA: Harvard University Press.

————. 2011. *Equality of Opportunity as Opportunity Equalization*. Discussion Paper. New Haven, CT: Yale University, Department of Political Science.

Stark, Oded, J. Edward Taylor, and Shlomo Yitzhaki. 1986. "Remittances and Inequality." *Economic Journal* 96 (383): 722–40.

VASS (Vietnamese Academy of Social Sciences). 2008. "Participatory Poverty Assessment 2008." VASS, Hanoi.

————. 2011. *Poverty Reduction in Viet Nam: Achievements and Challenges*. Hanoi: World Publisher.

————. 2012. "Opportunities for Children in Vietnam." Background paper for the 2012 Programmatic Poverty Assessment, World Bank, Washington, DC.

World Bank. 1999. *Vietnam Development Report 2000: Attacking Poverty*. Washington, DC: World Bank.

————. 2006. *World Development Report: Equity*. Washington, DC: World Bank.

————. 2009. *From Poor Areas to Poor People: China's Evolving Poverty Reduction Agenda; An Assessment of Inequality and Poverty*. Washington, DC: World Bank.

————. 2010. "Assessing and Monitoring Governance in the Land Sector: The Land Governance Assessment Framework." World Bank, Washington DC.

————. 2011. *Vietnam: High-Quality Education for All by 2020*. Washington, DC: World Bank.

World Bank, Embassy of Denmark, and Embassy of Sweden. 2011. "Recognizing and Reducing Corruption Risks in Land Management in Vietnam." National Political Publishing House, Hanoi.